Journey of the Gullphin

By Bert Milburn

While every precaution has been taken in the preparation of this book, the publisher assumes no responsibility for errors or omissions, or for damages resulting from the use of the information contained herein.

JOURNEY OF THE GULLPHIN

First edition. July 1, 2024.

Copyright © 2024 Bert Milburn.

ISBN: 979-8227186188

Written by Bert Milburn.

Table of Contents

Dedication

I write this book for the traveler within all of us and as a reminder to sometimes allow fate to shine a colorful light as a beacon for us to follow.

This book would not have been possible without the insights, patience, and collaboration of Angie (Geli), my beautiful German girl.

Notes about writing this book

Although my recollection is far from perfect, all events and facts in this book are accurate to the best of my recall. Nothing has been altered to exaggerate or embellish the events.

I contacted many individuals mentioned in this book and received their permission to include their pictures and events. After many years, those I could not find are referred to with changed names.

No matter how many final edits I made, I'm certain you may find a grammatical error or read a passage that could be improved. I've learned a ton from writing this book, more than I ever imagined possible. Learning never stops.

Special thanks:

Thank you to Andrew Lockett (an editor hired through Reedsy) for his developmental and initial copyedits. His suggestions made this book readable.

Dorothy Hall (Long-time friend) for her assistance with grammar, structure, and readability suggestions.

Sue Owensby (Pickleball buddy and avid reader) for her early read-through and excellent suggestions on what to add to improve interest.

Part 1
The Seagull and the Dolphin, Two Souls Meet

Chapter 1
The "Beautiful German Girl"

———

Weekday newspaper, Lake Park, Florida, April 2nd, 1975 (personal ads)

"Beautiful 19-year-old German girl wants to meet attractive gentleman for more information, write WeekDay 826 Park Ave, Box 46D, Lake Park ".

Teresa, the City of Palm Beach Gardens Recreation Department Assistant Director, reads the ad aloud, hands me the *WeekDay* paper, and says, "Here, this sounds like something you should check out." Katie, her secretary, says, "Yeah, interesting, and you need a little adventure in your life." I was a part-time student, taking evening classes at Palm Beach Junior College and working full-time as a janitor in the Palm Beach Gardens city hall complex. I had just quit my part-time evening job at Arthur Treacher's Fish & Chips and now had more free time. I had let my light brown hair and beard grow since I left the Air Force a year earlier but usually kept it in an acceptable ponytail for work. I thought the personal ad sounded interesting, especially since I was divorced over a year ago and hadn't met anyone or seriously dated since.

City of Palm Beach Gardens. City Hall 1975

The past year of hanging out with friends helped clear my mind of a time of bad choices and avoided responsibilities. We were all content to enjoy life in the sun, swim and snorkel in the ocean, listen to music, and attend a few concerts, all under the influence of some premium South Florida pot. I was starting to feel like opening up again and ready to meet someone, maybe even someone special. This change could be just what I needed.

Bert is ready to go snorkeling. 1975

I exited the Recreation Department air-conditioned office and headed across the second floor, open pavilion to my office/janitor closet. With the emerging morning sun shining through the pavilion opening to my back and looking at the parting clouds ahead, I saw a glimmer of color in the sky beyond the distant rain. It was the top arch of a developing rainbow. As I gazed at the emerging colors, memories of how I wound up here and where my life was going flooded my head, and I was full of doubts and uncertainty.

It seems like it was just yesterday. I'm barely out of high school, with no clue what to do with my life. After completing only one quarter, I dropped out of Ferris State College in Big Rapids,

Michigan in December, 1970. I bounced around several places, living for six months in Houston, Texas, working in the mobile home business. I lived with one of the business partners, who was a close family friend. After my steady girlfriend, Cindy said she had been "sort of raped" by her cousin at a wedding, I left Houston the next day. With experience in the mobile home industry, I was able to work a few short-term jobs while my life spiraled further away from stability. It turned out that Cindy just wanted her freedom. I would eventually abandon life in Michigan and move in with my older sister Joyce in Lake Park, Florida, for a few months. Finding no work, I returned to Jackson, Michigan, in the fall and got a job as a handyman for another mobile home business.

While working in Michigan that August, the draft board announced the 1972 military draft lottery selection. This lottery determined the order in which young men would be selected for military service. A person pulled out capsules with birth dates enclosed from a giant fish bowl one at a time. Those born on the date of the first capsule drawn were #1 and drafted first, then #2 through the last, #366 (1952, my birth year, was a leap year). When complete, everyone unlucky enough not to have a college or medical deferment knew their chance of being conscripted and how soon. On the day of the draft lottery, August 5th, 1971, I was at work setting up a mobile home and turned on my car radio to listen in on my lunch break. The lottery was a big event and even broadcast live on TV. Millions watched it over several hours.

I tuned in shortly after it began, and while eating my peanut butter and jelly sandwich, I mentally calculated my odds of being drafted. I figured my birthday would be selected midway through the lottery, close to 180 or, if I was luckier, 200 or higher. Such a high number would surely leave me undrafted and out of Vietnam. Media projections were that those with chosen draft numbers of 90 or less were likely to be drafted sometime in 1972. The odds were in my favor, and just as I was about to turn off my radio and head back to work, my birthday, "August 28th", was announced, and my lucky number was 37 out of 366. "Holy crap!" I said to myself. With the fighting in Vietnam winding down but body bags still being sent home, joining the war effort was not what I wanted.

During my short time with my sister in Florida, I joined 50 other potential draftees on a government bus headed to Miami to complete our mandatory draft physicals and determine our readiness to serve. The whole day was a joke. None of us wanted to be drafted, and we tried every trick in the book to get rejected. After a stern and intimidating introduction from a military sergeant, we followed our assigned colored lines on the floor to lead each to the proper health screening task. I passed a shaved-headed young man who remained seated with a catatonic expression. I coaxed him to get up, but he was frozen like a statue. With some prodding, he told me he accepted a dare to enlist in the Marines, shaved his head, and then freaked out. Before he got on the bus, he dropped two hits of acid, and now he couldn't move. While in the bathroom, filling up our small jars with our urine, several of us instead took urine from a man saying he had not slept in three days and heard that would make him ineligible for the draft. During my hearing test, I randomly pressed my left and right buttons, indicating when I heard high-pitched sounds from my headset. I still passed with flying colors and was pronounced 1-A, able to serve.

In October, back in Jackson, Michigan, I visited the local draft office to see about getting a conscientious objector deferment. When I told them my lottery number, they said I had maybe 'till the end of January before getting drafted and laughed me out of their office. I hung my head, walked down the hall to the Air Force recruiter's office, and enlisted. I'd leave for basic training on January 21st, 1972.

Then, to beat it all, around Christmas time, I agreed to marry a close friend, Peggy, who, as I found out later, was pregnant from her ass hole of a boyfriend.

Peggy and I had dated each other's best friend during my last year of high school. Steve went steady with Peggy, and I went steady with her best friend, Cindy. We double-dated every weekend for the whole year. Even so, I was pretty shy, with more than my share of insecurities and inexperience. Peggy and I connected when I left Joyce's in Florida and returned to Michigan. I was a bit surprised at how we became intimate so quickly and how the condom somehow ripped on that first date. It's hard to believe how naive I was back then. I just seemed to float through life without direction and accept each curveball life threw. Lucky for me, none of them hit me very hard.

I still had several weeks before basic training at Lackland Air Force Base in Texas, so Peggy and I hitchhiked to visit my sister in Florida. Peggy eventually told me she was pregnant and much later admitted the baby wasn't mine, as she had led me to believe. We decided we could still get married. She'd avoid the embarrassment of an unmarried pregnancy and promised to give the baby up for adoption. I could avoid the barracks and live off-base while receiving an extra $125 monthly for off-base family housing. This arrangement seemed like a win-win situation, and after all, we knew each other well and had lots in common. What the heck, why not?

After a few weeks in the winter sun, we hitchhiked from my sister's back to Jackson in mid-January 1972. My ship-out date was two days away, so we couldn't waste any time returning to Michigan. Our first big ride was "supposed" to take us all the way to Columbus, Ohio. What luck, we thought. Jerry picked us up in his Volkswagen Beetle, north of Gainesville, with his back seat packed with all his belongings and his well-behaved German Shepherd. Peggy and I squeezed into the passenger seat, and Jerry lit a joint. We stopped for gas in rural Florida just south of the Georgia state line. When I stood up quickly from the cramped seat, pretty well stoned, I got light-headed, passed out, and stumbled to the ground. My fall freaked out the young attendant pumping our gas, who promptly called the police as soon as we left.

Barely back on I-75 headed north, a cop pulled us over, leaned through Jerry's driver's side window, and, in a questioning tone, said to me, "Hear you had trouble standing up back at the gas station." I explained a low blood pressure issue I "supposedly" had, and the cop seemed satisfied. Just about to pull back out on the interstate, the cop's blue lights come on again, and another cop car pulls in front of us, lights flashing. Jerry quickly handed me two joints and said, "Here, hide these." In the next moment, he was yanked out of the vehicle, frisked, cuffed, hands in front, and escorted to the back seat of the trailing cop car.

Peggy and I sat there; no one seemed interested in us, but looking back at Jerry through the windshield of the cop car, I saw him motioning for me to eat the joints. Shortly before, we had frantically decided I should drop the joints between the front seats. With Peggy still sitting on my lap, I could see the two joints on the floor between the emergency brake handle and two heater levers, with barely an inch or two of space between the two front seats. I wriggled my hand around and past the obstructions to barely touch the closest joint. I pulled it up and out and popped it in my mouth while my hand returned to find the second joint. As my fingertips found the second one, the cop got out and started walking towards us. Just before he leaned in to direct us out of the car, I reunited the two joints in my mouth and began to chew. Scared, stoned, dry mouth, and acting on instinct rather than logic, I nodded in compliance with the cop's instruction to get out. The mouthful of pot froze in a bale of dry mass, and it was impossible to swallow. I frantically continued to chew it into smaller pieces as I slowly stood up and approached the rear of the VW. I knew when I spoke, I would likely spit pot all over the place, and that would be it for us. But like manna from heaven, Peggy handed me the Coke we bought back at the gas station, and I was saved. One big drink washed down most of the dry bale, and I smiled big as I responded to the cop's questions. Peggy later told me the chewed-up pot covered my teeth, but as we talked, the cop didn't seem to notice.

They let Jerry out, uncuffed him, and he explained how he "borrowed" a friend's parent's car license plates to make the trip as he had none. They reported this to the police, and here we were. With one cop car in front and one behind, we were to follow them somewhere. We were not just anywhere along some random interstate highway; we were in the Deep South, barely still in Florida, just shy of the Georgia state line, in an area renowned for their dislike of long-haired hippies and liberated females. Stories about secret hippie detention (rubber hose) camps in these forgettable Deep South Bastions were rampant.

Traveling along the interstate, maybe a mile or so, all three cars pulled onto the shoulder, not at an exit ramp, but to a worn path leading to a 10-foot tall, barbed wire fence with a locked double gate. Once inside, we seemed to enter a dense forest to an unknown but likely perilous fate. I could feel the rubber hose hitting my back as the cops howled with laughter at my well-deserved pain. It turns out this was a shortcut to the small town of Jasper, where we were locked up in the local jail/city hall house.

The Cops took Peggy one way in this old two-story brick house, and two others escorted Jerry and me to a large room behind a locked, rather hearty, screened door with a guard outside. I sat on a wooden bench with several others while Jerry used the pay phone on the opposite wall to plead with his friend in Miami to get his parents to drop any charges. Still relatively high from the pot and the excitement, a dirty-looking young man frantically beckoned me to call the guard to open the screened door. He said he would slit his throat and, "We'd all get outta here"! I freaked, turned, and ran up the cement stairs, only to hear someone yelling for me to come from a cell down a hall. I reluctantly approached the cell to see two other young men, with their heads shaved, pleading for me to help them. The one guy said they had been in this jail for weeks, their long hair cut, and they were not allowed to contact anyone. I ran down the stairs to find Jerry, and we waited to see what our uncertain fate might bring. A short time later, a cop brought me to the police dispatch office, where Peggy was seated. She told them our plans to return to Jackson, Michigan, quickly as I had enlisted in the Air Force. They had made some calls, and it checked out, so we were free to go.

With good fortune on our side and surviving a blizzard waiting for a 1 AM ride in Toledo, Ohio, we made it back to Jackson just in time for me to catch the enlistment bus headed to my next four years of patriotic duty.

———————

I was 19, and those two years married and in the Air Force were a blur. Peggy regretfully gave up the baby for adoption and shortly after became pregnant with our baby, Kimberly. I tolerated the Air Force and stumbled through to an honorable but early release after two years. Our divorce soon followed. I never really took family life seriously. Peggy tried to make family life work for us, but I never bought into the whole arrangement, and we split. Kimberly was only four months old. I sent Peggy $20 a week to help with Kimberly, but we would each move on with our lives. Then it was back to my sister Joyce's mobile home in South Florida with her two kids to start my life again.

Starting life over was not new to me. Growing up with my parents, we started over from scratch many times. I lived on my sister's couch for several weeks and was hired as a lunch cook at the Abby Road restaurant. On my way to hang out at the beach, driving my 1972 Pinto Runabout, I picked up a hitchhiker, and we hit it off right away. Steve had recently moved from New Jersey to live with a friend, but that didn't work out. I gave him a ride to his recently rented dive of a motel where he had spent the last of his money.

I didn't know anyone but my sister and a handful of more traditional type people at my new job. Steve was the first likable person I met with long, black hair with natural curls. He was, like me, an introvert with an open mind. We talked but didn't get into anything too heavy. We were both a bit funny and liked to laugh. Steve had this puppy dog look with big brown eyes that drooped just a bit. We were both looking to get a handle on a new life, and together, we did this with little fanfare. Neither of us was trying to impress anyone. We both wanted a simple life to enjoy and share with others.

Bert and Steve, in their duplex apartment in Lake Park, Florida. With Reefer, Bert's dog.

Steve soon found a job riding the trash truck for the city of Palm Beach Gardens and would get his first advanced paycheck within the week. Steve and I decided we had enough money to rent a cheap two-bedroom duplex apartment near his work and moved in together. We scraped by for a few months but finally stabilized our pooled finances and got our heads above water. Steve told me about the janitor job opening at the city hall complex in Palm Beach Gardens, and I quit my cooking job at Abby Road for this job with more flexibility and benefits. I received a letter from the Veteran's Administration explaining how to enroll in college classes and receive government assistance. By taking one night class, I would receive $100 a month, which I quickly took advantage of. This eased our financial burden and renewed my interest in continuing my education.

Feeling a sense of real accomplishment, we developed a stable existence with shared expenses and the reward of a fun life of simple pleasures. We shared music, food, philosophy, and hope for the future. We cruised through life together and thought how great it was to have a partner.

Steve had met another transplanted guy from New Jersey, Pete, who lived with a local Florida girl, Terri. Pete had the most infectious smile. He could charm anyone into a good mood. He had a round face with straight, blonde hair encircling his head with short bangs and the back touching his shoulders. He's what I'd call a "calm extrovert." Everyone liked Pete. Terri was the friendliest person and made it a point to get to know you personally. She was a fun person, a perfect match for Pete, and together, they pulled us in and made us a part of their lives. Terri had long, curly brown hair and always wore relaxed clothing. She flowed when she walked, just like her attitude.

When Steve and I came to visit, we never knocked on the door of their house in the scrub palms; we just walked in and called out their names. We were always greeted with warm smiles and soon-to-follow laughter.

The four of us became close friends and spent most of our free time together, hanging out, listening to music, and solving the metaphysical dilemmas facing the world through the lyrics of The Moody Blues and Pink Floyd. We became very close and bonded over our hippie philosophy and shared interests. Life went on like this for six months, then Steve met Marie. Marie visited Florida with friends from Brooklyn, New York.

She and Steve connected immediately, and she moved in with us to our duplex apartment. We were a happy group for the most part. Steve and Marie fell madly in love, and we got along pretty well. Once our living arrangement became a bit "crowded," we moved to a two-apartment house in West Palm Beach on 59th ½ Street, where I took the upstairs apartment and Steve and Marie took the downstairs.

1958 New Moon trailer in Sunset Village.

I eventually found living on my own too expensive and bought a small, owner-financed mobile home for $1,000 two miles north along US A1A in Riviera Beach. It was in Sunset Village, a retirement park with maybe two other couples under 30. The trailers were small and close together. After 8 in the evening, the residents were quietly tucked away in their metal-sided homes for the night. When listening to my music, I could play Cat Stevens barely loud enough to enjoy, but I could only play Led Zeppelin in daylight when there was enough background noise to mask it from the neighbors. I continued working my janitor job, kept up with my classes at Palm Beach Junior College, and finally settled into life in South Florida with an eye toward my future.

Chapter 2
A Suitcase Full of Letters

I was interested in the personal ad Teresa handed me. Still, I replied, "Right, even if the 'Beautiful German Girl' ad is real, who would place it in a paper devoted to the retirement set," where most read, "single mature lady who loves to cook interested in meeting a nonsmoking gentleman who likes to walk" or, "divorced man seeks a companion, 40 to 65 years young". If the ad was legit, the 19-year-old German girl must be either desperate or, how could I say, aesthetically challenged. I returned to the Rec. Department office, and again, Teresa and Katie prodded me to reply, "Come on, take a chance. What do you have to lose"? Interested but wary, I contemplated the possibilities and finally agreed, "What the heck, I'll give it a shot. If she is real, she may not even respond, and a thousand other lost souls are already responding to the ad". They gave me the newspaper, which I folded and stuffed into my back pocket. That night, I penned a letter to the unnamed beauty. I had no phone, so I would need to wait for any possible response by mail. A month passed with no reply, and the thought of an exciting encounter vanished. School, work, and adjusting to my new Sunset Village trailer park abode kept me busy.

Christhilde (Chris) and Angelika (Geli) sat on the floor in the pool house where Angelika lived, sorting through the last of a suitcase full of letters. They divided them into several stacks, one for Christhilde, the 19-year-old German girl who came to Florida as an au pair more than a year before, and one for Angelika, her close

18-year-old friend. Christhilde had invited her to work for a different Palm Beach family five months earlier. Another pile for those letters and pictures too inappropriate to do more than laugh about and maybe fear a little. Elsa, an older German acquaintance of Christhilde's who ran a flower shop in the area, placed the ad in the paper, which was unknown to the girls. She saw the two as young, beautiful girls isolated in a new land who spoke limited English. Elsa had no idea how many "attractive gentlemen" would respond to the personal ad. She had collected the suitcase full of letters to give the girls, minus the many extras she destroyed due to their disingenuous nature.

Chris's and Geli's adventurous but naive idea for their immediate future had always been to travel and discover this new country at their own pace before returning to Germany. Chris's six-month visa had long expired, and Geli's would lapse this month, making such travel risky. With this trove of letters came a new idea: they might find nice guys who would marry them, allowing them to obtain green cards and become resident aliens, then agree to divorce six months later. This arrangement was to be based strictly on friendship with no other benefits and allow them time to explore this vast country.

Chris and Geli had already called many and met with several suitors. Most were just very lonely. One even proposed during the first meeting with a diamond ring in hand. A few were just too strange. Some were much older, and more than one only had one thing on his mind. They both realized how lucky they were that nothing terrible happened at one of these meetings. Beyond a Platonic marriage and soon-to-follow divorce, neither put much thought into their immediate futures. They were young, had lived in small towns in Germany their whole lives, and were ready for a change.

Living in exotic Florida was different; they were excited to explore this new life. They each helped clean their respective host family's houses and take care of the kids. Watching American TV helped them improve their broken English and encouraged them to step further into the community. They made more trips to Burger King for American fast food, a Whopper, and a milkshake. They rode bikes along the ocean and Intracoastal Waterway pathways, a movie at a theater now and then, and brief visits with new friends had become their new lives, but it was still quiet for two so young and full of ideas and energy.

While sorting through all the responses to the "Beautiful German Girl" ad, they had put my letter at the bottom of the pile because I did not include a phone number, and they both felt insecure about writing back in English. With little opposition from Chris, Geli decided my letter sounded nice and would ask Tony, an American friend, to help her compose a response to me. After struggling to write her invitation to meet on May 11th, still two weeks away, she completed the translations, was satisfied with the content, and dropped it in the mail the next day.

That night, Geli lay awake for hours, thinking back to the many lonely people responding to the ad she had met and her life in Germany. She finished school at sixteen and immediately entered an apprenticeship to become a department store manager. There was no way she could stay at home much longer. Her brother, Manfred, and sisters, Christel and Jutta, were old enough now to care for themselves. Her parents, Ernst and Anita, were hard-working, and life was a continuous struggle to keep everything moving forward.

Geli, now seventeen, working her apprenticeship at a mundane job in a downtown department store, was ready for a change. Since leaving school, she made many new friends who, like her, were developing independent lives. They hung out in various places around Bad Kreuznach, drank a little bit, and smoked a little hash, but mostly, they just talked about life and shared their hopes and dreams. Life at this age was a group experience. Geli became close to a couple of guys over that year. Tobias was the nicest one; he was more intuitive and considerate. She felt safe with him. Conversely, Wolf was a more typical male with a strong will and a somewhat aggressive attitude. Geli once found herself alone with him in a tent and felt lucky he didn't force himself beyond her romantic boundaries.

Geli and others in this group once traveled to France for a ten-day vacation. They stayed five days with Peter Uhl's (Christhilde's older brother) Paris foreign exchange family, then drove south to Marseilles to camp on the Mediterranean coast. Geli visited Hallstatt, Austria, twice, but beyond these trips, she spent most of her time with her friends at one house or another in Bad Kreuznach. Christhilde's family house was a popular place to crash. Her parents were trusting of the five older siblings and left the group alone for the most part. Geli felt the most comfortable there.

It seemed the real underlying issue for Geli and most others was what to do with their lives. Sure, life was fun, and the strong group friendships were great. By sixteen, most young Germans were independent-minded and making their own decisions. They didn't believe their parents owed them anything beyond their stable upbringing. The question now was, what is next in life? The late 1960s and early 70s were different times. For many young people, following a typical path to marriage, children, and a secure but mundane job was expected, and they complied. This life was not appealing to Geli and her friends. They wanted new experiences and a different life than their parents. The question was, how to make that happen, and what would it be? For Geli, this was her driving concern. She was a bit lost and eager to act when Christhilde sent her the offer of an au pair job in exotic Florida. She boarded a plane at seventeen and cast her fate to the Western wind.

I finished my last exam of the Spring Quarter and, except for my full-time job cleaning the city hall complex, was free for the first summer break I had had in a long time. The beach and snorkeling awaited. In May, Florida was hot but still bearable. You could still walk barefoot on pavement or beach sand without burning your feet. The gentle breeze wafting through the palms and mango trees brought a freshness to life. Even in my little trailer park, life was good. Making a monthly payment of $100, I planned to pay off the trailer in a year, sell it, and move to a better place with the profit I made. Why waste my money on rent?

I parked my 1971 sky-blue Pinto Runabout in front of my 8-foot by 32-foot, faded green and white 1958 New Moon trailer. Ducking into the cool shade under my patio awning, I opened the mailbox mounted next to my front door. Wow! A letter, hand addressed to me, not just junk and sale ads. I didn't even take the time to change my dirty blue work pants and light blue short-sleeve shirt with "Bert" embroidered on an oval patch over my pocket. I quickly poured a lime juice and sat on my porch to decipher this German girl's one-page letter. Most of the words I could interpret through broken English. It said she had long brown hair and would like to meet me at Big Daddy's Lounge in Lake Worth. There was a chain of these bars in South Florida. She wanted to meet at 8 o'clock on, I think she wrote, May 11th, but the ones she wrote looked different, like the upside-down letter Vs. That's the way she wrote, just to be different. Big Daddy's was 50 minutes across town, and since the gas shortage a few years back, this meant a considerable expenditure of both money and time.

I still wasn't sure if I should take the risk. She signed the letter like nothing I had ever seen or heard. It looked like Augelika. I later learned her handwriting makes n's with two points on top instead of two humps, so the n looked like a u. Augelika. Hmm! Well, why not, I thought, really having nothing else going on, and now I'm intrigued. What if I met someone nice, and if she was, in fact, beautiful, that would be awesome! Naw, well, maybe. All week, I thought about the possibilities. I want to meet someone different, so what if she exaggerated the beautiful part? I've made no connections on the few dates since my divorce, so I am going to do it!

Chapter 3
Two French Girls, in the Corner?

———

That Sunday evening, May 11th, as I drove south on Military Trail skirting West Palm Beach, I thought I had finally figured out what was "really" going on but was afraid to believe I was wasting my time and money on a scam. As I turned east on Lake Worth Road, I figured I would know soon enough. I pulled into Big Daddy's bar around 8:20, running a bit late, and the welcome air conditioning pulled me in through the front door. I was shy or at least a closet introvert. I was not too fond of crowds or bars and didn't drink alcohol, so what the heck was I doing here? Maybe it was real, right?

I looked around, thinking it shouldn't be too difficult to scope out the reasonably large establishment to see if she was a real person and even still there after all this time. My eyes adjusted to the low lighting, and I looked around, but it wasn't easy. At least a half dozen girls with long brownish hair sat around the dimly lit bar. I wasn't about to go around and ask each one if they were, Auge-something. I wasn't even sure what to call her. My best guess sounded something like Aug-i-leeka. I knew that must be wrong. Wait, the barmaid has long hair, more blonde than brown, but her being Augelika made sense. She worked here, so that's why she chose to meet here. It was a safe place, and she knew everyone. My hopes were lifted, and she was, after all, beautiful. I approached the bar and asked her, "Is your name Aug-i-leeka?" with a bit of a stutter. She backed away suspiciously and replied, "Nooo". Realizing her apprehension, I divulged that I was here to meet a German girl and thought you might be her. With some relief, she said, "No German girl here, but two French girls are sitting at a table in the back corner." I glanced and saw one with blond hair. That wasn't her, I figured, but I ordered a rum and Coke and sat down at the bar to at least look around before I drove all the way home.

As I settled onto the bar stool to assess my options, the man beside me asked, "Did you say you were here to meet a German girl?" He told me he was also here to meet a German girl named Chris. I knew it. This meeting was too good to be true. As I looked around the bar at all the uncomfortable single people, I said to the guy, "I'll bet most everyone here responded to some fake personal ad and is waiting for that handsome or beautiful person to complete their lives. I'll bet this place is about to go bankrupt and came up with this scam to attract customers and keep this bar afloat". There was no sense wasting the two bucks I spent on this drink, so I sat and listened to Michael, who described his sad, recent divorce and showed me a handful of pictures of his souped-up Chevy Vega with the fancy paint job. No wonder he was divorced, I surmised. Just before 9:00, I finished my drink and was about to leave, but after so much anticipation and frustration, I said to Michael, "I'm goin' to check out the two French girls back in the corner."

Michael and his Vega.

Big Daddy's was starting to come to life. The rustle of people, background music, and the low din of voices as I maneuvered my way back to the table where a blonde-haired girl was sitting with another girl with, hmm, long brown hair, and she was "beautiful." "Pardon me," I interrupted, "I am supposed to meet a German girl here. I think her name is Augelika". Geli popped up from the table and said, "Ya, I'm Angelika!" Pronounced An-gay-lee-ka (hence the short name, Geli). With an immediate sense of shock, I blurted out two words before I could think to stop myself, "No shit" and, "Are you Chris" as I looked at the blonde girl? She nodded affirmatively. "Wait here. I'll be right back", I said as I hurried back to the bar. I told Michael, "They're for real, man, they're for real! Let's go".

Michael was hesitant, so I convinced him that joining the girls could be fun. Two-on-two was less uncomfortable than meeting one-on-one, even if this other guy had so many unresolved issues. We pinballed through the crowded room back to the German girls' table. After some quick introductions, they invited us to sit, and some light conversation ensued. We nursed our drinks over the next 30 minutes, asked questions, and shared brief stories about ourselves. There was enough time to assess each other, and we enjoyed each other's company. There were many smiles and enough direct eye contact to make everyone feel "relatively" comfortable, and there was a hint of attraction between Angie and me. I had trouble pronouncing her name, so she told me to call her Angie, to which I happily complied. Small talk had run its course, and before my masked discomfort with the bar scene became apparent, I suggested we all make the short drive over to the ocean to walk along the beach. Everyone agreed, and Michael insisted we ride in his super cool, two-door Vega.

After Michael took out his keys, unlocked and opened the passenger door for us, I pushed the back of the passenger seat forward, and Angie and I slipped into the small back seat. At the same time, he, like a good gentleman, ensured Chris was comfortably seated before closing the door. Angie and I exchanged more smiles, just a bit different than the smiles in the bar, enough to show each other that you're OK, kind of like, cool, this is alright.

Michael parked at the deserted dune lot, and we walked the short distance to the clean, white sandy beach. The moon showed enough light to see shapes and some detail but created a more intimate and natural atmosphere under the stars. The sound of the low tide waves gently lapping at the sand, the smell of the salt air, and the cool breeze on this hot night were pleasant, and everyone felt more relaxed. The absence of music, shuffling noise, and closeness of all the other people at the bar made it more personal between us all but somewhat uncomfortable at the same time.

After some awkward conversation, Chris laughed, almost dancing, and ran straight into the water with a spontaneous urge to change the mood. Playing waist-deep in the waves, hoping others would join her, she beckoned us in and laughed as her hands splashed the water. Angie and I thought about going in when Michael lost it and instantly became uncomfortable. "What the hell is she doing?" he murmured almost under his breath and mumbled about how weird she was, and now, "his car was going to get wet and sandy!" I, on the other hand, thought, alright! Chris is pretty cool and made a move toward the water. I didn't feel the same willingness from Angie, so I waited. Poor Chris. Happy turned to uncomfortable frustration as she returned to the group. Michael's body language changed abruptly, and the moment's mood became twenty degrees cooler.

The conversations turned back to meaningless small talk, and not wanting to let our fledgling new relationship fade, I asked Angie if she would like to walk down the beach with me. After maybe 10 minutes of strolling down the moonlit beach, we were one-on-one, still within sight of Chris and Michael. Our limited conversation was light but more relaxed. I could see we connected a little and wanted to test the water. Not the ocean water but the possible relationship water with Angie. The friendly questions and descriptive answers banter went silent for a few moments. As we stood there, looking out over the black ocean, we were each thinking about what to say next while examining our feelings. I leaned closer, lightly held Angie at her shoulders, and gently kissed her on the lips, lingering for just a moment. A bit startled by this bold yet tender kiss, Angie did not pull back but was stunned, afraid to send the wrong response signal. She received the kiss somewhat openly. She was not offended, definitely shocked, but now she was wondering and examining everything in her mind at an accelerated pace. I smiled, let go, reached down gently, and touched her hand. We slowly walked back, hand in hand, with fewer words spoken. Our feet progressed slowly back to meet the awkward pair, but our thoughts were traveling far ahead.

Rejoining Chris and Michael, things were different. Everyone could sense this. Angie's and my mood gave an air of mystery while Chris talked a lot to mask the uncomfortable time spent with Michael. Michael stood quiet and confused with his arms crossed over his chest. He had no clue what he wanted from this arranged meeting, but this was not it. He would have been more secure with a light dinner, a movie, and the possibility of a good night kiss from a quiet and reserved girl. A traditional date was not something Chris would ever be happy about. She was an exciting person and full of fun. She wanted to share laughs and be spontaneous. Being solemn and traditional was not her way of spending an evening.

Angie and I had returned in a softer mood and were perceptively closer. We shared a few simple comments and some light conversation as we walked back down the beach. Chris and Geli moved ahead of Mike and me and talked in German. Mike had little to say, but I was now enjoying my uplifted spirit and didn't hear a word he said. The evening for us all had run its course, and the ride back from the beach was quiet. Michael took off at Big Daddy's, leaving me to offer Chris and Angie a ride home. With a quick look between them, they accepted my offer. Angie's pool house was a short drive north along Federal Road to her quiet neighborhood.

Chris often spent the night with Angie. I quietly pulled into the driveway and parked by the pool. Angie and Chris talked quickly in German, and then Chris went ahead through the gate. Standing beside the open passenger door, I asked Angie if she wanted to go out again. She agreed and said next weekend would be good. I said I would pick her up at eight next Saturday. Smiles exchanged, and we parted ways. Life had changed. Chris and Geli talked the night away. I made my long drive home with a much different feeling than my drive there. I felt good, was happy, and thought, wow, she was real, and I liked her. Next Saturday is a long time, but I eagerly awaited it.

The following week was different than the time before I met Angie. My job at Palm Beach Gardens City Hall complex was easy. Empty the trash, dust a little, and sweep the tile floors for the police department, courtroom, mayor's offices, parks and rec, building department, and a center court plaza area. It would take me maybe 90 minutes if I didn't get distracted talking with the dispatchers or one of the cops. This pattern was great when classes were in session. The mayor appreciated me and had no problem with me studying or working on a paper as long as I finished my work. Palm Beach Junior College Summer Session didn't start until mid-June; for once, I didn't have a part-time second job. I now had extra time on my hands and lots of time to think. Many of my thoughts were of Angie; she was a beautiful German girl with her looks and character, and I liked her. She was quiet and pleasant, and when she smiled or laughed, there was a sparkle in her eyes that said more than words could convey.

One morning at work, Jeremy, a police lieutenant I got to know, asked me how my plants were doing. I shook my head, "What are you talking about?" "You know those three pot plants outside the jail's back entrance," Jeremy responded. Since I had long hair, Jeremy assumed I had planted them. "You're kidding me! Show me", I said. Sure enough, just outside the jail back door, where they escorted those they arrested, were three small marijuana plants neatly planted in a row. I said, "Check it out! Someone sure had some nerve." I offered to take care of them. Jeremy said, "Right, I'll bet you will." I carefully dug them up and replanted them behind a stand of trees barely off the city complex property, and I took a container of water to them daily.

Chapter 4
Flipper and Jonathan Livingston Seagull

———

In February, three months before meeting Angie, I heard about Richard Bach, the author of *Jonathan Livingston Seagull*, coming to the area to promote his newest book. Shortly before I left the Air Force, my friends Mike, George, Bob, and I were consumed with reading and analyzing *Jonathan Livingston Seagull*. It was more than just talking about the book. It was an enlightened transformation for us. First, George read it, then passed it on to Bob, me, and Mike. We "rode the range" as radio repairmen at Eglin Air Force Base in Fort Walton Beach, on the Florida panhandle. Our job was to drive a government, four-door pick-up truck to all the remote sites across the 50-mile-wide test range to swap out radio components or do minor repairs. Doing this gave us lots of time, riding those bumpy sandy trails through the arid shrub landscape, to smoke a little pot and talk. We traveled once or twice a week on these remote and restricted back roads to far-off workstations. We rarely saw another vehicle all day.

There was nothing on the radio except for local country music stations, which were twang and sob stories in those days, so we talked. After reading *Jonathan Livingston Seagull* and discussing how Jonathan broke free from his flock and found meaningful answers to life, we obsessed over analyzing the story. Though Jonathan was ostracized and condemned by the flock, he pursued his quest until he, alone, transcended the life of a seagull and attained a type of Nirvana. The revelations in this story led us through many stages of understanding life's secrets. We each experienced an almost religious transformation, and I finally felt I better understood why I existed and what awaited me in the next life. Since those days, I have become much more secure and comfortable with life. My transformation was all due to the rousings stirred within me by Richard Bach. I had to see him. I had so many questions.

I bought a ticket to attend an event at the posh Palm Beach Round Table Club. The club sponsored the luncheon for Richard Bach to promote his next book, *Wings of Flight*, a collection of earlier published stories. Bach's previous novel, *Jonathan Livingston Seagull*, compelled me to spend the $10 for the luncheon. $10 was more than I paid to see Eric Clapton and Joe Walsh at a festival the month before.

Money was always tight. When I lived with my best friend Steve, we survived on peanut butter and grape jelly, white bread from the discount bread store, 20 cents a loaf, and packs of Kool-Aid 10 for a dollar. My Pinto had a rotted muffler, and it sounded like a loud Harley Davidson. I also needed tires as mine were about threadbare, but I splurged on the luncheon to hear Richard Bach. It was a suit-and-tie affair, but I had neither. My best friend Steve lent me his corduroy jacket with patches on the elbows, and my other good friend, Pete, had a bolo, western tie, which was not a tie at all. It was more like a long, thick shoelace you'd wrap around your neck and clasp with a decorative slide. The only pants I owned were blue uniforms for work and Levi's jeans. The Levi's it was, and a button-down shirt under Steve's well-worn jacket.

It was a gorgeous, sunny day as I drove into the circle drive at the Palm Beach Round Table Club. With my borrowed coat and bolo tie, my hair pulled back in a neat ponytail, and a dog-eared paperback copy of *Jonathan Livingston Seagull* in my jacket pocket, I rumbled into the club. The night before, I re-read the book for the fifth or sixth time and jotted down a list of unanswered questions I had about the seagull's journey and life in general. No one might have missed my arrival at the club. Not only was my car the only Ford Pinto Runabout, but it was also the only car that didn't cost as much as a house and had no muffler. I made quite an opening impression. The ladies in their expensive summer wear and gentlemen in their light-colored suits stopped and stared, but they were not impolite, more perplexed. I left the car running while the valet slid behind the wheel and, with a slight smirk, revved the engine a bit before he took off. In the following quiet moment, I walked inside.

It was a massive room with a circular wall of floor-to-ceiling windows looking out over the vast waters of the Atlantic. Twenty-one-seven-person round tables faced the raised podium with the ocean as the backdrop. I arrived early, and a few people were already seated. The ladies at the reception table checked my ticket and reservation carefully. I noticed my name on a table diagram close to the podium, but with a subtle glance between two ladies, they redirected me to a table in the back. Disappointed but not wanting to press my luck, I did, after all, make it inside. I sat and patiently waited for the room to fill and for Richard Bach to approach the podium. The efficient staff served lunch, and I was hungry, but being a vegetarian, I found the meal less than substantial.

The people who joined me at the table were friendly but curious and asked me many questions. Thankfully, Bach arrived and proceeded to weave an exciting story about how he came to write his best-selling novels. I sat with rapt attention and was delighted to hear him say he would gladly answer our questions. My hand went up immediately, but Bach acknowledged several others first with questions like, "What is the highest you have ever flown?" from a retired pilot. Bach's response left the man and many others puzzled. Still, I understood what he meant when he replied, "The highest I ever flew was not in a plane, but while sitting on a rock, gazing over the ocean, my thoughts were coming together so fast I felt like I had escaped the bounds of the earth." Finally, I got my first chance and asked, "If a seagull's purpose, as promoted in *Jonathan Livingston Seagull*, is to fly with perfection, what is the purpose of man?" The questioning continued for maybe 15 minutes, and I asked my share of them from the far back of the room. There were so many that several guests asked me if I was a reporter or writing a book myself.

The club host thanked Richard Bach as we all applauded, and he walked to a back table to autograph copies of his new book. Twenty or more people meandered to the back, purchased a book, and formed a line to await their turn for the brief exchange with the famous author. I stood, and Bach reached for my tattered book, but I said I would wait and let all the others go first. I watched Bach exchange the same, "To whom shall I make the greeting?" And then he drew a quick sailboat and sun and an autographed greeting.

Bert's autographed copy of Jonathan Livingston Seagull.

With the last book purchased and signed, I, instead of handing him my book, shook his hand and said, "Thank you. Your book, *Jonathan Livingston Seagull*, has changed my life. I'd love to talk with you for a moment." Bach complied, and we spoke briefly as I relayed his book's impact on my life and asked a few more questions. As the host ladies were about to escort Bach to another private function, he took my ragged copy of *JLS* and drew a sea scene with boats, waves, the sun, and seagulls with a short, signed note to me. We smiled, shook hands again, and parted ways. My fondness for seagulls now became even more vital. They were always my companions at the beach, and Bach's Jonathan opened up a new understanding of life.

____

As Americans knew her, Angie watched TV with the Morgan kids. Reruns of *Flipper*, the same show she loved as a little girl growing up in Germany, but this time, it was in English, and the actor's lips synced with their dialogue. Angie picked up many words from shows like this and the rock and roll lyrics she memorized from The Bee Gees or Procol Harum albums. Flipper, the show's dolphin and star, appealed to Angie for many reasons. She was not just a cute mammal but super intelligent and intuitive. Flipper even communicated with those relaxed and fun-loving Floridian families who lived in their virtual paradise. Angie felt a special connection with the dolphin. They both existed in a world foreign to them and communicated through different languages, but only on a fundamental level.

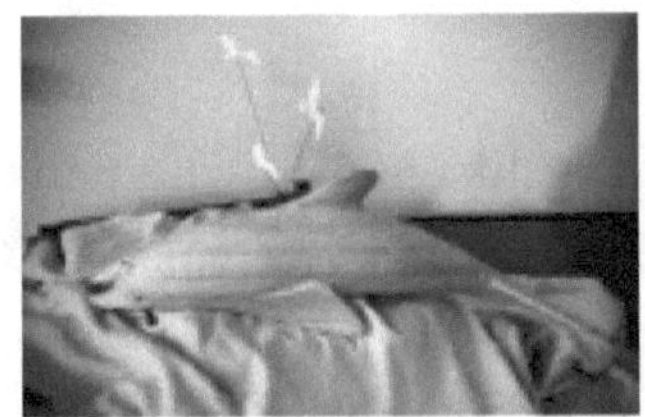

Angie wondered what subliminal influence the show, watched in Germany, had on her winding up in tropical Florida. She had even seen glimpses of several dolphins surfacing offshore as she walked along the beach over the last three months. She had never thought about it before, but like her coming to this new land, dolphins would break the surface to experience a new world, a fascinating world with different rules. The ocean was a beauty hidden from view. What lies beyond the surface, she thought. She might be a dolphin in another life, under the sea. Now, she lives in Florida and enjoys all the new things she has seen and experienced. People were so friendly here, it was always warm, and you could do many different things. Everything here was fresh and young. Germany was old, very formal, and often rainy and dark. She loved Germany, but Florida was exotic. Like Flipper, she learned to communicate with those she helped and loved the ocean's atmosphere. Angie shared a special bond with the concept of a dolphin.

When she arrived at the Morgan family home five months before, Angie spoke only the most basic English. Now, she feels more comfortable talking, and her English is improving, but she still has an accent, and many words she hears are unknown. If she understands some of the words people speak, she can fill in the rest to understand the meaning in context. Talking with the kids and watching *Flipper* did help improve her English.

———

Christhilde and Angelika had grown up in different small towns on opposite sides of Bad Kreuznach, West Germany. They both worked downtown at a department store, training to become licensed store managers after they had completed their public education. Chris was a year older, but they became fast friends and shared their hopes and dreams as they trained for their mundane career choice. Like all Germans, they both worked hard but wanted something more. They were unsure what, but Chris' opportunity came first when a neighboring family friend knew of a Florida family looking for a German girl to move to the States, all expenses paid, to help raise their kids and keep house. The move happened quickly; Christhilde was gone, and Geli was again alone at work.

Christhilde moved to Florida and sent many letters to her friend Geli, telling her all about the unusual, exciting things she saw and experienced living in her sunny tropical new home. Months passed, and Geli was still searching to find out what her life might become. Talking with her friends was essential to Geli, and they were all experiencing similar life questions. Ideas sparked some understanding, but big questions remained. Early adulthood caused a profound examination of understanding what life held in store.

Geli felt adrift and had yet to find answers to reveal the understanding of life she needed.

Then, a friend of Chris' Florida host family told her they would love to have someone like Chris to help them with their family. Chris sent Geli another letter, this time with the offer of a job in Florida. It didn't pay much, but the host family would cover all expenses, and she would receive some extra cash every week. Angelika didn't have to think long before she decided to take the plunge and venture into the unknown. Such a radical move wasn't like her at all. She thrived on the known and was comforted by knowing what to expect from most situations. Although just 17, she had two younger sisters and a younger brother she helped raise because her mother and father worked all the time to make ends meet and put away enough for any possible emergency. Could she leave her family and all the responsibility she carried?

Angelika was the oldest at home since her sister Rosemary, or Romi, married, so Geli was responsible for helping the most. Her sister Christel was 14, practically an adult in Germany, and was taking on more responsibility, so a daring move to Florida seemed feasible without abandoning her commitment to her family. It was time to stretch her comfort zone and take a chance. She thought this move would not be forever, and maybe her life would change for the better. Did she honestly want to manage the business of a department store year after year?

Her airplane ticket arrived in the mail, and on November 11th, 1974, she boarded her flight to sunny South Florida. Family and friends are left behind, and the hope of new adventures in a tropical land across the ocean awaits.

Chapter 5
Second Date Proposal

Angie's host family, the Morgans, was quite different from any typical German family. Mrs. Morgan was gone a lot, shopping, lessons, or taking care of the family business. Mr. Morgan was a dentist with a thriving practice and was gone most of the time. Angie was home with the children, ages five, three, and almost one, who were starting lives of American privilege. Mrs. Morgan was happy to have Angie's help, giving her the time and space to be more than a mother and family caretaker.

Geli and Christhilde biking along the ocean. Palm Beach, Florida, 1975.

During these times, Angie watched the kids and spent hours on the phone talking with Chris. She never had a home phone in

Germany. Her family never even had a car. When you needed a phone, you went to the local post office and paid to make calls. Buses and trains connected every town and city and would always run on time, so a car was unnecessary. Angie and Chris, whose host family lives 10 miles away in North Palm Beach, talked about everything on the phone. So much was new, and Angie could meet the kids' needs while on the 20-foot coiled cord from the wall-mounted phone in the kitchen, with the receiver held to her ear with her shoulder.

Angelika is enjoying ice cream. West Palm Beach, Florida

More than once, they discussed their most recently arranged date with Michael and me. Chris had no interest in meeting Michael again, but Angie explored the possible outcomes of Saturday's upcoming "date" with me. She was still puzzled by my bold move to kiss her on their short beach walk. She said to Chris, "Did he plan that? Was he truly interested in me or just female companionship? Is answering personal ads from the paper how he met all his dates? Was he possibly really weird and good at hiding it"? She thought not and said, "he seemed genuine. He was gentle and looked at you through honest eyes". She looked forward to seeing me again but was a little nervous.

The first time you are with someone, the newness of the friendship overshadows almost everything else about the other person. Beyond that first meeting, you start to see the actual person. If they are hiding something, the curtain begins to open. If they were unnaturally funny, they would start to get old. A second meeting would be good. She did feel safe with me and hoped she was right. Even though the language barrier would keep many conversations shallow, Angie was highly perceptive and knew she could trust her feelings.

Saturday evening arrived, and Angie waited in her pool house apartment. Just a big room, a foyer, and a bathroom but nicely appointed with sliding doors that opened to the shallow end of the pool. She saw me drive up and came to meet me at the gate. We smiled and talked about how cool living in a pool house was and how our meeting last week was a pleasant surprise. I briefly shared how skeptical I had been for a month before we met, and Angie hinted at how our first meeting turned out unexpectedly. We both seemed comfortable and looked forward to the night.

I had thought about what we might do tonight but didn't have a real plan. Probably find a casual restaurant to eat and return to the beach to walk and talk. A movie didn't seem like a good idea, and I wanted to talk and get to know Angie better. I planned to avoid the bar scene. One time was undoubtedly enough. The fake atmosphere and pricey beverages were wrong in so many ways. We talked about what each other might like to do that evening, and Angie suggested she would like to cook dinner for us at my place. I didn't read too much into the suggestion and agreed a simple dinner would be more relaxed and personal. We could get to know each other without the distractions of others and spend less time in the car, which Angie liked.

We arrived at Sunset Village, where I showed her around my New Moon trailer, which took only a minute. We strolled around the trailer park and then returned to sit on the awning-covered patio, where it was cool enough, and talked for some time. I didn't have any snacks, so we discussed what food I had that she might prepare.

Sunset Village, Riviera Beach, Florida

Since becoming a vegetarian seven weeks earlier, my menu had shrunk to little more than peanut butter and jelly sandwiches. For better meals, I boiled a pot of potatoes and a canned vegetable, then added cream of celery soup and wheat germ to create a modified quick casserole. That night, we settled for a box of macaroni and cheese with a can of corn and, of course, lime juice for that slight exotic flair.

The food was OK, but our conversation was fun. Almost every sentence that went deeper into any thought took some explanation and added description with hand gestures to overcome our language difference. Angie knew many words and could talk her way through the basics, but most of the details, which made the stories we shared more exciting and allowed us to get to know each other better, needed creative supplements to draw a virtual mental image. It was rather fun. We listened to each other attentively and laughed a lot. Angie shared her recent trip, a few hours north with the Morgan family, to see a "racket" and how amazing it was. "I don't get it, a racket. I know I'm missing something?" I said. "You know, a racket, lots of fire, and very fast," she motioned with her pointed hand as it shot up and away. "See, a racket," as she made a swooshing sound. "Oh! A rocket," I exclaimed. We both laughed and were now close enough that our hands, arms, and legs briefly made contact occasionally.

We enjoyed each other's company and became more comfortable together. We listened to soft music, definitely a Cat Stevens kind of night, and quietly talked. As darkness settled in, I mentioned the expected noise tolerance at Sunset Village. Then, I explained how the neighbors' proximity and natural curiosity about what we might be doing would attract their attention. Our laughs and labored but fun conversations turned to the more intimate side as we again held hands and shared some kissing. Nothing too heavy, but we both felt the warmth in each other's touch.

The night was beautiful, and our drive back to take Angie home was relaxed. Angie wrote down the Morgan's phone number for me and said to call her during the day. Mrs. Morgan had a slight issue with Angie spending so much time on the phone already. The line was often busy when Mrs. Morgan called home to check on things. I agreed to limit my calling to those times and would keep it as short as possible.

After midnight, we quietly pulled up to Angie's pool house. The windows were down, a gentle breeze floated into the car, and there was almost no sound beyond our exchange of the night's positive comments. It was an unexpected shock when Angie mentioned her desire to remain in the States longer by getting married. She explained how she and Chris had discussed doing this with someone, no strings attached, platonically, with a divorce after six months. A marriage would be just a piece of paper to keep from being deported before they had experienced more of this different land that was so compelling. I rarely react too strongly, but I was puzzled by her mention of a possible marriage. I wondered, was tonight a ruse? I thought not. I was genuinely starting to like her and didn't want this to end before it even started. I explained myself briefly and told her I had divorced from a misguided marriage barely a year ago and could not even think about doing it again. Angie let it drop. It was too much to ask. We said goodnight with one last lingering kiss, and we each slipped back into the night of unknown certainty. Our future was the unknown, and our feelings were the certainty.

I called Angie several times the next week, and only once did Mrs. Morgan answer the phone. Although it was easier to communicate in person, where facial expressions and gestures helped make sense of thoughts poorly expressed, these short conversations added to our fondness for each other. Then, we increased our time together to several times a week, and it wasn't long before Angie spent most of the nights with me at my place. We spent more time together: at the beach, walks to the Publix grocery store and the local Riviera Beach donut shop, and a long walk down A1A to the Twin City Mall, where we would splurge on a shared tuna sub in the air-conditioned oasis. Eventually, Angie talked with the Morgans about reducing her time helping and agreed to move in with me. I gave her rides back to the Morgans for a while, but it wasn't long before she stopped going altogether. Their arrangement was for Angie to work for six months in return for her plane ticket, and she did that.

Together now, for about six weeks, I was a bit concerned that Angie might get deported and finally brought up the possibility that it might work to get married. Just legally, so Angie could remain longer without looking over her shoulder. Her six-month visa had expired more than a month before. We would marry with the condition that Angie keep her $600 savings in the bank to finance our divorce after six months. That should satisfy the Immigration and Naturalization Agency, I thought. The marriage would be a convenient arrangement, not a lifetime commitment to each other.

We had become quite close and genuinely appreciated our growing bond. Meeting each other and spending this formative time together gave us both a sense of purpose and direction we both had been seeking. Angie was stable and practical and saw meaning in doing everything she did. I was adventurous and spontaneous and could lighten life with humor and fun. We weren't exactly opposites, but we were different enough to bring our other qualities to grow our relationship as we each discovered our desired path.

We filed the papers for a marriage license at the West Palm Beach courthouse and got our blood tests. A week later, I took the morning off, and we went to a justice of the peace and married in a simple ceremony. Ironically, this was the same place in Lake Park that notarized my divorce papers the previous year. The husband-and-wife justices of the peace officiated, and my good friends Steve and Marie joined us as witnesses. Pleasant music played as we stood before a podium with a large, colorful peacock wall hanging carpet as our backdrop in case someone wanted to take a picture.

Steve, Bert, Angie, and Marie at the marriage ceremony. Lake Park, Florida

It was not precisely a momentous day, but we dressed up to make it memorable nonetheless. Angie, in her jeans and simple white silk top. Her waist-long reddish-brown hair made her beauty even more radiant. I wore my favorite Levi's light blue denim, long-sleeve shirt with pearlesque snaps for buttons embroidered with a traditional Chinese red dragon across the back. This shirt went well with my old Levi's jeans, with dozens of patches I had sewn over holes and rips. Over the last few years, I learned to sew, keeping these pants in service with scrap material from wherever I could find something worthy. I dabbled in rudimentary, free-style embroidery of symbolic references like the pot leaf on my bell bottom pant leg. Sandals were always the footwear of choice for us both, especially on July 11th, in the heat of the summer.

Bert and Angie are officially married. July 11, 1975

With legal papers in hand, we went straight to the Port Authority of Palm Beach and answered some questions from a skeptical immigration official about the true nature of our marriage. We passed the examination and received the OK for Angie's green card application.

As soon as we exited the air-conditioned building at the Port Authority, we noticed a group of people gathered by the rocky jetty, pointing to the open sea. We all strained to see a water spout or ocean tornado churning offshore. The dark clouds and spout were visible, as was the beginning of a rainbow, which we agreed was a good sign for what we had accomplished that day—a beautiful act of nature to mark our choice. We thought it was a good omen, and we were right.

It was 11:30, and we looked for a restaurant to celebrate our special day. This lunch was somewhat of a big deal. We had never really gone out to a sit-down establishment; money, what little there was, was better spent on essentials. Today, we splurged. A Chinese restaurant along A1A caught our eye, and we stopped. We were the day's first customers and ordered a pot of tea and two lunch specials. This lunch was a special and unique experience for us both. When I mentioned to the hostess that we were just married, she insisted we keep one of the decorative tea cups with the restaurant's name on the side as a memento, which we did after thanking her.

Chapter 6
Becoming "(Un)Comfortably Numb"

After lunch, I dropped Angie back at the trailer and made it to work by one. When I mentioned the day's events to the mayor's secretary, she insisted I return home to be with my bride. I didn't think Angie was "my anything" possessive, but I cared for her now and gladly took the rest of the day off. The trash cans and floors at city hall would wait another day.

A typical day in the City of Palm Beach Gardens was slow, with few people who didn't work there entering the complex. It was mostly a place for the employees of the small city to take care of business or socialize. It was a great place to study after I completed my work. I often hung out in the department with the most activity, the police station on the ground level. I don't recall ever seeing a person locked up in either of the two jail cells, but the two radio dispatchers were usually busy, and one or two of the dozen or more cops would frequently stop to talk. The police chief was always in his office or on the road, and the plain-clothed lieutenant blended in with us civilians stealthfully. The sergeant ran the whole place and was always alert for anything unusual. I would stand and watch the teletype spit out proprietary information about possible criminal behavior or necessary police matters. Instructions to "be on the lookout" for missing persons or stolen cars, quickly typed across the paper scroll. But this day, I was returning to spend quality time with my new best friend and wife.

We lived together that summer in our cozy 1958 New Moon trailer through the heat of each day. The temperature would become intolerable by 10 or 11 each morning until the daily summer monsoon would arrive like clockwork and pour down for 30 minutes or more. Ah! The refreshing cool air and minor flash floods rolled down the street, and then again, the sun and heat turned the trailer into a sauna. The only place to be was under our covered patio surrounded by bushes, while the neighbors in their trailer, maybe 20 feet away, all closed up in their air-conditioned stupor, reflected more heat.

We fixed up the trailer more to Angie's liking, got rid of the pull-out, traditional sleeper couch, and, in its place, put a covered mattress on the floor. The stereo record player was on the built-in shelf over the front window with an awning. I organized my rock albums alphabetically on both sides of the stereo speakers. In our small bedroom, I built a two-by-10-inch board frame on top of thick plywood and cement blocks, which held our new queen-size waterbed. I traded a dime bag of pot to a friend of a friend for this waterbed several months before and finally took the time to set it up. It took three hours to fill the whole bed with water, which was cold. The cool temperature of the bed was refreshing during the day, but we needed several blankets under us at night to stay warm. The waterbed fit neatly, wall to wall, in our small bedroom with no more than a tiny, trapezoid-shaped floor space to access the adjacent bathroom or open the bedroom door. You could stand in one spot and touch the bed, bathroom sink, bedroom door, and outside back door, and with a bit of a stretch, open the old rounded-top fridge outside the bedroom door in the kitchen. It was pretty cozy.

I laid new carpet in the living room with so much left over that I extended it halfway up the walls and folded the top edge to make a soft loop on walls around the room at head level as you sat on the floor mattress. There was once an air conditioner in the window next to the front door that a simple glass pane had replaced with no curtain. This three-foot by three-foot, square solid glass pane provided an unfettered view of our living space at night. I couldn't afford and didn't want a typical window treatment, so I bought some art paints and covered the inside with a decent reproduction of the backside artwork from *Foreigner*, Cat Stevens' new album. It was a scene of a simple cabana supporting a hammock on the beach, looking out over the ocean with a table, bottle of wine, and two glasses. It looked nice and blocked out snooping curiosity, but at night, with the inside lights on, it looked fantastic from the outside. It was out of place for Sunset Village, but we loved it. I surmised that if I was careful, took my time, and made corrections when something wasn't quite right, I could accomplish something beautiful for which I thought I had no talent.

This adjustment would also become true with my maintaining a relationship. I was beginning to take my time with our relationship. I was being more careful and starting to consider my behavior and its impact before I acted more than I had in past relationships. Something beautiful was beginning to develop, and like my painting, it, too, was terrific.

Until I met Angie, I had no success figuring out what to do with my life or how to connect with anyone except my youngest sister. Joyce was almost eight years older than me and was always there for me throughout my life. I had two even older sisters who either left home or became independent at an early age and were not around much while I was growing up. Joyce came to my Little League baseball games, took me Trick or Treating, and even took me on some of her dates. She always remained close to my parents and me, even when she married and moved from Michigan to Florida. In my mid-teen years, I would fly to Florida and spend several Sumer weeks with Joyce and her husband, Frank. When she divorced, she returned home to Michigan while figuring out what to do with her life and her two kids, Stephanie and Chris. When I had no place to stay or wanted a fresh start, I went to live with Joyce. We were as close as I ever was to anyone. After I started making it on my own in Florida, Joyce moved to Texas, but we stayed close and called or wrote letters often. I was back in college and liked it, maintained a steady job, and was finally building a meaningful relationship with Angie. Life was looking up for me. I saw the path to follow, and it felt good.

Angie and I had many good times living in our New Moon trailer. One "mood-altered" night, we stayed up late conversing in nothing more than whispers for hours. We were quiet as mice, with the softest music playing on the turntable. Cat Stevens was barely audible, but we knew the songs so well we could hear the complete rhythm in our heightened, sensitive minds. After hours of almost silent, rushing conversation, we slipped out of the sleepy Sunset Village and stealthily strolled down A1A to the all-night donut shop. As cars hurried past and we were far from the sleeping Sunset Village, we realized we were still talking in an absurd whisper. My voice steadily rose as I joked around, not stopping at an acceptable level to exaggerated, booming exclamations, "WE WERE FREEEEE! to TALK AS LOUD AS WE WISHED!" Angie laughed without a care in the world until we both had tears of pent-up emotion.

We ran to the donut shop, a sprinkling of night people sitting appropriately distanced from each other as we slid into a booth on the same side, resuming our quiet, exaggerated whispers. Our melodramatic whispering made it even funnier, and we giggled non-stop until two donuts arrived. I assumed the lead role as the paranoid hippie and humorously convinced Angie that everyone was looking at us, and one was a COP! The bite of donuts we each ate stuck in our mouths and would not go down. Food? What were we thinking? We could not swallow anything. Money left on the table, we scampered out to the safety of the street, where our antics continued until, in exhaustion, we slipped back to the comfort of our new waterbed and held each other close until sleep finally came just before dawn.

Our life together did have some problematic issues. I would remain mostly oblivious and happy with our new life together, but Angie increasingly felt more alone and struggled with this uncomfortable feeling. Many nights, we lay in our waterbed while Angie tried to discuss her difficulties and get me to open up about my emotions. I would listen and try to understand how she felt, but I never really did and would retreat into a numb state. Our shared life fulfilled her material and physical needs, but I would too often isolate myself emotionally from her and repeatedly withdraw. I would escape to my music and smoke pot, and even though I was still present, Angie could not feel me. I wasn't seeing her the way she needed to be understood. There was this invisible barrier Angie sensed, and I did not. Angie was no victim, and any issue that stood in the way of our relationship, she would talk through it until there was an understanding or agreement of its crucial impact and an acknowledged plan to remove the barrier. She saw the future of relationships; if ours were to progress, it would require some fine-tuning.

On the other hand, I assumed my family's way of totally ignoring a problem and maybe, hopefully, not repeating the same error. Ignoring the issue did not work, and I would continue the same attitude or behavior again. Angie talked while I stared at the dark ceiling over the waterbed, focusing as much on the bed's motion as the deafening silence of my mind, which overwhelmed me to the point of uncomfortable numbness.

Trying to adjust to this new life, Angie deeply missed the connections she always had with her friends. Their late-night talks, making sense of the world around them and the feelings that came from starting adulthood, brought clarity to her and helped her understand the world. Adding our unexpected relationship to the mix here in Florida made her miss her friends even more. She had no one to talk her through things and help her see her path.

Even though she enjoyed this new life, she was starting to become deeply lonely. So young, barely 18, and far from home. We had no phone to talk with Chris, and everything here was new. The anchors of stability she had counted on her entire life, which kept her grounded, were gone. She felt her old life drifting away and could not replace her need for companionship with just me. I know how much she cared for me, but I wasn't enough to fill all the close relationships she depended on her whole life. Those nights in the waterbed, I became mentally exhausted and would fall asleep, issues unresolved. Angie would lay there depressed and wide awake. The deep loneliness seemed to have no bottom for her. The one-sided discussion would continue, not every night, but with increased frequency and no resolution in sight.

Life, for us, was still good. We spent weekends with my friends, playing volleyball or going to the beach, but still no deep connections for Angie. My friends were not the ones with whom she could develop a close relationship. She couldn't find that in such a short time. I was not doing anything to help her make those connections either, and we stumbled along. We were happy, but it didn't progress to the level Angie needed. So many things about America were superficial. The shallowness she was experiencing wasn't entirely negative, but my culture lacked the depth that had always been her foundation. Her relationship with me was fun and caring, but I would not open up to her and share my inner feelings.

I don't believe I ever opened up to myself in this regard; it wasn't my way. For all its positives, my life was superficial and prevented us from sufficiently cementing a solid base. She missed that. Still, Angie and I grew closer. She took care of me and cared for me. I kept things lively and depended on her emotionally and to share life. Our relationship grew with and from each other, but life was good. Angie's loneliness, however, did not go away.

Part 2
A Fork in the Road

Chapter 7
The Honey Half-moon

By late August, between my Second Summer Session and Fall Quarter, we decided to take off and show Angie more of the United States. The $600 Angie had saved for the divorce we instead spent on an almost honeymoon or a honey half-moon. We planned a camping trip to the Smoky Mountains in western North Carolina. Sunset Village neighbors Chris and Alan had friends who moved to that area and bought an old farmhouse on five acres near Asheville, North Carolina, for $10,000. The farmer still had more land to sell, so we thought we would stop by on the trip to dream a little. Alan loaned us all the needed gear: a tent, sleeping bags, a camping stove, and lanterns. Angie packed food and essentials in our cooler. I loaded the Pinto with maps, 8-track tapes, and gear and got the car road-ready for our two-week adventure.

After a pleasant day of interstate travel north, we spent the night in Atlanta. We lucked upon a quaint and inexpensive hotel right on Peachtree Street after only stopping at two others first. A quick inspection of these first hotels, model rooms, or the actual room where we would stay revealed some smelly or unsavory conditions, and we passed on them. After a quick in-room picnic from our cooler, we spent the evening at the bustling Atlanta Underground, a vast venue of shops, bars, and restaurants with an atmosphere reminiscent of a network of spacious caverns. The Underground was flush with tourists spending their money and keeping the local economy alive. In contrast, groups of long-haired young locals hung out in the side avenues, discretely keeping to themselves with the faint smell of marijuana punctuating the air.

We spent the evening window shopping, visiting a leather goods shop, a record store, and others. Meandering through the shadowy expanse, we splurged on a shared lime daiquiri in a commemorative pewter-like mug with a glass bottom. We stopped at a kiosk that put on a remarkable candle-making demonstration with the dipped wax, colored layers of the star-shaped column base, and the deft slicing and twisting of the still-warm edges into rainbow-like appendages. We watched in amazement for 30 minutes as the artists produced finished candles resembling colorful wax fountains. These candles were actual pieces of art and too expensive for our budget. Not wanting to spend the five bucks for the smallest rainbow fountain candle, we bought a lovely, simple candle as a memory instead.

Now tired from the long drive and activity of the Underground, we collapsed in our small but clean room on the third floor, looking out over Peachtree Street. We were excited about getting into the mountains and driving on slower country roads to enjoy the ride through rural territory. Our bond grew closer that night as we fell asleep in each other's arms to the light din of city traffic on the street below.

The following day, we got an early start, unfolding and analyzing our new map of the Southeast United States we had picked up from the free rack at the Gulf gas station before we left Atlanta. After a couple of hours driving through some busy towns, we entered the foothills of the Appalachian Mountains. The roads were now two lanes, and the traffic was moving slower. The cool morning was warming, so we rolled down the windows to enjoy the fresh country air and settled into the pastoral rolling hills of farmland and hardwood forests, canopied by a beautiful clear blue sky draped over the approaching mountains. As we drove up our first big mountain road, I pushed an 8-track tape into the player and turned up the volume to listen to the beautiful flute music of The Marshall Tucker Band's "Can't

You See." The finger-picked guitar intro to this song, followed by the flute solo, always gave us chills and, at this moment, would set the mood for our next three days of rustic camping in the Great Smoky Mountains National Park. We headed up the steep mountain and followed the music, "Gonna take a freight train... don't care where it goes...gonna climb a mountain, the highest mountain..." We listened to the song three times in a row before we let the 8-track continue playing the remainder of the album. Our trip was beginning to open us up to another level of appreciation for our new surroundings and each other.

The flute music serenaded us as we ascended the slopes and dipped through the valleys. We finally chose a campground from the many choices on our map and set up our camp in the National Park on the top of the highest mountain. I gathered some firewood while Angie prepared dinner from the cooler. She pulled out potato salad, macaroni salad, coleslaw, and bread and butter. After dinner, I took to carving our names on a large stick. I'm unsure what to do with it once finished, but it looked pretty good. When I showed it to Angie, she politely pointed out that I had misspelled her name. "Angilika", crap! I exclaimed, "Never could get the German spelling right."

Angelika, camping on their honey half-moon.

Darkness came early in the forested mountains. I built a fire, and we warmed ourselves from the cool air. There is something magical about a fire. We sat close together and poked at the fire with long sticks, whipping them around and making tracers in the dark. The hot coals turned to faint embers, and then we tucked in for the night.

Bert, hiking on their honey half-moon.

The next few days, life slowed down for us. We went on long hikes and had in-depth talks by a mountain river. A visit to the Headquarters of the Great Smoky Mountains National Park and demonstration village at the Blue Ridge Parkway's start proved informative and enjoyable. We drove through Cherokee, where I splurged and bought the first volume of the *Foxfire* books. These books were a local high school English class project in Rabun Gap-Nacoochee School in Rabun Gap, GA, that chronicled Appalachian Mountain life.

English teacher Eliot Wigginton had his student interview their oldest relatives to discover how they lived before this modern era. They researched hog dressing, mountain crafts and recipes, faith healing, moonshine, and many other ways of long-forgotten mountain culture. It was a way of preserving the past before it vanished and described a way of life we could benefit from in this modern world.

I was fascinated with the section explaining how to build a log cabin, everything from which trees to cut, how to strip the bark, and how to notch the ends to lock them in place. I dreamed of one day making one for us. These cool mountain days were nothing fancy or even remarkable; they were three days of easy living, back to nature, and just us. It was nice.

════════

We left the Smokies, stopped by our neighbors, Alan's and Chris's friend's farmhouse near Hendersonville, North Carolina, and talked with the farmer who had some land for sale but none with a house. Finding these friends was not easy, with only an address. Our map got us close, but we had to stop at two gas stations and eventually a Post Office to pinpoint their location. The friends were busy, but they had a phone and called the friendly farmer who came to meet us.

He drove us all over his land, which contained dozens of acres of soybean crops, and he described how these soybeans would be the big cash crop of the future. We had no idea what a soybean tasted like or how it could become so popular, but we did not doubt his wisdom. Most of the land we saw was unexceptional, and none had a house or other structure. The farmer did show us a small two-acre piece with a creek flowing through a grove of trees that was absolutely beautiful. We talked it over, then decided to buy it for $1,800 and gave the farmer a deposit of $100 with an agreement to make monthly payments of $50 until we paid it off. I signed his rudimentary, handwritten contract as a scared feeling developed in the pit of Angie's stomach. We had no long-term plans and the idea of buying land so far away from what was familiar set off too many alarms in her head. We knew no one here, and it was so far from our more familiar Florida.

Living in Florida was far different from her life in Germany, but this rural place would make her even more isolated. I loved this property's potential and talked about building a log cabin above the stream on a hillside clearing and maybe learning to live off the land. Although Angie was afraid, she didn't want to dampen my dreams and quietly agreed to the purchase. It wasn't a huge risk and might even be a good investment for our future. We would find out from our neighbor Alan that their North Carolina friends had called them and were upset about our purchase. The understanding was the beautiful two-acre parcel we were purchasing was to be a community common area. After our journey, already feeling somewhat overextended financially, I decided we were not ready to commit to this land purchase fully, so I wrote to the farmer asking to end the deal. He agreed and sent back our $100 deposit. Mountain life for us would have to wait.

The next stop on the honey half-moon I planned was to show Angie where I had grown up in Michigan. I wanted her to meet my grandmother, Fannie Kennedy, or Grandma K. We took I-75 north from Knoxville, Tennessee, through Kentucky and the flat lands of Ohio north of Dayton, then northwest through Ft. Wayne, Indiana, into Michigan.

We arrived first in Kalamazoo, where I showed Angie my old high school, Loy Norrix, and Milham Park, where I had many good memories of family picnics and evening hangouts with my high school friends. We spent the afternoon with my grandmother at her one-bedroom apartment in an old classic-styled house just off West

Vine and South Burdick Streets. I lived in Michigan as a child, and most of my relatives on my mother's side lived in Kalamazoo.

This side of my family included some of the founders of Kalamazoo back in the mid-1800s, the "Browns." My family moved from Kalamazoo in my junior year of high school, and I only returned a few times to see my grandmother. Even though Grandma K had probably 20 or more grandkids and many more great-grandkids, I always felt special around her, and I still looked for a piece of hard candy in her purse every visit. Now, with almost all my other connections in Michigan broken, I vowed to come back and visit her every year or so.

Grandma Kennedy and Angie, Kalamazoo, Michigan, 1975.

Grandma K took to Angie immediately, and they talked for an hour or so. Now in her early 80s, I wasn't sure if this might be the last time I'd get a chance to see her. This visit was more difficult than before, and our goodbye was more emotional, but I wanted to show Angie as much as I could of my past in these few days in Michigan.

Driving two hours east, we spent the day in Jackson and Clark Lake, where I lived during my late Junior and senior years at Napoleon High School. I showed Angie where we lived on Clark Lake, where my parents managed the sprawling Consumer Power Employee Club. Every Summer, employees, their families, and friends from all over the state came to enjoy the large clubhouse, manicured grounds, and plentiful activities in the shaded oasis on the lake.

We lived in a two-bedroom apartment above the large ballroom overlooking the lake. Below was a full-service snack bar and grill, two pool tables, shuffleboard and ping pong tables, and a massive fireplace. Twenty or more large round tables and chairs, all surrounded by floor-to-ceiling windows, provided a beautiful view of the shaded grounds, the beach, and the lake. There was an 18-hole mini-golf course, canoe livery, and a large sandy beach with a long dock extending into the water. The large swimming area was roped off, with a floating swimming platform and diving board a good swim from the end of the dock. The fenced-in grounds encompassed a vast picnic area under the shade of large oak trees with barbecue grills at dozens of tables.

From Memorial Day through Labor Day, the club was packed with power company employees from all over the state seven days a week. After the season, the employees used the clubhouse several times for parties, meetings, or special functions. Otherwise, it was just our home, to do with as we pleased. The two summers I lived and worked here were the best innocent times of my formative years.

I drove Angie by a country club pool where best schoolmates Ed, Danny, Jody, and I went for a clandestine midnight swim some years back. We parked a few blocks away in a nice neighborhood, jumped the tall fence at the country club, and swam in the cool water in early June. I remembered one of my friends taking Ed's underwear and running them up the flagpole. Deciding we had enough cold water, I found a golf cart next door by the pro shop with the key left in the ignition. Although none of us drank alcohol, we drove around hooting and hollering like a bunch of drunks, Ed and me in the seats and Jody and Danny sitting on the front fenders acting like turn signals as we plowed through a sand trap and skirted the green. Tired and cold, we returned the two blocks to my car in our underwear around 1 AM and found two police officers going through my car. Jody said, "I'm outta here," and took off in nothing but his "whitey tighties."

Danny, Ed, and I approached my car and placed ourselves at the mercy of the two police officers. I had left my keys on the back tire to avoid losing them in our high jinks. We left our clothes in the back seat. The police found my keys and searched my car for identification or possibly drugs. Upon our return, they were friendly and reasonable about our late-night mischief and let us off the hook with a stern warning. We were still 20 miles from home, so we drove slowly around the neighborhoods, looking for Jody for 15 minutes with no luck. What would he do because his clothes and wallet were in my car? Just about to give up the search, in the pitch dark, I saw Jody running after my car, waving his arms over his head in the faint glow of my tail lights. Jody said every set of headlights he saw were the cops. He ran between houses to hide when we drove by, thinking I was a cop. The night was good for a laugh and would be the last escapade of my high school years.

We drove right past my ex-wife's parents' house in Jackson, but I had no intention of stopping. They were great people, but I figured they wouldn't care to see me since the divorce. Then I showed Angie the "strip" where all the cool dudes drove caravan-like in their souped-up cars. Each Friday and Saturday night, a parade of vehicles slowly progressed from the drive-in root beer stand at one end of West

Michigan Avenue to a McDonald's parking lot on the east end of town. The parking lot overflowed, and a few even went inside to purchase a hamburger and fries. Each car was filled with three or four boys full of life, wasting time trying to impress carloads of girls or push the hired police just far enough to make them mad or laugh; it was a fine line.

Two days in Michigan was enough, and then we pulled out our stack of free gas station maps of the states following the Mississippi River to plan our route south. Once we returned to Florida, I wanted Angie to meet my good friends, Andy and Audrey, near Tallahassee but, most importantly, meet my daughter Kimberly in Fort Walton Beach. She was 18 months old, and the last time I saw her, she had started walking. First, we would travel south to Ponchatoula, Louisiana, to surprise my best Air Force buddy, Mike.

Chapter 8
Bayou Country

We drove through the night with a brief stop in St. Louis, where we walked along the Mississippi River park and visited the famous St. Louis Arch, Gateway to the West. We decided the dollar trip to the top was too much, so we just looked around, then stood with our toes and chins touching the inside of the arch, looking up the colossal curve till we almost fell backward. It was time to continue our journey south to Ponchatoula. I drove as late as possible, and then we slept in the car in a rest area in Mississippi before getting to Ponchatoula around ten the following morning.

I looked up Mike in the phone book, hoping to find his address so we could surprise him. I hadn't seen or talked to him since my discharge from the Air Force almost two years before. I didn't find Mike's name in the book but recognized his father's, so we stopped there. Mike's mother listened to my surprise plan and told me how to find Mike and Linda's new house. Within a few minutes, we were knocking on his door. "Surprise! Guess who?" I exclaimed, and Mike said, "What the he-ell, you son of a bitch". With my two years' worth of long hair and full, untrimmed beard, Mike took a second to figure out what had happened. We reminisced all day and into the night while Angie and Linda got to know each other.

The next day, Mike took us on a fast, motorized Jon boat ride through the swampy bayou to his grandmother's small house on her tiny, remote island. We saw several alligators lying in the nearby rushes and many people fishing and trapping, but no water skiers, imagine that. "You could get lost out here," I mused, "You sure you know where you're goin'? You're not paying me back for this surprise visit, are you? You got enough gas in this boat?" After maybe 40 minutes on the water, we pulled up to a rickety, short dock and walked up an overgrown path to a small, weathered, wood-plank-sided cabin. Spanish moss hanging all over the place, weeds, grass up to your waist, dense bushes, and a canopy of trees overhead made it so dark it looked more like 8 in the evening than 11 in the morning. The heat was sweltering as we walked through the broken screen door of the almost dilapidated porch.

"Memaw!" Mike yelled several times to announce our arrival, likely so as not to get shot. Mike led the way into the dark, surprisingly cool house, and Memaw called out, "At you, Mikey? Why you a doin' way out he-ah?" Mike introduced us to Memaw, who seemed happy to meet us. She then went into her small kitchen to fetch some bitter lemonade and offered us a snack. Mike and his Memaw mostly talked while we listened. He hadn't been to see her in over a year. Memaw lived alone; she must be in her late seventies, but she seemed to get by all right. A nearby relative would stop in to bring things and check on her. She had no phone, only an old generator for the fridge, a few lights, and a fan. She kept the generator going during the day until supper was over, then shut it down and kept the small fridge closed till morning. A cistern well provided enough fresh water for herself, and she washed her clothes in an old wringer washer and used an outhouse down a short path in the backyard. When I went out to relieve myself, I chose to pee in the weeds. The smell coming from the outhouse on that hot day was offensive.

Angie tried to join the conversation with Mike and his Memaw, but the Creole dialect was cryptic to her. You could clearly understand some individual words she said, but the rhythmic cadence and exaggerated inflections were more like a song and nearly impossible to decipher. I gave up taking part as well. Mike and Memaw enjoyed seeing each other again, though, and hugged and kissed as Mike promised, "Not to stay-way sa lang, nes time." Angie and I were amazed. It was like stepping back in time. The beauty of Memaw's place, the language, and the preserved culture that was as strong as it was unique made a memorable impression. We wished we had brought the camera.

Linda had fixed a dinner of crawfish etouffee by the time we returned. This meal was not what you would call fast food. Linda spent most of the day going to market, boiling, cleaning the tiny crawfish, chopping the veggies, and sautéing the sauce. She talked about how this traditional recipe was passed down through generations of her family and served on special occasions. It was a real delicacy, she exclaimed. Their two young daughters joined us for dinner, and our conversations continued all night. Angie never felt very comfortable at Mike's and Linda's. She spent time with Linda, who was very friendly and hospitable but more of a traditional homemaker, and it was clear they were pretty different, with little in common. I enjoyed reminiscing with my old buddy, but Angie felt she was just along for the ride and was glad when we left the following day.

As we left, we thanked Linda and Mike for their kind hospitality, good food, and once-in-a-lifetime experience on the bayou and hugged. Mike promised to repay the surprise visit sometime when I least expected it and smacked me so hard on the back that I knew it would be true. As we drove off, Mike looked quizzically at a bumper sticker on the rear of my Pinto that said, "Support your local police." Mike shook his head and told Linda, "The last bumper sticker he had on his old van said, 'Beautify America, shoot a redneck.' I can't figure that guy out." When I worked for the city of Palm Beach Gardens and had several cops as acquaintances, I willingly accepted the bumper sticker they gave me as a joke. I put it on my rear bumper, feeling It wouldn't hurt if I ever got pulled over, with long hair and all.

The half-day trip along I-10 and US Highway 98 brought us into Fort Walton Beach, Florida, around two in the afternoon. I would finally have Angie meet my daughter, Kimberly. Who, with my ex-wife, Peggy, were still living there, or so I thought. Peggy had a phone, and I had left several messages with her housemate saying we planned to stop by sometime in early September. I hadn't seen Kimberly since Peggy left her with me for three weeks after her injury from a motorcycle accident in February. I was excited to see how much she had grown, and I shared many stories of the relevant history of my failed marriage and Kimberly's young life with Angie.

We pulled into a driveway at my most recent address for Peggy. With some apprehension but excited with joy in my heart, I knocked on the door, only to be greeted by Peggy's former housemate. She sadly informed me Peggy and Kimberly had recently moved back to Michigan to live with her parents. Thoughts swirled around in my head: they're not here. We left Michigan the week before 900 miles away. When could I see Kimberly again? Why didn't Peggy answer the damn phone when I called? Sorrow and anger filled my heart as I drove away to find the nearest pay phone. I still had Peggy's parents' phone number in my small, black address book, and after a few rings, Peggy answered the phone.

The operator said, "Hold, please," and asked me to "deposit 95 cents for the first three minutes". I struggled to sort the change I had placed on the small shelf before me to insert the proper amount. Peggy could sense my frustration, hurt, and anger almost immediately but didn't seem to care, and maybe she was even a touch happy.

Peggy had good reason to be resentful. We were both young and had married without good cause. I was never really into the new arrangement and did too many stupid things, causing it to fail, including my one-time infidelity after we separated. Peggy had tried to embrace family mode, but I never followed. The bickering and bad times overtook the better times, and Peggy moved out. The marriage ended shortly after Kimberly was four months old, and I left to live with my sister. I never looked back except to check on or visit Kimberly.

Peggy almost enjoyed telling me she had passed me on the road in Michigan near her parents' house last week. She somehow thought I would stop by, which I never did, and she could not contact me when I did not.

I hung up the phone, returned to the car, and explained what had happened to Angie. I was lost, torn between being angry and sad to have missed seeing Kimberly. It would have been nice for Angie to meet her as well. I could do nothing now except return home, where school's fall semester would start in three days.

Angie, sensing my pain, leaned over and hugged me deeply. Even though I tried not to show the hurt as much as the displeasure, she intuitively knew how I felt inside and said, "I love you." I was shocked. I had told Angie I loved her several times but never heard this from her. She was very much in touch with her feelings and knew love was much more than being with someone and enjoying each other. She had held off, telling me she loved me until that moment. Now, she felt it and meant it. Wow! I now had another layer to add to my current state of mind. At least, this was a profoundly satisfying layer I hoped would lead to a stronger relationship. Deep down, this was good; my feelings gained some clarity, and I could move forward. A focal point that was not there before was coming into the picture. Sadness moved back a step, and hope moved forward. We drove on. Few words were spoken, but so much was said.

After a two-hour drive, we pulled into Marianna, a small town an hour northwest of Tallahassee, and stopped to call Audrey for directions to her house. Audrey told me she and Andy had separated but were still good friends. I connected with them briefly before I left the Air Force. We had developed a close bond during my last months in the Air Force, and they were who I depended on most during my rough separation from Peggy. We kept our long-distance friendship active through random phone calls and letters to Audrey (Andy never had a phone).

A few miles north of town, I turned down a dirt road to a mobile home in a grove of tall pines, where Audrey lived. It was late evening, and Audrey was so happy to see me and meet my new wife as she escorted us into her trailer. We talked for a long time, and then Andy arrived in his old 62 Ford pickup truck, followed by a cloud of smoke. Andy left the Air Force shortly after I did and had also let his hair grow out. Andy was a talented radio repairman but survived by doing many odd jobs to bring in a little money. He never managed to save any of it, though. Creditors were on his tale all the time. He had not lived with Audrey for several months but was there to help her with repairs, and she gave him money when she could. Audrey cared for 17 severely disabled children at the state mental hospital near Tallahassee. One other young woman helped her, but it was quite a handful feeding, dressing, changing diapers, and sharing her love with this group of forgotten, older children who lived in their unique realities.

Audrey had to work the next day, so Angie and I tagged along with Andy. We picked okra from an acquaintance's property and stopped along the roadside to sell as much as possible from Andy's pickup.

We sold barely enough to buy a pint of blackberry brandy and two quarts of beer for the night's consumption. While we all talked into the night, Andy finished a wood carving of a walking stick handle he had made especially for Audrey. It was a remarkably accurate replica of a penis. We joked about all the obvious implications and teased Audrey. Angie liked Audrey, and if we had had more time, they could have become friends, but we were leaving in the morning.

We still had a little trip money left. Gas and food might cost $20 to get us the rest of the way home, so I offered Andy 20 bucks. Andy said he could not repay me, and I was OK with that. I thought Andy was a great guy and felt bad for the situation he got himself into. As we drove off, waving and a long honk of the horn, I hoped Andy would get back on his feet and finally start to live up to his potential.

Even Though Angie got along with Audrey and thought Andy was funny, my friends weren't the same as Angie's friends. Before she left Germany, she was in the prime of developing close connections with the people she knew. They hung out constantly, talked, shared their lives, and established a mutual trust not experienced here in the States, except for her bond with Christhilde. Then, right amid her new developing life, she moved to Florida at Chris's invitation. It was so exotic and exciting. Then she met me. We got along well, had lots of fun, and developed this close relationship, but it was hard for her to get close to my friends. They were friendly and tried to include her, but it was not the deep relationship she craved. The language was a barrier, but this lack of any closeness was dispiriting. She felt sad and became more and more isolated. I could tell she loved me, but I could still not share the closeness she needed. It would be good for her to get back to share it all with Christhilde. Her friend was her anchor here in Florida.

Chapter 9
Paths Diverge

We arrived home, opened the windows to our stuffy trailer, and got ready for the coming week. The fall quarter started the next day, and I had textbooks to buy. Angie would find a job in a lens factory, operating a polishing machine. Our neighbor, Chris, worked there and would give Angie a ride every day. The extra money she earned would be good, but, as she would find out, the work was mundane, and the strict environment sometimes made it hard to get motivated. Before we left on our honey half-moon, I had quit my job with the City of Palm Beach Gardens and now relied on the $300 I received from the GI Bill each month. This money would cover my tuition and textbooks and be enough to pay our basic expenses. With Angie's added income, we could survive as well or better than before.

Over the next couple of weeks, we would decide to sell the Pinto to avoid the $93 a month payment, not to mention insurance, repairs, tires, and gas expenses. The city bus stopped on A1A, right outside the entrance of Sunset Village, and one change downtown would get me to the Palm Beach Junior College campus. Angie got a ride to work with Chris each morning, and the Publix grocery store was a short walk down A1A, so not having a car seemed a workable idea.

Angie felt good back in our cozy home. I had become comfortable with Angie's physical changes to our trailer, and it felt nice here. I still had my black light and strobe light mounted in the living room, but when turned on, Angie was uncomfortable, so I rarely used them. My life was also changing, and the effects of the black light's fluorescent glow or the strobe's trippy flashing light had become a bit juvenile.

Angie made friends with Mrs. Murdock, who lived in a newer, big trailer directly behind ours. She was in her 60s but talked and, more importantly, listened to Angie.

Patrick and Tom, at Chris and Alan's. Bert's and Angie's, Sunset Village, next-door neighbors.

The couple next door, Chris and Alan, were our age and had become a welcome addition to our happy life. We would spend two or three evenings a week visiting on their porch. Their friends, Pam and Tom, would stop by and hang out, but we had less in common with them. Alan's brother Patrick was cool. He was a bit younger but a thoughtful, nice guy. He and I hit it off pretty well. Yes, life was pretty good here in Sunset Village. We called it home, which suited us both, but was it enough for Angie?

Starting the Fall quarter at school, I noticed my life moving in a new direction. My old friendships with Pete, Terri, Steve, and Marie were beginning to fade. We lived farther apart, and having sold my Pinto, I didn't get around much anymore. I had Angie, and this relationship had become the most meaningful focus of my life. No one but Pete had a phone, but I rarely called. We all gradually drifted apart. Someone would pop by occasionally, but the close, day-to-day hanging out was gone.

I made several new friends in an English Literature class that would meld into a new group—Mike, who grew up in the West Palm Beach area, and his friend of a few years, Leonard. Leonard was one of the many northerners who came to live in Florida for a change in life. Like so many other young hippie types, we decided to try college after a time of fun in the sun to find a productive direction and make something positive of our lives. Mike still lived at home and owned a 1960 VW microbus, which provided transportation when it wasn't broken down. We often hung out at school, Leonard's apartment, or on the beach whenever Mike could transport us. Angie got along well with Mike and Leonard, too. An evening at the beach was typical, sometimes with a bonfire. The fire tended to draw the police or customs agents, as this was a usual way to signal small drug boats wanting to drop their loads. None of us drank alcohol. We just sat, talked, smoked a little pot, and enjoyed the cooler nights with the constant rhythm of the waves.

Leonard and I reminisced about crazy times in our past when it was quite common for friends to up and take off on a cross-country adventure. Before I joined the Air Force, I sat around with friends listening to Black Sabbath late at night. Sammy and Brad decided to hitchhike from Michigan to California with no more than the $7 and change we scraped together for them. I wanted to go with them but had a new job and needed the money. Sammy and Brad were gone for six weeks, and no one heard from them until they returned with $20 and an ounce of California pot. I always regretted not going along.

We tried to convince Mike to take us all in his VW microbus cross country the following Summer, but his bus was old, and Mike hesitated, so that never panned out. Our time hanging out was spent studying or listening to music. Their taste in music was a bit different than mine. Mike was really into Joni Mitchell, and I, too, gained an appreciation for her but never bought one of her albums. Leonard loved Art Garfunkel's solo albums, and I did buy a few of those. All three of us were laid back and introverted. Over the next year, we became good friends, and Angie liked them too. We shared a common focus on school and figuring out what we would do with our lives if or after graduating.

As Angie was putting the pieces of her new life in perspective, Christhilde moved, which shook Angie's foundation. Christhilde had become unhappy working for her Florida family. She had been with them for over a year, and expectations changed as the kids transitioned to their pre-teen years. Through a mutual friend, she found a family living in New York who wanted Chris to move north and work for them, so she did, just like that. She wasn't ready to return to Germany, even though her visa had expired long ago, and she would like to see other parts of the United States. She hated to leave Angie but needed to make the move. They could still write and sometimes talk on the phone.

It didn't take long for Angie to start missing Chris. They wrote to each other all the time, and eventually, Chris invited us to visit over the Christmas holiday. Without a car, we would have to see if we could figure out how to make it happen, so a visit seemed a long shot.

With Chris gone, Angie turned to a couple of other young German acquaintances who had married American soldiers stationed in Germany. Of the two, Christy was the more responsible friend, and Monica was on the wild side. They got together now and then but never became close. Once, Angie and Monica met at a bar near Sunset Village. Monica had too much to drink, and Angie tried to get her home and keep her out of trouble. Monica's husband had been looking for her and caught up with them walking along A1A back to Sunset Village. Angie was doing her best to keep Monica vertical when her husband saw them and stopped. After a quick outburst of accusations and insults, he planted her in his car and drove off. That was the last she ever saw of Monica.

Angie developed a better relationship with our neighbor and now co-worker, Chris, but she never found the closeness she needed. I would also hang out with Alan, and the four of us spent many evenings on one porch or the other. Alan's younger brother Patrick came over a lot, and we typically spent the evenings talking on the porch or down at the "clubhouse," an oversized garage, playing ping pong. Life was peaceful but mundane; for Angie, the loneliness again made her feel homesick for her friends and culture.

As fall turned to winter, the weather in Florida cooled to manageable temperatures during the days, and at night, sleeping was comfortable for a change. Angie came with me to campus one day. I wanted her to sit in on an interesting English Literature class I had told her about. The instructor was Watson B. Duncan III, who was unique, or more likely, a bit eccentric. He sometimes wore a large gold metal S on a chain around his neck, representing Shakespeare, one of his heroes. Professor Duncan would talk about the three famous former students who kept in touch with him. The actor Burt Reynolds, who had him play cameo roles in a film or two; Monty Markham, a TV role actor, and Terry Garrity, who wrote "The Sensuous Woman," a best-selling novel for females who "yearn to be all woman."

Professor Duncan would start each class differently. As 70 or more students settled into the lecture hall, he would silently act in an absurd but funny caricature until he had everyone's attention and then began. On the day Angie visited, he entered, looked at the restless class, placed a pencil in one ear, looked quizzically, and then another pencil in the other. Several students were now paying attention, but not all. Next, he hunched over like a bunny, not easy for a 70-plus-year-old rotund man, and hopped around with the funniest facial expressions. By now, everyone was not just paying attention but laughing and sharing the moment with their neighbor. He then exclaimed, "Now that I have your attention, let me tell you about what it means to wear an albatross around your neck," and quickly went into a theatrical presentation of a memorized passage of the "Rhyme of the Ancient Mariner." Time in his class always flew by, and he made the dry course enjoyable with detailed stories of Samuel Taylor Coleridge's Kubla Khan and Xanadu and the satire of Jonathan Swift.

Toward the end of the quarter, my Sociology instructor gave a packed auditorium presentation about Exo-sociology, or how humans will respond when extraterrestrials visit Earth. He described our dilemma: to fight or learn to greet them peacefully. The Vietnam War was now over, and much of American society was in a more peaceful state of mind, so maybe we would not need to destroy these arriving aliens from some distant galaxy. During this campus-wide presentation, standing next to me in the aisle was an announced visitor to campus who was an up-and-coming Australian media mogul. The middle-aged man had recently purchased a couple of British tabloids and was starting to gain some notoriety. His name was Rupert Murdoch, and he stood in the aisle during the presentation with his small entourage for maybe 10 minutes, then left. I guess that was enough experience and information to publish his tabloid article. Like always, he would sensationalize the topic to attract readership or, more importantly, make money and garner attention. Over the coming years, he would revise this philosophy but still manage to use persuasive hyperbole to influence people while enlarging his fortune.

Chapter 10
NYC or Bust(ed)

As winter break approached, we searched for a way to visit with Christhilde. We wanted to make it to New York and stop to spend Christmas with my parents, who now ran a Best Western motel in Washington, North Carolina. Having no car and taking a train or a bus to North Carolina and New York was not practical or affordable. Hitchhiking might work, but the cold weather made that less appealing.

Having seen a billboard at a car rental place down A1A looking for people to drive cars north, I walked the mile down A1A to talk to them. Many snowbirds rented cars to go south, but not many went the other way. I could get a car with no rental cost. We only had to buy our gas, which sounded like a good deal. It turned out the gas cost us as much as bus tickets. Two days into winter break, I signed some papers and picked up a large Oldsmobile station wagon. We threw our meager luggage, my duffle bag from the Air Force, and a small suitcase of Angie's in the back seat with a cooler of sandwiches and drinks and hit I-95 north.

This trip would lead us to new territory for Angie, and I enjoyed showing her new places. This trip would also be the first time Angie and my parents would meet. When we married, I wrote a letter informing my parents of the hasty arrangement with a German girl. I included a picture of Angie slumped on our couch (mattress on the floor) with a beer in one hand, a cigarette in the other, and half-open eyes. My parents were happy for my independence and life on my own, but what was I thinking? And no doubt, what were they to think of Angie?

In their later years, my parents started managing a progression of motels for a living, usually staying with one motel job for a year or a little more before moving on to greener pastures with another motel. That's the way it was for me my entire life. My mom stayed home and raised the family, and my dad was a salesman for different companies over the years I lived at home. I rarely lived in the same place for more than a year. Once, I counted 31 locations I had lived in my first 19 years. Managing motels was my parent's late-in-life job, out of necessity to make a living, but my whole life was interrupted by my dad, a pretty good salesman, frequently changing jobs. It was either better financial opportunities, avoiding pestering debt collectors, or my mom's unhappiness with life at a particular location. It was easy to make a fresh start with no past in a new place, sometimes in another state. The reasons we moved so often were never discussed with me; it was just time to move again. My three older sisters experienced some of this, but the moving became more frequent after they had moved out.

We made it to their motel in North Carolina, and my mom and dad were thrilled to see me again after so long. My parents tried to see me once or twice a year, but it had been the previous Christmas since we had last met. They were accepting and cordial to Angie but had their suspicions about the quick marriage. My dad, the ex-WWII Marine, was shocked to see my long hair and beard but gave me a bear hug, and his eyes lit up nonetheless. When my parents visited my sister Joyce and me before I joined the Air Force, he practically demanded I cut my hair with a tear in his eye. Under his sometimes-gruff exterior, he was a loving and caring person. Even with my long hair, he loved me more than you could measure. After a pleasant visit with good food and shared stories, we continued to New York City, Brooklyn, to be exact, to drop off the car.

Murray and Norma Milburn, with Bert in North Carolina.

As we maneuvered through the Friday evening traffic in New Jersey, light snow turned into a mini-blizzard. The roads, slick with the new-fallen snow and bumper-to-bumper traffic, made finding our way to the destination dangerous and scary. The night was falling as we arrived at the address following the written directions of the car agency.

We were surprised to arrive at a private brownstone row house instead of a business, where we were to drop the car. We parked on the tree-lined street, retrieved our bags, and went up the long brick stairway to knock on the door of the "residence."? We were shocked to find a group of a dozen or more 30-year-old upper-middle-class people having a party. After explaining who we were and thinking some wires had crossed, the friendly host exclaimed, "Excellent! We've been expecting you." The man quickly excused himself and ran out to "inspect" the car. He was back in a short minute, quite happy, and offered us a drink or hit from a pipe. I wanted to stay, but Angie was uncomfortable, so we left, walking through the light accumulation of snow to a nearby bus stop. Angie said she was sure we had unknowingly delivered drugs to this Brooklyn brownstone address. We caught a bus to a subway stop and headed to Manhattan, where we were to meet Chris at the base of the Empire State Building.

This visit was our first time in the Big Apple, and in 1975, we were in for some eye-opening experiences. New York City was a dynamic, thriving city, but there was a strong undercurrent of the unstable danger of life here. The people we met along our way were extreme, both on the strange but true side and nice and friendly. Our bus ride to the nearest subway stop was short and uneventful, but as we ascended the long, covered metal stairs to the elevated subway, a violent fight broke out between two young women. With fists flying, we skirted the battle and walked up the platform with relief. Glad to get on the subway and out of the cold, we sat on one side of the packed car, facing elbow-to-elbow people on the opposite side. As the interior lights constantly flickered with the clacking of the train's motion, a group of intimidating thug-like people moved slowly through the trains, looking for an easy mark to extort money. We looked like we had no money, so we received no more than a glance from them.

A man and woman got on at the next stop and sat right across from us. The woman looked warily at the man and slid uncomfortably away several times. Two older men sitting next to them kept smiling at me while they talked to each other. The one man looked like an artist with a goatee, beret, and a bag at his feet containing rolled paper tubes. Maybe artwork, I thought. They gave me a slight wave, then a nod, and smiled. Then the artsy-looking man passed me a hastily scribbled note, which said, "Did anyone ever tell you that you look like Jesus Christ?" I shook my head affirmatively and smiled at the man. The train was noisy and crowded, making conversation across the mid-aisle difficult. The man passed me another note asking if I would consider playing the role of Jesus in an ongoing Christmas play. I was flattered but indicated I was not an actor, nor did I have time, as we were merely passing through. At the next stop, the man and woman who seemed uncomfortable with each other got up, wrapped arms around each other, and exited the train. Angie and I exchanged looks. What the heck was that all about?

We exited the subway inside Grand Central Station. Observing a bank of 20 pay phones on five center posts, four phones on each post, north, south, east, and west facing, while a group of bag ladies evenly spaced walked around each set of phones, checking the coin return. As each got to the end of the pay phone groupings, they returned to the start and repeated the journey. Many people used the pay phones in between, and some undoubtedly forgot their few coins returned if their call ended early.

As we exited the station, we looked at landmarks and our city map to navigate our way to the Empire State Building. When our necks weren't cramped from looking up at the monumental tall building towering over us, we noticed, beyond the rush of hurrying masses, raggedly dressed homeless people hanging around the entrance to the station, seemingly isolated in their made-up fantasy world. With several layers of clothes and mismatched shoes, one mumbled to himself while he walked in a circle, kicking a paper ball for at least ten minutes. We escaped this odd circus of sad behavior and continued down the cold street to look around until it was time to meet up with Chris.

After a 15-minute walk down 5th Avenue, we arrived at the Art Deco Empire State Building amidst the flurry of snow. We huddled against the building just outside the lobby, waiting for Chris to arrive. It wasn't long before we recognized her, bundled head to toe, with her bright smile beaming above her scarf. Angie and Chris hugged, and their eyes lit up. Chris always wore her emotions for all to see, and when she was excited, it was contagious. Her face showed the joy in her heart, and her voice inflections skipped happily along as Chris told Angie how much she had missed her and how delighted she was to see her. You could see the same in Angie; her voice was happy, and she started to bounce on the balls of her feet with excitement. Chris and I spoke briefly and hugged, but the two "beautiful German girls," as the ad said, had so much to say and share I was more of an afterthought.

Christhilde Uhl in New York.

An Empire State Building admission stand employee graciously allowed Angie and me to stow our bags in a store room before we rode the elevator to the top to view the city below from the cold, windy observation deck. After 30 minutes on top, we decided it was enough, and it was time to find somewhere to sit down out of the cold and maybe get a warm drink while we reconnected. Not knowing where to go, we meandered back along 5th Avenue toward Grand Central, a couple of blocks to a side street, looking for somewhere to sit and talk.

Geli and Chris walked arm in arm, with a spring in their steps, as they talked like they hadn't seen each other in years. They had so much to share. The wind-blown light snow swirled around their feet as they led the way into a rather dark place with maybe a dozen shabby tables on West 36th Street. Few people were there, so we didn't feel too bad about only ordering coffee and sitting in a four-person window seat that looked out on the street scene. Sitting here gave me something to do besides making comments now and then while Geli and Chris caught up. The people in the establishment took little notice of us. Some were speaking Spanish, with some broken English intermixed.

We sat and talked in the warmth of the window booth for a while when a homeless-looking man tried to strike up a conversation with us, frantically prophesying about the wonder of some religious ideal. We tried to ignore him without being rude, but the scruffy man was not to be deterred. I explained to the man that we hadn't seen each other in a long time and that he should move along. When he attempted to sit on the top of my overstuffed duffle bag, I physically brushed him away to stop him from crushing our unseen sandwiches and snacks in the top of my bag. The man was offended and started to react with anger and outrage when another man, likely the owner, came over and spoke harshly in Spanish to him. Whatever he said calmed the man for the moment. Then he pulled a transistor radio from his heavy, ragged overcoat and mumbled about something incoherently. He placed the radio in the center of our table, exclaiming this gadget was a miracle of miracles, and snapped it on full blast. At the same time, he waved his hands over his head and mumbled/chanted some aimless chatter. The owner hurried over and brusquely tossed him into the street. I thanked the owner and then suggested to the girls that we wait maybe ten minutes and leave to avoid a possible repeated confrontation with this delusional man.

Warmer from our brief stay indoors, we returned to Grand Central Station, where we boarded a train to Greenwich, Connecticut, near Chris's new home. She had a friend, Jeff, with a car who picked us up at the station and took us to Chris's host family's house in Pound Ridge, NY, 30 minutes away. The family was on their way out of town, and Chris would have the place to herself. Angie and Chris spent two days catching up with each other while I got to know Jeff. It was odd for a financially well-off family to have so little food in the house. Chris said they either went out, ordered a delivery, bought just enough for a meal, and never saved leftovers. Chris and Angie did what they could to prepare some simple meals, but we stayed hungry most of the time.

It was a quiet two days, which Angie and Chris didn't seem to mind, but I became restless. Most of our time was spent sitting around catching up. We took short walks in the foot-deep accumulated snow. Pound Ridge was a beautiful small town, especially with all the snow and Christmas lights, but there was not much else for us to do, especially with little money. We should have enough money to return to Florida if we do not encounter any problems.

Bert and Angie are ready to hitchhike from New York State to Florida.

After our two-day visit, Chris and Geli had a tearful last goodbye. Jeff gave us a ride over snowy roads to Port Chester, where we would catch our first ride home on the Cross Westchester Expressway across the Tappan Zee Bridge. The expressway skirts around New York City and connects with I-95 northwest of the city rush.

We were lucky hitchhiking for the most part. We caught one ride around New York City and two more to get to Philadelphia. Several rides and too many hours spent on the cold entrance ramps finally got us past Baltimore and one more, past the Capital. Night fell, and we found a cheap motel in Southside, Virginia, at an I-95 exit. The weather improved as we made it farther south the next day. One long ride to Savannah, Georgia, and a half dozen more brought us back to Riviera Beach. We walked the last mile down A1A to our warm New

Moon trailer in Sunset Village. Exhausted but safe, we settled in and prepared ourselves for two more months of relatively cool weather in South Florida. We still had a week before the spring quarter would start for me, so we spent time at the beach, this time in sweatshirts, and enjoyed having regular everyday meals in our cozy nest.

Chapter 11
The Ranch

Sometime in February, Angie found out about a job on a wealthy Palm Beach veterinarian's estate that sounded perfect for us. The Lockwoods were looking for a couple to help with light housework, some after-school child care, and help on their ranch. They currently had Zeke, who helped Mr. Lockwood, but he was leaving for a better job the following week. Mrs. Lockwood wanted to find a couple to help with the house and kids and on the ranch. If hired, Angie was perfect for helping with the housework and kids, and I could take care of the four horses, assist in the stables, and tend to the ten heads of cattle.

We borrowed Patrick's car and drove to the Lockwood ranch for an interview. The ranch was about eight miles west of West Palm Beach off Southern Blvd., on the rural edge of the developed area on the fringe of the Loxahatchee National Wildlife Refuge.

Entrance to the Ranch, Cyprus Woods.

We found the ranch in an out-of-the-way neighborhood of big houses, small farms, and ranches. Each was on about ten acres or more. We drove through the rustic, western-themed entrance, with a "Cypress Woods" sign suspended above, then down the long sandy drive. The driveway ended at a sprawling, modern, ranch-style home with a large screened-in pool area, a barn, stables, and old-growth trees dotting the property. The Lockwoods greeted us as we parked and led us into their house.

The interior was beautiful and well appointed, but as we entered, we were shocked to see mounted animal heads of boar, zebra, jaguar, and some other horned animals. Exotic hides draped over couches and served as rugs on the floor. Two 6-foot-high elephant tusks stood like sentinels on each side of a grand piano. Mr. Lockwood was a big-time game hunter who traveled the world to hunt exotic animals. It seemed an odd hobby for a veterinarian, I thought.

We sat in the living room and exchanged light pleasantries; next came several questions about experience and background. The Lockwoods seemed happy with us and then gave us a tour of the grounds. Mrs. Lockwood first showed us the screened-in, large pool area with a bar, ample seating, and potted plants everywhere. We were then shown the stables with ten stalls for their four horses. One was an extremely valuable racehorse from a prominent lineage. Finally, we were shown a one-bedroom apartment with air conditioning on the far end of the stables. What a luxury for whoever would fill the position. Across a large wooden privacy fence, next to the apartment was a neighboring farm with several acres of orange groves. The Lockwoods had about three acres fenced for the cattle and a few more acres of grassy area for leisure and horseback riding.

We briefly met their two children. Their "tweenage" daughter, Sarah, loved her horse, Stormy, a pure white temperamental stallion that was only to be ridden by her. A trainer would come to the ranch to give her private lessons several times weekly. The slightly younger son, Preston, would typically be occupied with sports and other after-school activities, so it looked like they would need caring for only periodically. They both attended a private Palm Beach school and were busy most days and evenings. Mr. Lockwood was gone all day at his practice and spent most evenings at a private club. Mrs. Lockwood led an active social life, then picked up the kids and joined her husband at the club in the evening.

As the tour ended, they offered us the job. This offer was an exciting opportunity that we discussed and quickly accepted. The thought of living at this ranch with all its amenities and peaceful environment was a surprise neither of us expected. We would save money with no rent or utilities to pay, but we would need a car for this new job to work. Zeke, the departing ranch hand, would be leaving in a week, so we had a little time to prepare for the transition.

The following week, I found a 1961 VW Beetle for sale in the local *Trading Post* sales paper. $400 was a reasonable price, and Angie spent the rest of the money she had saved for our divorce to buy the car, and I put the trailer up for sale. Our 1958 New Moon trailer quickly sold for $1,200, and we again had a nest egg for our future. My bet paid off, and the money I would have spent on rent we would recoup in the sale with a profit. We now have a new, shared job with a flexible schedule, a nice place to live with air conditioning and a car, and I was closer to the community college. With no furniture to move, it took us three trips in our new VW Beetle to move all our worldly belongings into the apartment at the end of the stables on the Lockwood ranch as another chapter in our life together began anew.

Living on the ranch was quite different. The apartment was much bigger than our trailer, and we could now play music at night at a reasonable level without disturbing any neighbors. We did not have neighbors within earshot. The Lockwood house was closest, maybe 100 yards away. The next ranch was not even visible. Our furnished apartment had a television, but we rarely turned it on. At night, when the lights were out, we would hear the light pitter-patter of tiny legs running across the kitchen linoleum. Palmetto bugs (Florida cockroaches). These palmetto bugs were giant, some two to three inches long, with antennae constantly probing as they scurried from behind the fridge or any small space to their preferred dining point where unseen crumbs had fallen. When we turned on a light, along with the palmetto bugs, wolf spiders were on the move or clinging to walls. In the dark, these spiders took over the place. They were about three inches around and an inch or more tall, with fat, hairy legs. They scurried around, feasting on smaller bugs.

Night time for the first several weeks consisted of Angie rousing me from bed to rid the apartment of these nocturnal invaders. When I entered the kitchen and flipped on the light, the palmetto bugs would scurry for safety, knowing a shoe was about to disturb their evening search for food. Looking closely, I could count upwards of eight wolf spiders frozen on the walls and floor. At first, I would take a small container and cover a spider, then slip a piece of cardboard stealthily underneath to trap them and release them in the nearby woods. This method worked a few times before the other wolf spiders would retreat into hiding before I could trap them all. The spiders I did release found their way back for the same routine the next night.

Life on the ranch was quiet and private, but never alone. After several weeks, Angie became more tolerant of the wolf spiders. They were ugly but harmless. The palmetto bugs, on the other hand, were disgusting. Florida was their land, and they intended to outlast us, humans. They crawled where they wished, and gravity did not affect them. You could even see them crawling on the ceiling. They could fly short distances, five to ten feet, and their reproductive capacity was prolific. They were there to stay. Spray and stomp them to death, but more were always waiting to take their place.

Angie became familiar with the Lockwood house and the family. She efficiently handled the work expected of her. The housework was light, and when the two kids came home from school, they were busy with their hobbies or schoolwork. Mr. and Mrs. Lockwood were gone almost every weekday, so there were no interruptions to us getting chores done. I would clean out the stables, shovel manure, feed the cattle, and complete a few other tasks on the ranch, but I had plenty of time for my schoolwork and studies.

Bert and Nanny play in the goat pen at the ranch.

I became best friends with Nanny, a goat who welcomed my new companionship. We would play chase games and butt heads in the penned area, permanently barren from Nanny's ravenous appetite. Nanny was also a master escape artist. Much of my fun with Nanny stemmed from my many attempts to chase her down and get a rope around her neck to lead her back to her pen until her next escape. Nanny would keep me company while I cleaned the stables and when I took the golf cart to feed the cattle. I brought the cattle their daily powdered antibiotic hormone supplement, which caused them to grow twice as fast and larger. Animals being pumped full of such hormones was one of the primary reasons I became a vegetarian in the first place.

Our days at the ranch were pleasant and peaceful as we completed our jobs. By March, it was warm enough for Angie and I to swim in the pool when the Lockwoods were away and relax in the large screened-in area. We'd put on a good radio station from their Marantz receiver in the main house, connected to a nice set of speakers near the pool, swim, and then relax in the comfortable lounge chairs while we listened to some good music. The Lockwoods did not mind but did not want anyone there while they were home.

A few times while the family was gone, I took the unwarranted liberty of riding Stormy, the daughter's white horse. One of my chores was to walk him on the days Sarah did not ride him, which became three or four times a week. Stormy was a spirited animal, and I didn't bother with a saddle. A saddle would be more comfortable, but I didn't want to take the time and maybe get caught. The short rides were as exciting as they were challenging, and Stormy liked them, too. There was a trampoline on the lawn outside the pool area, which I also loved to use.

I occasionally ran errands for Mr. Lockwood, so he allowed me to hand pump gas for the VW from the 500-gallon gas tank behind the stables. Free gas meant we rarely had to spend money to fill the VW, another saving. Life was quite enjoyable on the ranch. It was easy to contribute our part to maintaining the farm, as we had few other pressures. The Lockwoods were descent people who liked their privacy and respected ours.

Working on the ranch was also a time to observe and learn. Watching Dr. Lockwood perform acupuncture on the racehorse was interesting. He would tape an electrode over a sore muscle on the horse's knee or ankle, then use another electrode connected to a metal box to probe an area on the shoulder, upper back, or chest to find a connecting nerve. He would then snap a short needle precisely in that spot. When complete, the horse had a dozen sharp needles stuck in various places where they would rest for maybe a half hour. The racehorse never complained, so I guess this worked.

Another job I enjoyed was robbing honey from the beehives. Dr. Lockwood would take the lead, wearing protective clothing and screened face shields. I dressed the same. Slowly, I smoked the bee hive with the handheld smoker while Dr. Lockwood carefully pulled out the honeycomb frames. Small honey bees would cover our suits in spots. A few even managed to crawl up my sleeve or land on my exposed neck. As long as you were calm, they would not sting. We placed the combs in a hand-spun centrifuge, drained the honey into a vat, then opened a tap to fill bottles. Life was interesting here; there was much to do, moderate work, and decent pay.

With all the many benefits of ranch living, it was still lonely, especially for Angie. We shared chores and spent time together, but this wasn't enough for Angie. I was in school every day and always had a paper to write, notes to study, and occasional visits with my new friends. Angie was there all day, every day, alone. The Lockwoods had a phone, but to call Christhilde would be expensive, and they did not want us making long-distance calls. Several times, Angie took a small pile of change to a pay phone booth at the nearby gas station to call Chris. These calls helped, but talking for 10 to 15 minutes over the pay phone was not enough time to share as much of her pent-up feelings as Angie needed.

During these lonely days, Angie had all day to think. Living here in isolation, without friends and being unable to drive, made her too dependent on me. She was homesick and lonely, and the complications of our new relationship were becoming more emotional. She missed her closeness with friends and family and yearned to return home. It was becoming hard for her to be happy at the ranch. For me, life was good. We had friends that I got along with, but Angie never made the same connections. I couldn't understand her growing despair. I kept ignoring the issues, but they wouldn't disappear. I was too preoccupied with school or ranch work, but I mostly didn't know how to relate to her loneliness or understand its depth. Something would need to change, but what, how?

Chapter 12
The Sisyphean Burden

My classes at Palm Beach Community College were going well. They were tougher this quarter, and after four previous quarters of a part-time turned full-time load, I was slacking off a bit. As a C high school student, I was surprised at how well I could do as a more mature college student. The GI Bill attracted me at first. I received $100 a month for taking just one class, which I did for the extra money. Back then, housemate Steve and I shared a meager existence, living in our duplex apartment on peanut butter and jelly. I took a US History class and earned a squeaker of an A. The course wasn't so bad, it was even enjoyable, I decided. The next quarter, I took two evening classes, Psychology and English 101. After that, I carried a full-time load and never earned less than a B through it all. This quarter was different. I struggled to get the algebra pass/fail credit through a self-paced course with modules that were to make progress more steadily at my own pace. I only earned two of the three credits. I earned a 'C' in Zoology, which was manageable, but the terminology was challenging. I dropped an electronics course because of my math deficiency. Music Appreciation didn't turn out as I had hoped either. Classical music was not my cup of tea. My Philosophy class, however, was fascinating.

I earned a 'C' in Max Agee's Philosophy class, but I enjoyed it the most of any class I had ever taken. Mike, Leonard, and I decided to take the class together as an elective. The ideas presented in this class related to thoughts and conversations we had experienced over our young lives, but the depth and the insight I learned blew my mind. The 50-minute class, Mondays, Wednesdays, and Fridays, went by like lightning. Max presented arguments about values, morals, and infinity that involved the whole class to the point several would remain after class to continue the debate. The course provided material for many conversations between Leonard, Mike, and myself, leaving us wondering even more about the topics covered in class. We discovered no definitive answers, but doors of awareness always cracked open.

Max, our instructor, became a friend outside of class as well. We often talked in the library or the campus cafeteria/game room. Max eagerly accepted my invitation to a party Angie and I were throwing to celebrate the start of Spring. Max had received his master's degree in philosophy at a University in Bonn, Germany, several years before. He shared many stories of his fraternal experiences, involving large quantities of beer consumption and sometimes a little fencing. Max was eager to meet Angie and speak German with a native speaker again.

The night of our Spring party, I suspended a large tarp from the lower branches outside our apartment and built a fire in a makeshift pit. I borrowed the Lockwood's charcoal grill to prepare dogs and burgers, and soon, about twenty people arrived, ready for a fun evening. I rigged up speakers in the apartment windows to set the rhythm of the evening. My stereo pumped out Country Rock music from Charlie Daniels, The Marshall Tucker Band, The Allman Brothers Band, and heavier Led Zeppelin and Jethro Tull music.

Friends arrived as evening dusk turned to the black of night. Headlights penetrated the darkness as cars rounded the stables and parked by the barn. The fire and the outside porch lights created a warm atmosphere for our den of social activity amid our vast, dark surroundings. As more people arrived and placed their wine or beer in a tub of ice, the level of conversation rose, and the music retreated to the background. I started the charcoal, and Angie arranged the salads she had prepared and the condiments on a table. Others added their prepared dishes as introductions, connecting some of our older friends with our new friends and Zeke, the Lockwood's former ranch hand.

The day before our party, Christhilde had flown in to visit Angie and her former Florida host family. Angie perked up and was beginning to smile a bit more often. Together, they prepared for the evening. Max arrived at the party early and was happy to speak German with Angie. They mixed in English to avoid rudely excluding others in the immediate grouping. Angie stayed busy with arriving guests but gave Max the attention he wanted. She did want to interact with others, but the more beer Max consumed, the more German he wished to speak. It got to the point where I felt Max's attention toward Angie was getting a bit excessive, and I tried to steer the conversation my way. Leonard and Mike jumped into the conversation, but Max, now quite intoxicated, seemed almost fixated on Angie, which produced a more uncomfortable atmosphere.

Angie, however, was sullen and quite distant from the party in general. Her loneliness and isolation had become deep-seated, and it showed on her face. She listened to Max and briefly talked with others, but she was unhappy. Christhilde sensed her depression.

The Lockwoods were out of town that weekend, and as the evening progressed, Angie took Chris to the Lockwood house for some private girlfriend talk. Geli explained her loneliness to Chris and how I never spent time discussing our feelings about each other. The ranch was so far from everything, and there was literally no one to open up to except me, and I was just not there. Oh, how she missed Chris. The tears streamed down her cheeks as she let her pent-up emotions all out. Chris consoled her and cried as well. She felt so bad to have left Geli so alone.

Chris would be returning to New York tomorrow, and as much as Chris hated leaving, it would not be possible for her to stay longer. She hoped this all would get better for Geli and promised to call her more on the Lockwood family phone. She said Geli could call her "collect" or reverse the long-distance charges. After releasing all these pent-up emotions, they recomposed and returned to the party. By this time of night, no one noticed their subdued mood shift. People started leaving in the hours after midnight, and the party ended. Angie enjoyed being with all our friends, but she craved closeness as she had with Chris and her other friends back home.

Still lonely, not alone, but lonely. I loved Angie, and she loved me, but I was not providing what Angie needed. She would talk to me night after night, trying to explain how she felt, but I did not understand. Angie needed a relationship with depth that I had never experienced. She needed someone to seriously listen to her thoughts and emotions and discuss the depth and intricacies of our love. Angie would feel more alone through these almost nightly conversations, and I would get more frustrated. We had so much fun and truly cared for each other, but our divide never closed.

During a long break between classes, I would sit by the large pond on campus and try to pull our relationship together in my mind. I had a hard time getting in touch with my feelings. I started writing poetry to Angie about this divide between us, comparing our emotional distance to the physical distance between our cultures. It was easier to express myself through the abstract words of poetry. Poetry allowed my words to convey my feelings through simile and comparison. My composed words aimed to define my feelings and open up to Angie, but she needed more, and our divide persisted.

M eanwhile, back at life on the ranch, our little Volkswagen was perfect for us. The gas mileage was great, plus the Lockwoods provided most of our gas. Angie was eager to learn how to drive, so we would head out to the sandy backwoods for her to practice every chance we got. Not too far from the ranch, going inland, were miles of back roads, barely big enough for a vehicle, that mostly followed the miles of symmetrically laid out canals. The Army Corp of Engineers dredged these narrow canals in the 1930s and 40s to drain the swampy land and bring fresh water from Lake Okeechobee to southern Florida. These canals and roads were the only sign of human activity in the otherwise pristine forests with heavy undergrowth. Few people knew about this area. It was an excellent place for Angie to learn to drive and master the stick shift.

Angie parked at the ranch, preparing for a driving lesson.

W e went through some pretty tight spots for miles, and if we weren't careful, we could get stuck in the pure sand pits, which appeared out of nowhere. When one appeared, you had to keep enough forward momentum and not allow the car to bog down. If it did, the car would sink to the axles in no time flat. You could feel it start to happen, and once, I had to jump out of the still-moving car before it bogged down and pushed while I directed Angie to steer over the low bushes on the left to get some traction. The possibility of getting stranded made us think about what might happen if we did get stuck. Miles away from Southern Blvd., the main road, we'd have quite a hike to get out of this wilderness. Each time we returned to civilization, we made it a habit to pick up the first piece of trash we spotted on our return to keep this area pristine.

Once, as I was driving west on Southern Blvd. for a new round of driving practice, Angie spotted a wolf spider just over her visor on the passenger side. She never screamed but made it perfectly clear she was not hanging around with that spider in the same car. As I quickly pulled over and attempted to stop, Angie was out the door while we were still moving. I had to trap and release the spider before Angie even considered re-entry. The spider freed, and Angie thoroughly inspected the entire car before we proceeded to our backwoods driving course for another exciting venture into the Florida wilderness.

Spring quarter was ending, and with my grades slipping, I decided not to sign up for summer classes. Summer would begin, and our only responsibility was to continue helping the Lockwoods. I would have enough credits for my Associate's Degree with a few more classes, but I knew we both needed a break. I didn't know what we might do, but we needed to do something. My solution to any problem or difficulty was moving or at least traveling. Moving on wasn't an answer for Angie. She was still lonely and did not know how to fill this void in her life.

Chris was in New York, and Angie had no other close friends within 4,000 miles. She loved me, but this was not enough, so she finally decided to return to Germany. I know how much Angie cared for me, but being only 19, she was overwhelmed by our growing relationship and isolation. Angie needed to reconnect with her friends from home and the culture she left behind. It was painful, but she knew going home was the right thing to do for her, and that had to be what guided her.

Her decision crushed me, but I was not entirely surprised. We talked it through as much as I was able. For many months, these nightly discussions – Angie never argued – had become a Sisyphean effort for her. She worked hard to roll the boulder up the hill, only to have it roll back down each night. I felt the unseen boulder at a weight that invisibly crushed my soul. I tried to listen and understand what Angie was saying, but the gravity of her burden was becoming too great for me, and the love we shared wasn't enough anymore. I could have been happy with a life of some insurmountable differences as long as we loved being together, but for Angie, it was clear she needed a more profound connection than just our shared good life. This fun but superficial life Angie found in the United States had caused her to lose a part of herself that was important to regain somehow. By returning to Germany, she hoped this would happen. She wasn't sure what her plan would be, but she had to return to her homeland to figure out precisely what it could be.

Chapter 13
Into the Clouds

Angie booked her flight to leave in late April. I was confused; I was happy with our life. Angie was more than special to me, and I believed I loved her. My problem was that I did not know what love genuinely was. Our time together was the closest I had ever come to what I thought of as love. I knew I would miss her, and neither wanted to end our relationship, but everything seemed to have stalled. Angie needed more and knew she would not find it in Florida. We both knew our marriage was initially a convenience, and we were both so young with no idea what our future might hold. This separation would be, maybe, for the best. As painful as this decision was, we agreed fate would determine our future relationship, and Angie would go back to Germany to return to her roots.

For me, going with Angie to Germany was never considered. I couldn't speak the language, had no real marketable skills, and had no money to embark on such a journey. Angie needed her space, and I would not fight her, even though I knew I would miss her terribly. As our time together was coming to a close, I planned to take my savings and the VW and move to San Francisco once Angie left. I had no connection there and knew very little about the place other than San Francisco was the chosen new home of many other hippies. With my meager savings from selling the trailer and continuing college with the GI Bill, I could survive there until I figured out what I wanted to do with my life. I thought maybe six months to a year, and who knows, Angie might decide to return.

We told the Lockwoods of our plans to leave, and shortly after, they hired a young man to fill the spot at the ranch. We packed up our things and moved to a weekly motel/efficiency apartment to spend our last days before her flight. I still had no definite plan to leave the area myself, but I'd figure it out after Angie was gone. Our last few nights together were special. We joked and held each other close as we tried to ignore our coming separation. We went to a final dinner together at the Abbey Road restaurant, where I had worked before we met. This time together reinforced how much we meant to each other after all. Angie's plans were in motion, and she was all packed. There was no turning back.

The ride to the airport was quiet, but we both could feel the hurt deep inside. The uncertainty of what was to come was deafening. Angie was going back to her home, family, and friends. She hoped to do nothing more than clear her head. Only then would she start to develop a firm plan for her future, whatever that might be. My plan was nothing more than a vague idea that could change with the wind, but there was no doubt that I loved Angie.

Angie's Air Bahama plane waits to take her back to Germany in April 1976.

Angie checked in for her flight, and we walked to the tarmac to say our final goodbye. We hugged each other tighter than before and held our kiss longer, afraid to part. Angie turned and walked up the rolling stairway to disappear onto the airplane. I retreated outside the fence, got the VW, and pulled up to the curb near the runway. I stood before the car, leaning on the front fender, as her plane taxied to its spot in line to take off. As the aircraft accelerated toward and then passed me, I waved, not knowing if Angie was on the side facing me or not. Then, in a few seconds, she was gone. She was up in the clouds of the overcast day, on her way to a transfer in the Bahamas and then home. As the wheels left the runway, a few tears streamed down my face, and I knew immediately that my plans would not take me west but east to regain what I just lost. I didn't know how, but I would not retreat silently into my uncertain future when one, so bright, so right, just vanished right in front of me. I would return to the same West Palm Beach courthouse where we got our marriage license and apply for a passport on Monday. I was going after her. The language barrier, no job prospects, and the cultural divide didn't matter. I knew in my heart that my soul was incomplete, and to make it whole, I would follow my lost half across the ocean.

Part 3
You Say Hello, I Say Goodbye

Chapter 14
Reflections

Lying on the bed in the motel apartment, I had never felt so alone. I struggled to sort out what happened as the darkness outside descended over the window: no music playing, no one to talk to, just me and my thoughts. Over the last year, not only had our life together changed so much, but I also thought I was changing and maturing as an individual. I understood Angie's loneliness but never understood my role in making her feel like she was not alone. Angie needed the closest connections in a relationship, but such a deep closeness was never a part of my life. She had depth and an earnest desire to share a life with others, me included. Compared with Angie's, my life was superficial and lacked the need or commitment to share such depths.

Now pitch dark, it was more than loneliness that consumed me. I was not complete, and my feelings reverted to the times in my life when I was alone with no one to share my life. More than lonely, I was empty. I knew I wanted to be with Angie again, but how? I could physically make this happen, but my mystery was how I could reach into myself and harness the true feelings. My life was my life, and my connections with others were typically shallow. I suspect this comes from never living in one location long enough to develop strong emotional bonds. I hoped I could again be with Angie and follow her lead to a deeper place where I could understand and share the life she needed. My past inability to connect with others had always been there, but I never realized its more profound impact on my ability to get close to others. Any difficult emotional situation was quickly glossed over and locked away in my formative years. You moved on to something happier and shut out bad feelings. Ignorance was bliss.

It was time to learn, to listen, and to share myself. Not just with Angie but also with anyone with whom I was close. I was always looking outward in my relationships to the worldly. Looking inward and focusing would be an unfamiliar path but one I must learn to regain my life with Angie. Maybe trying to open up with my friends would be a place to start. It was time to listen to them, ask questions about their feelings, and share my own. I feared karma would continue to give me only what I had given if I did not learn to do this. Could I do this? I hoped with all my heart I could.

It wouldn't take long for my saved money to run out. It would happen quicker than I could imagine. I had saved most of the money from selling my New Moon trailer, but with no job and $20 a day for the motel, car expenses, food, living expenses, and the anticipated cost of going to find Angie in Germany, I would need to make some changes. It was time to look seriously at my financial and emotional situation. I had lived poor often enough and could make do with a bit of good fortune. I could live on the cheap and manage my finances if I pulled my plan together and acted quickly. My emotional challenge was going to be more daunting. It was time to listen to others and share their feelings. That's what I did not do enough with Angie. It was time to focus.

Over the next week, I planned to rearrange my life to make my reunion with Angie happen. Getting a passport would take time and a big chunk of money, and the cheapest one-way airline ticket to Luxembourg was with Air Icelandic or Air Bahama, the same company, costing more than $300. I stopped and talked with the same travel agent Angie used to buy her airplane ticket. I reserved my travel date for May 29th. The travel agent completed some paperwork, and I gave her a $100 deposit, agreeing to pay the remaining $225 within three weeks. With a firm date for my flight, I wrote to let Angie know my plan and flight details as quickly as possible. Angie's parents had no phone, so writing a letter addressed to her parent's house was the only way to reach her. I included Pete's address so she could reply, as I have no idea where I might live these last four weeks. There should be plenty of time for the letter to get to Angie, and if all goes well, I hope to get a response before I leave. Overseas mail was slow, so maybe not.

How would she feel about my coming? I hoped she would be happy, but I was not sure. In my letter, I described how I miss her and my emptiness. I explained to her that as her plane took off from Florida and left me standing there, I knew nothing else mattered to me as much as her, and in my entire life, I had never known love like my love for her. I would arrive in Luxembourg on May 29th, and I hoped she could find a way to meet me at the airport. Hearing back from her in this short time was not a certainty, and more importantly, I wanted to know she was feeling the same about me, but some part of me feared the worst. Thoughts rushed through my mind that she might find it better to get on with her life without me by returning to her home and friends. Deep inside, I believed we shared a bond; neither would give up too quickly.

Luxembourg, where its precise location is, I wasn't sure. I pulled out my "Introduction to Political Science" textbook and looked at a map of Europe in the appendix. Angie lived near Bad Kreuznach, Germany, but I didn't see that on the map. I knew it was close to Frankfurt, which wasn't too far from Luxembourg. It seemed reasonable that Angie should have the time to arrange a way to greet me at the airport.

While waiting these long weeks to hear what I hoped would be a joyful response, I needed to find a way to both stop spending money and even earn some more to make this trip possible. $20 a day for a place to live quickly emptied my wallet.

A friend from Air Force days, Troy Smith, also lived in West Palm Beach and offered me a place to stay if I would chip in some money for rent. His long-term girlfriend, Robin, had been living with him. They recently broke up, and she moved out, which devastated him. I didn't know Robin well, but it was clear how much Troy loved her, so I listened to Troy as he shared his heartbreak over his lost love. I asked him questions and kept my focus on his feelings and what he hoped for as time moved on. I also went into more detail about my experience with Angie and its similar impact on me. Typically, I would hear this type of emotional sharing and think I was a good friend by merely listening attentively. Diving deeper with Troy made me realize I was pretty shallow regarding others. These few conversations with Troy were a good starting point for me to address my shortcomings and brought Troy and me closer.

Troy and I were never that close back at Eglin Air Force Base, but we knew each other reasonably well and started hanging out toward the end of my Air Force days. It was a strange twist of fate how we reconnected. I was living with Steve in our duplex apartment, and with my car in the shop, I hitchhiked home from my job at Arthur Treacher's Fish and Chips. I'm anxious to catch a ride and get home when I see a car with a custom yellow paint job coming my way. I recognized the car and thought, no way, that can't be Troy way down here in South Florida. But it was him! He didn't even look at me on the side of the road with my thumb out. I stepped off the curb and waved as he passed, going 45 mph. I briefly chased after him, waving my work smock over my head, but nothing. The Florida Turnpike was less than a mile ahead, and I thought he was gone. A few months later, I parked two blocks from the Florida Driver's License office to get mine renewed, and I saw Troy getting into his custom yellow car two blocks down and thought, "crap! There he is, and I'm gonna miss him again." I raced full speed and caught him just sittin' in his car, studying for his driver's test. Out of breath, I banged into his driver's door and...

> Before I describe his response, you must understand. Troy was always, I mean always, the most laid-back dude. He wore oval, light-rimmed, tinted glasses that, when he looked up, would do so over the rim at you. Like most of us Airmen at Eglin AFB, he wore his military hair as long as possible, which meant covering his ears (off duty only) with a shaved tapered neck. He still looked the same.

Troy Smith

I hit his window, excited and panting like a wild dog, and he calmly looked up from his study manual, slowly rolled down his window, and said, "Bert"! That's it! Then he's quiet. I hadn't seen him in over a year and hundreds of miles away in a different culture. All he can say is Bert!

Troy's sister lived in West Palm Beach, and he came to work for his brother-in-law after his discharge. Now, living in the same area, we have developed a stronger friendship over the past year. Staying with Troy these next four weeks would be a massive help for me and would slow the money flow from my wallet into some motel cash register.

Chapter 15
The Puzzle of "Home"?

Angie stepped out of the plane in Luxembourg, all tanned from her year and a half in Florida. She wore her most comfortable, long turquoise dress, carrying her backpack and guitar over her shoulder. Geli now descended the rolling stairs with little sleep after a long flight. Her mind never stopped thinking about the life she was leaving and how it would be, reunited with old friends and her family. Angelika was just tired. She was too deep into her thoughts and needed to rest her mind. Geli hoped this would be possible.

Angie's Passport issued when she was 17 (1974, September).

Once through customs, she saw Gabi, whose shining, long red hair, natural ruby lips, and green eyes lit up when she saw her. Tobias, Geli's once boyfriend and still a good friend to everyone in their close-knit group, was there, along with Heinz, Christhilde's younger brother.

Geli saw their smiles as they waved at her, and her feelings of belonging and trust flickered anew, but still, it felt strange. They hugged and kissed on the cheeks and had so much to say. As they walked through the airport terminal, Geli felt the familiarity of home and the differences between herself and her earlier life. She had been gone quite a while and knew she had changed, but she could sense that her friends had also changed. She left when she was 17, and those following formative years brought changes to everyone. It was good to be back, and she looked forward to settling in and taking some time to rest before she could sort everything in her head. Gabi and Geli's childhood friend Helga would be there to listen and share with her when the time came.

As all her friends knew her, Geli quickly resumed her rapport with Gabi, Tobias, and Heinz on the four-hour trip back to Bad Kreuznach. Gabi had borrowed her father's car, and as they made the long journey home, Geli shared much of her recent life in the U.S. with them. They made a few stops on the way home, and eventually, some quiet time set in, so she rested her mind a bit. They arrived home in the dark and dropped her at her parents. Gabi gave Geli an open invitation to come to her new place in Asbach with her new live-in friend, Rudi, and a phone number of their communal living neighbors across the street. Geli said she would visit but was not sure when. She also told Heinz she would come to Hargesheim in the next day or two to see the Uhl family (Christhilde Uhl being the second oldest of 10 kids) and other friends.

Her parents were happy to see her, but her brother, Manfred, and two sisters living at home, Christel and Jutta, were the most excited. Christel had moved into Geli's old bedroom upstairs with the balcony, so Geli put her bags in the other small upstairs bedroom and spent the rest of the short evening catching up with her family and eating some much-needed, familiar comfort food. Finally, she settled into bed and fell asleep, thoughts of all that had happened this long day still swirling in her head. That night, Geli would have a solid, uninterrupted sleep, which was rare for her. Her thoughts mostly kept her awake or an unfamiliar noise, but tonight, she slept, mostly from pure exhaustion.

Over the next couple of days, she fell back into everyday German life, taking care of basic needs, eating, doing laundry, helping around the house, sitting out on the patio, and taking short hikes with a sibling or two, but mostly just living and letting things rest. It was good to find time to relax. The feeling of being stuck between two worlds would be hard to overcome.

After two days at home, she took a bus to Hargesheim, a village north of Bad Kreuznach, and stayed with the Uhls. No, Christhilde, her best friend, but Peter, the oldest, Marietta, Heinz, and Haribert still lived at home along with five younger siblings. *Herr* Uhl was always at work or in the garden, and *Frau* Uhl was the sweetest, kindest mother and was especially busy with her younger children. Even with such a large family, it was a relaxed household. Everyone did their part, and every visitor was welcome and made to feel at home. For Geli, this was a second home. In the evenings, other friends like Tobias, Thomas, or Wolfgang, Marietta's boyfriend, would stop by. The older "kids" would hang out in Peter's or Marietta's room while the younger kids played outside and went to bed early. The Uhls, a Catholic family with ten children, meant receiving a substantial monthly per-child *Kindergeld* payment from the German government. Kindergeld was a generous state subsidy to promote an increase in the German population after the devastation of World War II. This benefit meant Frau Uhl could afford to stay home and manage the large family. The older kids would stay up late talking and maybe listening to music. Peter and Marietta worked in the mornings, and Heinz and Haribert went to school half days and worked their trade in the afternoons, so everyone was asleep by 11.

Geli's best friend since *Kindergarten*, Helga, is now married and living a few hours north. She returned to Bosenheim to reconnect with her long-absent friend. Growing up, Helga and Geli were inseparable. They did everything together, usually arm in arm. Even eating an apple was a combined effort for the two. Geli could never take the first bite, so Helga had to do this for her. At age 14, Helga was in a bad motorcycle accident, which meant Geli started her apprenticeship while Helga took time to recuperate from her debilitating accident. For the first time, they went in different directions. Geli began her job in the city and became friends with co-worker Gabi. Helga and Geli remained good friends but were no longer inseparable. Before leaving for Florida, Geli was Helga's best friend at her wedding, where she married Ewald, a friend from their group in Bad Kreuznach. Ewald had been serving his mandatory time in the army, and they had a son, Swen, who was now four months old. Geli had become his Godmother.

Helga offered for Geli to come and live with her, Ewald, and Swen near *Köln* (Cologne). Ewald had recently completed his last year of military service and began a new job managing produce deliveries at a large company. Geli did not want to live at her parent's home. So, after being home for more than a week, she took a train north to live with Helga and her family. She would sleep on the couch of their two-bedroom apartment while she sorted out her new life back in Germany. Helga welcomed Geli into this new family life, where she and Helga spent every day together again. They talked all the time and reconnected quickly. She shared with Helga how lonely she had felt, especially during her later times in Florida living at the Ranch.

Geli still felt stuck between two worlds and thought she didn't belong in either. Everything was still so strange. It was taking longer to get used to being back than she thought it would. Her life with me was always on her mind, and she still wasn't sure life without me was what she wanted.

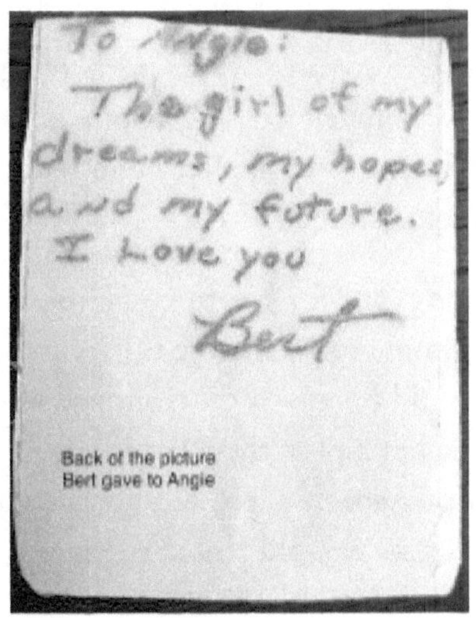

Bert's note to Angie on the back of his picture for her to remember.

Helga knew a woman who owned a small Bratwurst restaurant in town, just one big room, that was now out of business. She said she would reopen it if Geli agreed to work there. Geli needed money and had to start somewhere. She learned how to make curry wursts and fries and operated the business for the owner. She eventually rented a bedroom in a nearby older couple's house. She moved off Helga's couch and settled into her new life. She'd work the daytime and spend most evenings with Helga. She wrote letters a few times but did not have my address, so she sent them to Peggy, my ex, in Michigan. None ever made it to me.

After two weeks in a strange town with Helga as her only friend, she felt isolated again, and her life was getting wishy-washy. She received a phone call from Gabi at Helga's inviting her to live at the house in Asbach, which she shared with Rudi. Gabi explained how it was a beautiful country village with farmlands and forests and how friendly the people were. Their house was a 100-year-old *fachwerk* (timber frame) fixer-upper. Instead of paying rent, they agreed to make some repairs. After three weeks with Helga, it was time to try something else. Geli felt terrible about leaving the bratwurst restaurant and backing out on the lady who reopened it. But it was time for her to do something different.

Geli and Gabi made plans for her to come to Asbach in two days. Geli would first go home to pack more things and tell her family her new plans. Gabi would borrow a car from a neighboring commune of "friends" to pick her up at the Darmstadt train station, about 45 minutes north of Asbach. Geli said goodbye to Helga and her family. She left her one-week-old rented room and new job and took a train home to Bad Kreuznach. She was to catch the train the next afternoon to meet Gabi, so she spent one last night with her friends in Hargesheim. She would stop by her parents to collect her things the next day on the way to catch the train.

On her two-hour train ride back to Bad Kreuznach, she had time to think about her feeling of belonging to two different worlds and wonder how and what I was doing back in Florida without her. She loved me so much. I was her first true love and longest relationship. She had a few previous relationships, but none ever lasted too long. Friendship and having fun with her friends were always more important than being isolated in a relationship with just one person. Now, she needed to have time to decide what was the right path for her. Maybe she could begin to do this in Asbach. Find a job and eventually get a place to live. One step at a time, she thought. After a year and a half with me back in Florida, she was now lonely in a different way. She missed the closeness we had shared but knew leaving Florida was the right thing to do. Returning to her familiar surroundings did seem to establish a possible new way forward for her.

Chapter 16
Arranging The Pieces

S aturday, the day after Angie left, I managed to move my life's accumulations from the motel to Troy's. My VW died the night before and still sat on the side of the road near Pete and Terri's house. I took a bus to Mike Carroll's in Delray Beach to get his help moving my stuff. Luckily, he was home. He drove me back to my motel room, where we loaded his VW Microbus with my belongings. We took most of what I wanted to keep and would bring to Germany to Troy's. We left the rest on his bus to sell at a flea market we would attend at an old drive-in theater back in Delray Beach the next day. I hoped to sell my stereo, stacks of albums, bass guitar, kitchen stuff, assorted posters and pictures, a fencing helmet and foil, and other odds and ends to make some extra money. We split the $10 setup fee for the flea market space.

Mike crashed on the couch at Troy's, and we overslept. We arrived late and were assigned one of the last available spots in the back of the drive-in theater. It was the beginning of a hot summer day, and the flea market had no shade. At first, it was a hornet's nest of prospective buyers, but soon, the summer rains started, and the people dried up. I didn't sell enough to cover the setup fee and gas there. What a disappointment. I decided to leave the remainder of my belongings with Mike and the understanding that if I did not return from Germany, he could keep it all. Mike took me back to Pete's house, and we got my VW running again. They pushed while I sat in the car and popped the clutch. It took us three attempts, and they were exhausted, but it finally started.

As I was wrapping up my life in Florida, I found spending 50 cents for bus tickets whenever possible cheaper than driving. After settling in at Troy's for a few days, I took the bus to the courthouse in West Palm to apply for a passport. They informed me it would take at least six weeks to process and referred me to their Miami office, where I could request an expedited one, taking only a few weeks. It's not a great day so far, but I will settle my affairs and set my plan in motion.

I found a phone booth, pulled out all my change, and called the Miami office. They told me to bring my birth certificate, two passport photos, and $65. I found a photography studio not far from the courthouse to have my pictures taken. I could pick them up the next day. I already had my birth certificate, so I was all set for tomorrow's 90-minute trip to Miami.

Car trouble, again, delayed me a few days, so I decided to wait till Monday. I spent Saturday snorkeling with Leonard. I still needed my car for a few more weeks, but then I hoped to sell it to Leonard. I knew he needed one. He was moving back to New Jersey soon but had already decided to buy his neighbor's old Nash Rambler instead. He knew I would be selling my VW, but we had no agreement, and the Rambler cost him only $200. I needed the cash and wanted to sell the car for $350 or more before I left the country. If I sold the VW to a dealer, it would only bring $200, so I hoped to find someone to buy it for a lot more. Without a phone, I could not list it in the *Trading Post*, so putting a for sale sign in the side window is my best option now.

On Monday, I stopped by Tom's, an acquaintance, to collect the $15 he owed me and decided to leave the VW running as it might not restart. Before I drove to West Palm Beach and picked up my passport photos, I got a friend at my local gas station to tune up my

VW. It was now after 2 PM, and Miami would have to wait another day.

Tuesday, May 11th, was Angie's and my anniversary of meeting at Big Daddy's lounge. It's a good day to travel to Miami and start the passport process. I was counting on this expedited passport process to work and be ready to pick it up in two weeks. Fighting the Miami morning traffic and using the city insert map on my Florida state map, I found my way to the passport office. After completing the paperwork, they asked me where to have the passport mailed. I was shocked and assumed I would return to pick it up. I didn't know Troy's address, so I gave them my parent's address in Fort Walton Beach. I guess I'd be making another trip up to see them.

Sitting down and writing out my budget and thinking about how many more days I had till my flight, I calculated that I should be able to stop at my parents on the way back from Michigan, where I would visit Kimberly once more before I left. I had less than three weeks before my flight, and my plans would only work if I could earn more money to add to my leftover savings. Selling the VW for a fair price would also be essential.

Troy told me about an "employment agency" he once used to earn cash for day labor. Following his instructions, I showed up at a specific street corner early Wednesday morning and joined a growing group of a dozen, mostly Hispanic men, for a chance to ease the strain on my budget. A man pulled up to the group in a big van, pointed to six of us, and we piled in the back. The driver dropped us off at a rail yard where we unloaded car after car of boxes, dog food, turtle food, fertilizer, and who knows how many other bags of assorted 50-pound sacks onto dollies to fill waiting tractor trailers. I worked at this site for the temp agency for two more full days, moving heavy bags, before I felt I had enough money to get by for my last two weeks. With all the lifting, I hadn't been this sore since high school football (double days) practice. Now, I felt pain inside and outside.

Before I left for Germany, I wanted to visit Michigan to see Kimberly, but that would be expensive, and even if I slept in my car or stayed with an old friend, it would cut me too short on time and money. Several times over the last two weeks, I went to a pay phone to call Peggy at her parents' house in Jackson, Michigan. It was nearly impossible to reach her. Either there was no answer, or I briefly talked with a parent who said they would tell Peggy I called and when I planned to call back. We finally connected the week before I was to leave for Germany. Peggy was still cold toward me, and our conversation was short. I told her I was no longer working and heading to Germany. When I mentioned I didn't know when I could send her more child support, she told me she was getting some government assistance and could manage it so they would get by.

As the curt phone call ended, I wrote Peggy and Kimberly a long letter to express my feelings since I couldn't do this on the phone. I loved Kimberly and felt terrible I was leaving for an uncertain future, and I had to let her know this. I trusted Peggy would somehow let Kimberly know my feelings. I called the Credit Union I formally used in Jackson, Michigan, to close my account and send the $125 balance to Peggy. They explained what to include in a letter to them, and they said they would close my account and send Peggy the balance.

I closed my checking account at my bank in Lake Park and converted all my money to traveler's checks that I could spend almost anywhere. Since a visit to Michigan was now out of the picture, I would have the time to make my trip to my parents in Fort Walton

Beach without rushing. I included a stop to say goodbye to my friends Andy and Audrey near Tallahassee.

Before my early but honorable discharge, my last three months in the Air Force were with a new group of Airmen. One of the radio technicians was Andy, who was not only an excellent radio repairman but also a master at ping pong. Every day in King Hanger, it seemed all we did was play ping pong. The overstaffed repair shop had very few radios in need of repairs. Everyone was waiting for orders to ship out to a new duty station.

In these last three months, I spent all my off time working on a financial discharge. If I could document that my expenses were more than my paycheck would cover and that I had a job offer that paid more, I would be granted an early, honorable discharge and not need to complete my four-year enlistment. No one had used this type of financial discharge since the end of the Korean War. I knew this Chief Master Sergeant from Hurlbert Field, adjacent to Eglin AFB, who helped me through the process.

During my last six months in the Air Force, Peggy and I managed the Mansfield Motel (nightly, weekly, and monthly stays) while trying to find a way to an honorable and early discharge. The owner offered us more money if I could get an early discharge from the Air Force. The Chief Master Sergeant was a regular Patron of the motel bar and seemed to like me. With his guidance, I was out a couple of months after collecting a stack of signed affidavits. Ironically, within the month after my discharge, the Air Force allowed anyone who enlisted during the Vietnam wartime to sign a simple release and get out. Andy took advantage of this, as did several other friends. During these last months, Peggy and I had become good friends with Audrey and Andy. As Peggy and I finally dissolved our relationship, I leaned on Audrey and Andy quite a bit. I was going to Tallahassee to see them before leaving the country.

Chapter 17
Saying Goodbye

When I called Audrey to plan a visit, she said she and Andy were still separated. He had moved to Statesboro, Georgia, but said we'd find a way to get together. She was excited to have me up for a visit. I left West Palm Beach after lunch, hoping to get to Audrey's before dark, but my VW Bug broke down at a small truck stop north of Gainesville. I looked under the hood on the back but had no idea what to look for, so I called Audrey, and she agreed to drive down to get me the following day. I spent the night hanging out with the two young guys working at this small, rural truck stop, playing pinball and talking. I fell asleep in my front seat around 5 AM.

Audrey arrived in her old Dodge van with her dog Cowboy at 11:30. She said she rarely went anywhere without him. Cowboy was a mixed breed medium-sized dog with a calm and pleasant disposition. Maybe a cross between a Husky and some smaller dog with a cute, curled tail. She brought an old tire to strap between our two vehicles and some rope to tie the two cars together. She and Cowboy would tow while I sat in the bug to steer. As we connected our two vehicles with the rope and a dozen knots, a man, coming out of a nearby diner, asked what was wrong, and I explained. He asked if he could look at the VW's engine. After less than a minute, he reconnected a wire that came loose and said, "Give it a try now."

I jumped back in the seat, and what do you know, it started right up. I didn't have much, but I gave the man $5 for his timely expertise. We untied the rope, threw the tire back in Audrey's van, and followed her a few hours back to her place. We spent the afternoon at Audrey's catching up, then headed out in her van to Statesboro, Georgia.

With Cowboy perched in the backseat, we cruised the back roads through northern Florida and southern Georgia, reminiscing until dark. I asked Audrey about Andy and the issues that had separated them. Audrey and I were close friends, so her sharing their problems was not out of line for my inquiry. I listened to her and asked questions about her and Andy's sentiments. I focused on placing myself in each of their shoes. It was easy for me to relate because Andy and I were similar regarding "not talking" about emotional issues. When Audrey talked to me, I focused on her feelings and what Andy might be going through.

My few comments and observations made Audrey feel comfortable. Why couldn't I have done more of this with Angie? Angie and I were so close, whereas I only saw Audrey a few times a year. Regardless, I made little past progress with Angie but held out hope for a time when I could be with Angie again, to do more than listen, to engage. I wished to get more opportunities to do just that with Angie if I could find her.

Along the way to Andy's, we picked up Bill, a hitchhiker in his 70s. Bill entertained us for miles with 40 years of hitchhiking stories he had lived through. Had Bill lived 50 years earlier, he would have been just another hobo riding the rails looking for telltale chalk X marks in people's driveways to beg for food. Bill sat with Cowboy in the back seat, who seemed to like him, so Audrey and I also took to him. When we dropped him off at a Salvation Army shelter, we bought him food and a pack of cigarettes and said farewell.

Delayed by a coolant leak for three hours and a self-patch job with a roll of electrical tape, we finally arrived in Statesboro wanting to surprise Andy. Like most of us, he had no phone. Audrey thought she remembered where he lived, but we spent hours looking before finding his house at about 3 AM. As soon as we pulled into his driveway, Audrey realized she had left Cowboy at the last place we asked for directions, so we raced back and found him sitting, perfectly calm, waiting for us. What a relief.

After the long drive, we spent Sunday catching up with Andy and relaxing in his backyard until the summer heat became unbearable. That afternoon, we visited the local bar for happy hour, 15-cent beer, and a shot pool in the cool air conditioning. Later, we went to the university campus to watch a cheap movie, Blazing Saddles. While Andy was at work, on Tuesday, Audrey and a friend of Andy's, Georgia Anne, cooked us all a nice dinner. I spent most of that time curled up in a chair, trying to finish Albert Camus's *The Plague*. I connected the plot of understanding and fighting the plague with my struggle to understand and remedy my emotional pestilence with Angie.

———

As our dinner was finishing, Andy said something teasing to Audrey, who responded with the remains of her glass of water thrown in Andy's face. Andy said nothing, got up, went to the bathroom, and returned with his own water. He stood behind her and slowly poured water over Audrey's head. She sat there unmoved with a scowl as the water followed her long, straight, blonde hair and completely soaked her body. What Audrey had thought, without looking to see the source of this waterfall, might be a glass full, turned out to be a pail full. When the cascade of water refused to stop, she picked up the stick of butter and threw it at Andy's face, who caught it in the palm of his hand and smeared it all over Audrey's face, hair, and ear. Georgia Anne and I laughed till we cried.

Andy's and Audrey's make-up sex, soon after, loudly proclaimed they were, in fact, still close friends.

Audrey, just before the water fight, Statesboro, Georgia.

After tearful goodbyes in Statesboro and again back at Audrey's, I drove a few hours west to Ft. Walton Beach to surprise my parents. I hadn't told them I was coming. In their later years, my parents managed motels and had recently moved to Fort Walton Beach to run the Econo-Travel Motel. Coincidentally, my parent's motel was a block down the street from where I managed a different motel (Mansfield Apartments and Motel, Daily/Weekly/Monthly) while stationed at Eglin AFB.

I spent most of the next day visiting with my parents, telling them about my plans and how I hoped my passport would arrive at their place soon! My dad and I played golf in the afternoon, which we had done many times since I was a teenager. My mom had a nice home-cooked dinner waiting for us that evening. The next day, I tried to contact my old friend and karate instructor, Jim. I called 7 or 8 Rodriguez in the Fort Walton Beach phone book before finally reaching him. We met with Wanda, Jim's long-time partner, and spent the night on the town until 4 AM.

The following day, I got the VW ready to sell, washed and waxed it, installed some new carpet, placed two for sale signs in the windows, and parked it in front of the motel. While I was looking for the title in my stored boxes, a couple stopped and fell in love with the car. They planned to add extra insulation inside the doors and travel to Alaska. I explained the missing title, and the man, not too concerned, said he'd stop back in the morning. Sure enough, the man stopped by at 8:30 AM the following day. We drove to the DMV/tax office, and I completed the paperwork for a lost title and completed the sale. $350 richer now. With this sale, I wouldn't have to ask my parents to borrow money, which had been my backup plan. The day improved; my passport arrived in the mail, and I could now prepare to wrap everything up in Florida and begin my new journey.

Everything was falling into place and starting to get real. No turning back now. My sun was rising in the east, and I felt more confident and comfortable with my evolving plan. Would it work, I thought? My efforts were coming together now, and I was nearing my departure, a few days away.

After dinner that night, I talked with my mom about politics and religion, as we had done frequently since high school. This rambling discussion devolved into morning hours of hearing of Mom and Dad's troubles, co-managing a motel. These alcohol-endured misgivings from my mom were similar to our previous talks when I was younger and still living at home. I forced myself to "not" dismiss her complaints and still give her my honest appraisal. My mom was not an emotional person unless she had a few drinks. I asked her some questions that went deeper than I thought, and she opened up more. All the while we conversed, I was thinking about my problem, followed by engaged talking, leading to not really solutions but at least progress or, at some point, clarity. I was starting to see my past inattentiveness as more than ignoring others for not caring, but more because of my impatience with their lack of progress. In my quiet mind, I rarely dwelled on a problem and decided what I might do quickly or, more likely, just left my fate to the wind and moved on.

After a long night, the 25th started with a big breakfast, which was my dad's specialty (and would also become mine). Lots of advice and expressions of quiet love came with a big hug from Mom. Finally, my dad took me to the airport for a three-stop flight back to West Palm Beach. From the airport in West Palm, I hitched a ride to Troy's place only to find him gone and the doors locked. I Walked several blocks to a pay phone and called Peter, who picked me up and took me back to his house.

Chapter 18
Big Bambu

I spent the last few days before leaving the country with friends as often as I could manage without having my car. Without Angie, it just wasn't the same. It seems we have all changed over the past year. We played volleyball, went to the beach, and hung out at someone's house every evening, but with Angie's absence, it wasn't as much fun anymore. Good friends Pete and Terri had decided to break up amicably. They still lived in the same house, but Terri began seeing an old sailing friend. Jerry had grown up in the area and, coming from a family of long-time recreational sailors, was well known to the local customs patrols. With this relationship, he managed to run quantities of pot through customs on his 40-foot sailboat without being challenged. Terri and Jerry stayed paranoid and were no longer much fun. My former house-mates, Steve and Marie, were deep into their relationship and couldn't be happier. I visited with them and had a good time, but their relationship was more about each other, and like everyone else, I was a mere distraction from their dedication to each other. Everyone's lives were changing, and I knew it was time for my life to move on.

With my passport and plane ticket in hand, the day finally arrived for me to go to the International Airport in Fort Lauderdale and begin my new journey. I asked Pete if a letter from Angie had come for me. Nothing had come, no word, which was concerning but not wholly unexpected. Considering the slow postal service for overseas mail, hearing back from Angie might take several weeks. Did she get the letter I sent a month ago? Did she not know how to respond? Maybe she realized it was all a mistake and resumed her life in Germany, seeking a new path alone or with someone else.

I knew we had a real connection, but should I follow through on this momentous, life-altering plan and chase after Angie? Casting my fate to the wind, I knew in my gut this was the moment to listen to my heart and take the leap. There was no turning back. I longed to be with Angie again, and if this failed, then I would at least know for sure to move on and try to rebuild my life anew. With all my soul, I hoped there would be a passionate reunion to reunite us again.

Bert, in front of Pete's and Terri's house, on his last day in Florida.

Terri, Pete, Pam, and Jerry offered me a farewell ride to remember in Jerry's small car to commemorate my exit from Florida. Pete and Terri (you rarely spoke one name without the other, even after their separation) wanted to make my 60-minute trip unforgettable. Terri picked the route off the interstates, and music and Pete rolled a joint for the road that would last almost the whole hour. We couldn't even finish it. He used the rolling paper from a Cheech & Chong record album, *Big Bambu*, which was the size of the album. It took about a half ounce to make it work. That pretty much describes our ride to the airport. Pete and Terri hugged me at the departure drop-off. They both excitedly jumped up and down. We exchanged lots of advice, and then, poof, I was all alone on the sidewalk in another world.

Pete, Terri, Pam, and Jerry begin a ride to remember, taking Bert to the airport to start his journey to regain his lost soul.

The sun was baking down, and people were everywhere, rushing this way and that but inhabiting different worlds. There I stood in a temporary daze, with my long hair and beard, wearing my patched jeans and a long-sleeved jean shirt. My faded blue shirt was something special, and I paid a friend to embroider an elaborate Chinese dragon across the back. I shouldered my Air Force duffel bag and lifted Angie's homemade (from an older pair of white jeans) cross-shoulder satchel over my head, placed my ratty straw hat on my head, and made my way to the Air Bahamas ticket counter. I patiently waited in line while I gathered my senses, the few I had left.

I told the young woman ticket agent I wanted to check in for my one-way flight to Luxembourg. The agent asked me why, one way, and with few exceptions beyond German nationals, everyone had a round-trip ticket. I briefly explained my situation, and after a side conversation between the agent and her supervisor, they both questioned me further and explained the financial and political dangers of buying a one-way ticket. After a phone call to a likely customs official, they said they could let me board with the one-way ticket IF I also had the money for a return ticket. It was not unheard of for a person to be rejected from entry to a country and forced to return, and in this case, it would cost another $325, possibly leaving Air Bahama on the hook. I knew I didn't. I had less than $50 but said I had the money. Luckily, they did not ask to see the cash. Ticket in hand, sea bag checked, and homemade satchel over my shoulder, I followed the signs to my gate and eventually boarded the plane.

Stepping onto the plane was a transformation of old life fading, space becoming confining, air cooler, air pressure denser, and almost everything changed. Life would never be the same. The cabin door closed. I had no home to return to in Florida should I be refused entry into Luxembourg. My parents' motel in the Florida panhandle had no place for me. My closest sister, Joyce, had moved to Dallas,

Texas, with her kids, but I had no desire to go to Texas anyway. Nope, nothing here to keep me or make me want to return. My path was set onward and, literally, upward. Short hop to Nassau for a three-hour delay before the long flight to Europe. With little money left, I'd sit under a big ceiling fan, looking out through the wall of windows at another tropical paradise.

The flight across the ocean mainly was sleep. I was lucky that I could sleep anywhere. As soon as we attained cruising altitude, the in-flight meal arrived. As a vegetarian, I had little to eat and was fortunate enough to have no one next to me, so I stretched out and started reading one of Hermann Hesse's books but mostly slept. Others might stress or fret about the uncertainty of my plan, but I was not one to "ponder the question too long," to quote Jimmy Buffett.

I rarely stressed about things, even the big stuff, like this trip and if I would find Angie again. I learned this trait from my parents, who, although primarily stable, were constantly moving and rarely had financial security. They often lived life expensively on the cheap. In other words, they had little money, but when they did, they spent it and had a lavish good time. Never worrying about tomorrow, they knew time would take care of them, or they would do without or move on. Somehow, they always seemed to manage. This attitude I inherited was the opposite of Angie's outlook on life. Her upbringing made her anticipate almost everything. Not in a negative way, just your typical German way. Think ahead, prepare, and determine the best, most efficient path. She never forgot a thing either, as I could attest. She was also never judgmental and saw everything surrounding her life as an objective opportunity or sometimes a hurdle. Angie was what I needed now, and as each day went by without her, I knew she was the one to complete my life. With the seat next to me empty, I stretched out and drifted off with a warm feeling of hopeful things to come, nothing specific, just feelings.

Part 4
Into the Looking Glass

Chapter 19
Down the Rabbit Hole

Luxembourg

The captain announced over the P.A., "We are now entering European air space and will be landing at Luxembourg International Airport in 37 minutes. Prepare for arrival...etc., etc.". With the air pressure beginning to change and the sounds of lots of people shuffling to re-stow their gear, stewards readying the cabin for the descent, I awoke this final time to look out the small window and start to hope at what I expected to greet me very shortly. Clouds began to part, and a large land mass appeared below. Green hills, yellow fields, rivers, and lakes reflected sunlight as we slowly descended. Between the scattered clouds, I could see a smattering of small villages but no cities. I buckled my seatbelt and brought my seat upright as directed. My ears could now sense the changing altitude. This and the pit in my stomach over what the anticipated reunion would bring finally made me feel uneasy yet hopeful.

I imagined Angie and a few close friends, who had driven several hours, waiting for my plane to land, then seeing each other, running to each other with an embrace that would last a lifetime. This would be followed by frantic introductions, new languages and accents, handshakes, and hugs of new friends, followed by a long, comfortable ride to Angie's home in the back seat of a friend's car, holding hands and savoring the mutually welcome reunion. Yes, this would be perfect, I thought.

The wheels touched down, and the rush of the brakes grabbed hold as the airport came into view. Scattered planes on the tarmac were taxiing to and fro while others, lined in neat rows, were offloading passengers down stairways. Several hundred meters beyond, a large two-story wing of a building, with a rooftop outside viewing area, crowded with people looking at all the disembarking passengers. I strained to see a glimpse of Angie. I knew she must be somewhere in the large group of onlookers, but everyone looked similar from this distance. Finally, I was out the door and down the stairs to the tarmac. Straining some more, I looked to find my lost love. I must keep moving with the anxious, embarking passengers; everyone has places to go and people to see. Surely, I'll find her when I get through customs and comb the crowds. Soon, I would see my "beautiful 19-year-old German girl," as the ad stated, with waist-long reddish-brown hair and eyes that could see into the depths of my soul, only minutes away.

Bert's passport, stamped by the Miami Customs Office.

Passport stamped and seabag over my shoulder, I moved along and through double doors to the rush of people. I stood tall to see over the crowd of people ahead of me who were shouting and moving in and out of each other's way. I saw smiles, hugs, tears, excitement, and people pushing through to find their way. It was all so exciting with so much emotion, but no Angie. I looked everywhere and thought maybe there was another exit point, or probably, with such a long drive, there was some delay, road construction, or whatnot. I wandered around, eyes constantly searching, heart pounding, and brain imagining all the possibilities. What if she did not want me to come after her and was glad to have left me in Florida? No, I decided. Our goodbye at the West Palm Beach airport was only a month ago, and I knew the tears we shared then meant more to us both. She would not leave me abandoned and alone.

Angie's note to Bert on the back of a picture for him to remember her.

Having walked almost everywhere at the airport, I decided to find a conspicuous place to wait. How long should I wait, an hour, two, or three? I had nowhere else to be. I didn't know how to use the phones – even so, Angie's parents had no home phone, and I had no other contact. I had one address in my tiny black address book, which I kept in my wallet. This address didn't even make sense. I couldn't tell which was a street or town name, and the numbers were unclear. So, I'd wait. International flights were all in, and the airport slowly paced down to a less hectic atmosphere. A couple of hours passed, and still no Angie.

I struck up a conversation with a young French man who spoke a little English. We went for a beer while time passed. I related my unfortunate situation, but he never understood the depth of my despair. While we struggled to understand each other's small talk, my mind was in overdrive, with many questions needing immediate answers. I knew Angie lived somewhere near Frankfurt, but how could I get there if Angie didn't show up? How much would it cost? Bad Kreuznach would be farther still and cost more. Then, could I even find her house with the address I had? I still have $40 and change; I must make it last. My new friend told me where to find a group of buses destined for several major Western European cities parked outside the airport fence, and they would all be leaving soon. He said I was three to four hours from Frankfurt, so I donned my straw hat, loaded my shoulder bag and sea bag, and headed for the busses.

I found the bus for Frankfurt, paid about $18 for a ticket, and settled into a seat for a long ride. No one I encountered spoke English except the French guy at the airport bar. I was beginning to realize my mushrooming loneliness, which wasn't settling well with me. I looked out the window at a different world passing by. We traveled along narrow, curvy roads, past houses of stone with red tile roofs and so close together. The people I saw on the streets dressed differently, and the towns and villages looked nothing like places I had ever been. As my window to this new world passed through village streets, shopping and industrial areas, and quaint neighborhoods, I felt almost like I was falling into an infinite spiral, spinning as I fell. I saw forests and hilly terrain, but the endless villages kept appearing. I was traveling through a maze of never-ending communities, each different than the last, with unpronounceable names. It all blended in my mind as if it were another dimension where I would lose myself. Only the anticipation and hope of rejoining Angie kept me going.

The bus eventually passed larger urban areas on *Autobahns* and entered the Frankfurt inner city, so I moved up and sat right behind the driver. When it stopped at a signal light, I asked the driver if he could let me off close to the train station. He spoke some English and said he had to drop everyone at the same stop, a long way from the train station. The driver noted the scared concern on my face and, a few blocks later, turned and said, "Be ready, jump quick, when I say. At the next signal, two blocks from the train station. You go quick". With a sense of relief, I acknowledged my good fortune. He stopped at the next signal light and said, "Quick, go there, short distance, the trains." "GOOD LUCK"!

I bolted out the door onto the busy 5 PM street, engulfed by tall buildings. Masses of people going every which way. Walking down crowded sidewalks, first, one block, then another, looking in every direction at each corner, I wondered what a train station might look like. I kept going and found the Frankfurt *Hauptbahnhof*, with multiple open-air entrances and thousands of people who knew exactly where they were going and how many minutes until they arrived to catch their train. I knew neither. I shuffled around in a daze; everything looked mysterious, and I had no idea what to do or how to communicate. Finally, I saw a large, glassed, walled room with impatient people lined up under a sign that said INFO, among other unknown words. First, I stood in the wrong queue and asked if anyone spoke English. The hurried man said *Nein* and pointed to another line where I waited till another young man forcefully slowed down to help me buy an equivalent $8 train ticket to Bad Kreuznach. He directed me to track number 7 to catch the train, leaving in a few minutes! Yikes, pushing my way through and down steps to the passage under tracks 1 - 6 and up to the right track, I was starting to feel like everyone else.

2-inch-tall train ticket from Frankfurt, through Mainz, to Bad Kreuznach

I boarded the car on the train with Bad Kreuznach on the engine marquee, sat with my bags, and hoped I had followed directions correctly. As the train pulled out, the conductor stamped my small ticket with a date and time and, in broken English, told me we would arrive in exactly 58 minutes. What a relief. Now, I was feeling better and had some time to anticipate what would be next.

My knowledge of all things German was nothing more than what Angie shared the past year. She had taught me to count to ten, say the days of the week, *hallo, auf Wiedersehen, bitte,* or excuse me (I thought), and that was about it. I assumed Bad Kreuznach would be a small city where people were familiar and knowledgeable about each other. I could likely find someone who could look at the address and point me directly to Angie's house and our happily-awaited reunion. I thought, ah, the funny story to ensue about car trouble on the Autobahn and how they got to the airport just after I found my way to the Frankfurt bus and their long, tiring journey home, arriving shortly before I was to get there. Right, that's what must have happened.

As the train pulled into Bad Kreuznach, I realized this was no small city like I had imagined, but one of a hundred thousand or even more people. The sun had set, and it would soon get dark, maybe 8:30, as I walked through the empty station and out to the street with my bags in tow. The cool air was refreshing, and all the smells were new. Many people, who looked Middle Eastern or maybe Turkish, were waiting outside the station. Everyone here was hurrying, but nothing like they were in Frankfurt. Feeling better, I checked my money before deciding how to proceed. Down to less than $20. Where to now?

I saw some of the awaiting people crowding into taxis and leaving. Walking over to the driver of an empty cab, I pointed to Angie's address in my little black address book. The driver didn't speak English but motioned me to get in the front seat. I trusted the driver knew more than I did, so I climbed in. I waited as he loaded more passengers, none speaking English or German. An older woman, a scarf around her head with a young child, got in the back, followed by two men, not with the woman and child, and yet one more man got in the front seat with the driver and me. The taxi traveled all over, dropping each in different locations over the next half hour. After driving another 10 minutes, he stopped in a small village and said, "Bosenheim"! I looked again at the address, and sure enough, Bosenheim was a word in the address. I asked, "But where is this house?" and pointed to the address in my book. The driver shrugged his shoulders and repeated, "Bosenheim"!

Now dark, I get out of the cab, collect my bags, pay the driver $8, and he's gone. Standing there looking at the quiet but long street traversing the town, I contemplate my options. Standing at the sweeping curve of this two-lane main street with one somewhat dim street lamp hanging over the road, I take a long look in one direction, then turn and stare down the other. The entire length of the street consists of three-story houses, all connected and remarkably similar looking. The places were all made from concrete blocks, stucco finishes, orange ceramic tile roofs, lace-curtained windows with shutters on each side, and usually a window flower box. All windows were well above my head so I could see little within.

As I stood there assessing my dwindling options, a loud noise behind me startled me back to reality. The large window just above my head slammed shut as a covering rolled down to seal the entire window. Some houses had courtyards behind tall gated walls, but you couldn't see inside. A few lights were on behind the closed wooden gates, and I could hear people moving around in the courtyards. I looked in each direction and saw side streets intersecting the road with more houses and wide sidewalks on each side of this main street. No grass or trees were present, and the few cars coming through did so quickly and disappeared into the blackness. Not a soul in sight. My world suddenly became an empty small town with one dim street light and no visible people. Each direction seemed to lead nowhere. My mind became as lost as my body, and my carefully planned trail ended.

Chapter 20
A Crack in the Rolladens

There I stood, $10 and change in my pocket, in a town I think, I hope, is Angie's hometown. I don't speak the language nor see a soul on the now pitch-dark, deserted street. What to do? I knock on a wooden gate, wait, and with no response, move to another and knock on it. Finally, behind a closed gate, I hear, "*Hallo*." I say, "I'm looking for Angie, Angelika Weyell," and ask for help. I hear some confused talking from the unseen resident in German (behind the closed gate), trying to gain any comprehension with no success. I move on, and another "hallo?" More of the same. No one has a clue who I am or what I am saying. At one point, I remembered a German word and replied with bitte, which I incorrectly remember as meaning "excuse me," as in I'm sorry, but it means, please say that again. So, I would speak, the German resident would speak, I would say "bitte" and attempt to move along, at which point the resident would repeat him or herself, and I would again say "bitte." After the third time, I walked off while someone was repeating himself. Never once did anyone open their gate to where I might attempt face-to-face communication.

I walked ten minutes down the long street, searching for any sign of life to continue my quest for help. With the end of the houses up ahead and the single dim street light far behind, I spot a small neon sign, about the size of a placemat, in a lower window of one of the row houses and notice the gate is a bit bigger than all the rest. With no traffic on the dark street, I walk across and listen from below the window. I can't look in because the window is maybe 2 meters above the sidewalk. I hear voices in social conversation, so I knock at the large gate several times. No answer. Bravely, I lift the gate handle, and the gate swings open. I enter a courtyard with a small car or two, a farm wagon, and the entrance to the building under a large overhang. The large door has ornate glass; I think it may be a business, bar, or restaurant. I knock twice with no answer but hear the conversational voices within.

Finally, a young woman, a bit startled, opens the door and speaks to me in German. I go through a brief explanation in English to no avail, but the young woman says, "Ah, English, *einen moment*," and motions me into the bar/restaurant establishment to wait while she fetches someone. Inside, a handful of patrons sit drinking beer around a large table, and all conversation stops. They look me over solemnly, and no one says a word. There I stand, tired and a bit unkempt, with my large seabag, satchel over my shoulder, and straw hat covering my long hair. I nod to them and give a subtle wave, but no one responds.

An older man arrives, who turns out to be the young woman's father, and remembering some English from the war (WWII), says, "*Guten Abend*, can I help you"? The nice man talks to me in German and some broken English. I explained how I came from the United States to find Angelika (I think I am finally pronouncing this halfway correctly) Weyell. I say Weyell like Y-el. The man ponders this for a bit and murmurs, "Y-el, Y-el," but there is no understanding. I pull out my address book and point to Angie's name and address, and in a moment of reckoning, the man states more succinctly and exclaims, "Ah Weyell," as in the correct German pronunciation, "Vi-ell." With a broad smile, he rapidly speaks to me (in German), explains something to his daughter, and then leads me to his small, old station wagon in the courtyard. He lifts my duffle bag into the rear compartment and motions for me to sit in the passenger seat.

Opening the big gate, we head out on the main street. All the while, the nice man tries to engage me in the most basic conversation. I try to understand or even to pay attention, but at this point, I am so exhausted I can barely think straight. A few turns and two minutes later, we drive up a rough, short, dusty lane to the third house from the end and pull into a dirt driveway in complete darkness. He parks at the beginning of this driveway, holds up both hands, signals for me to wait while he goes up the steps, and rings the doorbell.

After a moment, a yellow porch light comes on. As I watch through the windshield, a short, older man answers the door. There is an exchange of conversation, and a taller, somewhat heavier woman directly joins the conversation. Now, around 10:00, they talk while I'm sitting out of hearing range in the passenger seat of the small car. Every once in a while, one of them points toward me, and they chuckle or gesture in a friendly way. Finally waving at me, the driver motioned for me to come up and join the group. Mostly relieved and tired, I get out and, amongst the chatter, ascend the short stairs. The three are talking in German, of course. There are no handshakes or hugs but many smiles, and I wonder if I have found the correct address or am at the wrong house and now just the central topic of some odd event in this small village.

There was no Angie; she would have surely come running for my rescue if there. After an eternity of probably 2 minutes, I was invited into the foyer while the driver collected my duffle bag. More indistinguishable conversation, and just as the driver was about to abandon me, I saw a picture of Angie and me standing on ocean rocks with the sea to our backs on the living room wall through another door. Our wedding photo. Hurray! I scream inside my head. This picture was the first familiar thing I had recognized since I stepped on the plane in Fort Lauderdale the day before. But where is Angie? I was relieved to have arrived somewhere I hoped I would find, but I was disappointed there was no Angie.

The driver was gone, and I was escorted from the stairwell through the short hallway to their small kitchen. We sat at the *Eckbank* (corner bench), where lots of talking ensued but little from me. The mother, Anita, brought out a board of sausage, cheese, and dark bread with plenty of encouragement for me to eat. I did not eat meat, but I ate some bread and cheese. The dad, Ernst, spoke a few words of English, but communication was minimal. He offered me wine, which I did have, a small glass. Speaking louder, Anita brought out more and more food for me to eat. I understood nothing Anita said, but she talked nonetheless. I focused on where Angie, "Angelika," was and if she would return home. All I got out of the attempted conversation was that "Geli" was far away, which disappointed me tremendously.

Finally, after maybe 45 minutes or more of incoherent communication and sampling of heavy bread and cheese, Anita showed me to a bedroom up a wide spiral staircase, through two more doors, where I crashed on the bed with thoughts of where Angie might be and how I might find her. I was soon fast asleep and slept like a baby until maybe 10 or 11 the following day. Understand, German windows are covered outside by Rolladens, roll-top slats that interlock when you roll them down, letting ZERO light into the room, so I never noticed daylight and slept late into the morning.

Angie had returned from Helga's and spent the night at the Uhl's house in Hargesheim. Before catching the train to Darmstadt to meet Gabi and move to Asbach, she would stop at her parents to pick up a few last things. The moment Angie walked in the front door and saw my duffel bag, she knew I was there. Shocked, Angie raced up the spiral stairs and opened the door to the dark room.

I was in that semi-waking twilight that begins to stir you awake, not yet conscious but drifting from dreamland to awakened reality. The darkened bedroom door bursts open, and Angie falls into bed, arms wrapped around me in the most welcome, massive hug I have ever experienced. We said nothing for what seemed an eternity, then questions, answers, more questions, and answers, recollections from the past month's absence, more hugs and long kisses, till finally, we decided to join the world around us again. Angie raised the Rolladens a tiny bit to let in some light. Life, in my mind, was beginning to sort itself out.

Back in the downstairs hall, just above my duffel bag, on a small table, sat a letter from me, addressed to Angelika Milburn, unopened, which had been forwarded, first to Helga's house, then returned to her parents due to being undeliverable. The letter never caught up with Angie until this day to be opened the day after I had arrived.

Chapter 21
Bosenheim

Over the next several days, Angie introduced me to her sisters, Christel and Jutta, and her brother Manfred. Christel,16, three years younger than Angie, was finishing *Hauptshule* (secondary school) and about to begin her nursing co-op. Christel was a quiet and intuitive person who looked up to her older sister even more than she did her parents. When Angie left for Florida, Christel quickly assumed the role of primary helper in the household but always remained somewhat reserved. Always thinking but rarely speaking out, she protected herself from the argumentative discord of her parent's life.

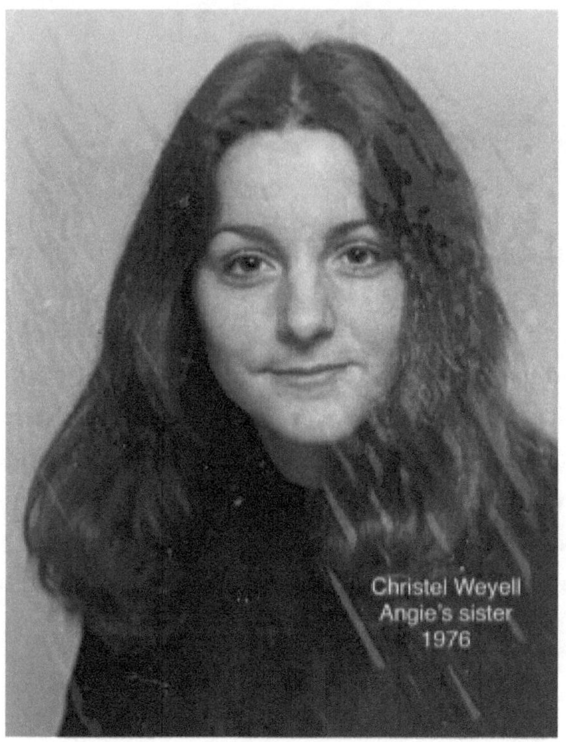

Christel Weyell, 1976

Manfred, 13, was starting Hauptshule and devoted much of his time after school to helping in the fields and vineyards. He always seemed to look at life with a smile. With an outgoing personality, he was the one who tied the family together with his jovial love of life. Mother Anita favored him, and he became the positive force in the family dynamic. He was a teenager, learning to properly use farming tools bend drive the tractors, which was exciting and fun. Working with his hands on motors or anything mechanical gave Manfred great joy.

Manfred Weyell 1976

Jutta was ten and still in *Grundschule* (primary school). The youngest of the Weyell children, she was happy to begin the transformation out of childhood and take on more family responsibility. She was content to follow the family's daily routine and keep time to herself, developing her young life. With sparkling eyes, she laughed easily, but more was going on in her head than she let on. Where Manfred was more of a pleasant leader, Jutta was a happy follower.

Angie also had a sister six years older, Romi, who married and lived in Sprendlingen, a nearby town, raising her family. With three young children, a restaurant with rooms for rent, and a husband with a quiet demeanor, she grew up quickly and put everything she had into building a stable, successful life. Even though Sprendlingen was only seven kilometers from Bosenheim, she was too busy to return home often. Life after the war was getting more manageable, but people had to work hard for everything they needed. They had to rebuild their lives, starting with very little, including Romi and her family.

Helmut, Romi, and Ernst. Angie's father, older sister, and her husband.

Karl Hans was the oldest, ten years older than Geli. He was their half-brother who hadn't lived at the Weyell home since Angie was six. In those turbulent years after the war, he was the child of Anita. The father promised he would marry young Anita but disappeared instead. Since Anita's birth mother died from TB when she was just a baby, and her father disappeared from her life shortly after, Anita was raised by a kind woman, her informally adopted mother, in Bosenheim, who ran a working farm by herself after the death of her husband. By Karl Hans's birth, it was just the older woman, Anita, and her young son.

Ernst, Angie's father, was from Appenheim, 20 kilometers north of Bosenheim, with a mother, father, and one brother, Erich. Together, they worked the family farm. As the oldest son, Ernst was conscripted into the army during World War II. Erich, the youngest and only remaining son, was exempt from conscription and stayed home to help with the farm. Ernst was captured by the Russian Army somewhere near Ukraine during the Russian counter-offensive in 1944. The Russians routinely executed German POWs, but a nearby British battalion, fighting alongside the Russians, was given the captured Germans, and he eventually wound up at a British POW camp in Egypt.

Ernst, on the left, with POW mates in an Egyptian POW camp.

Prisoners were treated well at the camp, and the young German soldiers could start believing in humanity again after living with fear and threats for such a long time. He was released from there in 1948, three years after the war had ended.

The Weyell family farm in Appenheim was now in the hands of Ernst's brother Erich, who had married and started a family. Erich continued to run the family farm after the war and would eventually buy out Ernst's share with a small settlement.

Now a free man, Ernst returned to the ruined German landscape and decimated economy. He placed an ad in the newspaper seeking a wife to build a new life from the rubble after the war years. Anita, also looking to find a decent husband, answered the ad, and they united to forge a better life together. Ernst, Anita, and Karl Hans lived with the adopted mother in Bosenheim until some unfortunate decisions caused her to lose the farm. The new family rented a place on the main street in Bosenheim, and the adopted mother rented the place downstairs. This was the Weyell home from 1950 until Manfred was born in 1960.

With the meager settlement Ernst received from his brother and help from the young German government, they bought a plot of land outside Bosenheim and built a large house for the growing family. Karl Hans would remain with the adopted grandmother until he joined the German Army a few years later.

This new family home was a large two-story, sturdy, cement block structure with a stucco finish and a red terracotta roof. A large unfinished basement contained an oil furnace that provided steam, radiator heat for the house, and a cool room used as a root cellar to store potatoes and canned vegetables. An oversized garage housed their tractors and equipment. Most of their food was grown in their garden or their nearby fields. A pig was slaughtered twice yearly to provide the growing family with a constant supply of meat and sausage. The meat was stored in the local community center freezer, where space could be rented inexpensively for the year. Angie's parents had never needed the luxuries of a home telephone or an automobile. The town Post office had a phone for occasional needs, and mass transit was readily available.

Angie's father, Ernst, worked for years at the Boehringer pharmaceuticals plant about 15 kilometers from Bosenheim. A company bus came every day to provide transportation. His passion, however, was farming. Every afternoon, the work bus dropped him at home around 4:30. He ate a snack, changed clothes, and worked in the fields until dark. He worked all day on Saturdays as well. Only on Sundays did he stay home.

Anita Weyell 1977

They had grape vineyards, potato fields, and a large vegetable garden behind their house. Anita worked all week in the vineyards, completing one chore after another to ensure a fruitful grape harvest. She managed the home and family and took care of the shopping at the two local, small grocery stores in Bosenheim. She made morning trips to the local bakery for fresh bread and an assortment of *Brötchen* (rolls) for breakfast. Later, when the first Aldi (grocery store) opened up in Bad Kreuznach, shopping was done once a week in the city, a 15-minute bus ride away. Dragging the heavy grocery bags home was difficult, so one of the children had to accompany Anita to assist.

Breakfasts began with a fresh Brötchen or two for each, with cheese, meats, or jam. Everyone also ate a soft-boiled egg or two and had coffee. Around 1 PM, there was a big meal, followed by coffee and homemade cake in the afternoon. There were always one or two freshly baked cakes in the formal dining room. This room was closed and dark to keep the temperature cooler for the cakes. I made several trips for a slice of plum *torte* or a thick cut from the hazelnut cake with the glazed chocolate icing. I wished for a cold glass of milk, but that was not to be had.

Quenching your thirst was quite different in Germany. You rarely, if ever, drank tap water. Not so much because it could be dirty, far from it; the chlorinated water made tap water unappealing. The next-door neighbors had a side business selling *Sprudel* or carbonated water and *Limo'* (*Limonade*), a sweetened carbonated soft drink. These beverages came in glass liter bottles you would return to redeem a deposit. Juice was rarely an option, and milk came in one-liter, unrefrigerated, waxed boxes used more for coffee and baking, so Sprudel was the sustenance beverage with Limo' on special occasions.

Ernst always had several small glasses of wine each night. He kept his small wine glass on the back of the sink and made many trips to the kitchen, so he likely drank more, like 5 or 6 small glasses. Anita watched closely and gruffly told him when she thought he had enough. I learned to enjoy cellar-temperature German *beer* and marveled at how many Germans would sip a beer at work anytime. People working on re-bricking a new street take a beer break. The man in a toll booth would have a beer by his register. Even on TV, when the *Bundestag* (Parliament) was in session, many representatives had a beer in front of them. But in every case, they all had a stopper closing off the bottle until they were ready for another sip. This stopper preserved the carbonation and kept potential bugs out. People would nurse their beer for hours, and you would never see someone drunk at work. You could also legally have an open beer in the car, but if the driver blew a .08 blood alcohol content, they would lose their license. You could even buy beer from *Automats* (vending machines) in Autobahn rest areas. Amazing. With freedom comes responsibility, and Germans are responsible people, like

99.9% of them, and they do this willingly as a matter of custom. Truly amazing.

All three of Angie's younger siblings attended school a bus ride away. Some upper-grade levels even required a short train ride. From Kindergarten *through Grade 5, students typically walk* to the local village school. After Grade 5, they used public transit alone or with a friend to get to school. Parents trusted them to follow customary behavior patterns and assume this responsibility with increasing confidence and maturity. It was not unusual to see adult passengers scold young students for getting silly or unruly on the bus. These public warnings were an acceptable community responsibility, and the children would most always comply.

Most afternoons and every weekend, family members helped in either the fields or up on the *Bosenberg* (Bosenheim's big hill or small mountain) in their vineyards. There was always work to do. Life was all about financial stability. There was little extra money, but their basics were secure. Social medicine ensured a healthy population and public transportation was readily available to get you anywhere in Europe at a reasonable cost when needed. The Weyell family rarely, if ever, traveled beyond Bad Kreuznach or only a few kilometers away.

The Weyell's did have a family television in the living room that broadcasts three German channels from 4 in the afternoon till the test pattern froze on the screen at 11. Before 4, everyone was busy at work or doing housework, so there was no need for TV, and after 11, well, you worked early the following day, so you went to bed. At first, I was shocked by this schedule, but I did like that all TV programs ran uninterrupted, from start to finish. Five to ten minutes of commercials came on between shows, a perfect time for a snack or a bathroom break. Between commercials, to keep your attention, they would show cute little 10-second cartoons. Even I could understand these. All programming was in German, even the American series like Bonanza and Charlie's Angels.

With not much TV to watch, I was glad to find a bookstore in Bad Kreuznach with a selection of English books. Angie always had a book or two she was reading, and I now spent more time reading. Family time at home was spent joking and teasing each other while doing chores or working in the field. Communication was difficult for me, but everyone understood teasing, which helped me connect with them. I developed the practice of rearranging the hundreds of Knick-knacks Anita displayed around the house. My creative antics pestered Anita, but it made a light connection between us where the communication barrier seemed insurmountable.

The house itself was an adjustment for me. Although typically German, to me, it felt closed off and partitioned. No large open spaces, and every room had a door. The doors were solid wood framed, most with large, rippled glass panels that would let light through, but you could see no details. Kitchens were relatively small with small appliances. There was always an Eckbank or corner bench where most all meals happened with a radio in the back corner behind the seat softly playing some 1950s traditional German pop music. Anita loved this and would hum along. I would change the station to Armed Forces Radio, which played rock and pop American music but was quickly switched back to German Pop music each time Anita returned to the kitchen.

Angie and I made a few trips into Bad Kreuznach to look around and maybe get a treat from one of the many bakeries. Angie showed me where she used to work, go to school, and hang out with her friends. There was a sizeable pedestrian-only shopping district that went on for many blocks. Multistory department stores like Kaufhof, with accessible and free public toilets, were as busy as an anthill. Like most German cities, these large pedestrian areas had bakeries, coffee shops, butcher shops, candy stores, flower shops, watch repair, shoe repair, book stores, specialty clothing stores, and tons of shoe stores. Fast food restaurants and sidewalk kiosks were everywhere as well. Some tiny kiosks with glass walls from top to bottom were full of miniature bottles of liquor for sale—hundreds of different brands. Many Germans need these shots of *Kreuter* or spiced liquor to settle their stomachs after lunch. Some required 2 or 3, mostly men, but a few women also imbibed.

One of the things Bad Kreuznach was known for was its *Brückenhausen*, or bridge houses. A stone bridge arched over the Nahe River, and four three-story, several hundred-year-old stone houses stood right over the water on each side of the bridge. Parks, pathways, and eateries stretched along the river in each direction.

From 7 AM to 5:30 PM in the city, people were everywhere. Elbow to elbow, every store was packed with people bustling every which way. Time was valuable, and efficiency ruled. People were not rude, or at least their intention was not to be rude, but I was not used to this pace of urban life. When making a purchase in a busy store, I quickly learned to have my money counted out and ready to pay immediately, no small talk, no polite gestures, know what you want, do it, and move on or at least out of the way. Smiles were subtle. Holding a door for the next person was never expected. Everything was done with a purpose, quickly and efficiently. Then, promptly at 5:30 PM, almost every store closed, and the city emptied. Many people who lived in city apartments skirting the pedestrian areas were still present. A few late businesses and restaurants remained open, and the train station stayed busy for a while, but what a remarkable change. It was almost like someone flipped a switch, and everyone turned and left at 5:30.

Angie introduced me to a few friends from Bosenheim: Helga, her childhood best friend, and Oli (Olivia), another schoolmate. Malita, who had recently lost both parents, lived alone in a room behind their neighborhood grocery store. It now stood closed and empty. I knew her recent loss of her parents and now living alone in the empty store had a terrible impact on her attention to reality. When visiting Malita, we hung out in a back room, resembling a cave with mattresses on the floor and black light posters on the wall. Malita was friendly and spoke broken English to me. With the recent loss of her parents and now living alone at 19, she was losing her focus and often retreated into a melancholy funk, which made our visits uncomfortable.

We spent most of our "friend" time with Christhilde's Uhl family, Angie's closest friend still living in the United States. Her family was two bus rides away in the village of Hargesheim, north of Bad Kreuznach. Christhilde had nine siblings. Peter, the oldest (now living in Brittany, France, with his girlfriend), frequently returned home. Then, Marietta and her boyfriend Klaus who was always present. Heinz came next with his long, straight, beautiful red hair, and then Haribert or Hari, who would become my best friend in Germany. Five other younger brothers and sisters were around, but they were all busy with little kid stuff. We stayed a night or two when we visited Hargesheim, which was frequent.

A host of other local friends from Hargesheim would also join us frequently. There was another Geli and Thomas (pronounced Toe-Maas), the only other left-handed person I knew in Germany. He lost several fingers on his right hand and was allowed to become left-handed. Then there was Olaf with his long blonde hair, thick, bushy mustache, and perpetual, inviting smile.

When Angie and I visited, the group would walk down to the local *Wirtschaft* (pub) for an evening of beer drinking and joking around. Here is where I learned about the custom of sharing a beer from a *Stiefel* or large boot-shaped glass. The clear glass boot would hold about three bottles of beer, and we would each take a sip, pass it to the next around the table, and so on till someone would take the last drink, meaning the person before must buy the next boot. Sharing a Stiefel became a game of skill to take the tiniest of sips or a colossal gulp, and no chugging was allowed. And when the beer in the boot barely covered the turn below the ankle, you would place the boot in front of the next person with the toe pointed away from them. When they drank, as soon as the beer allowed air to flow into the toe, a rush of beer would splash them in the face, making everyone laugh. People wised up quickly. After drinking a couple of boots, we would sing traditional drinking songs with arms locked with each neighbor, swaying left and right with the music.

A walk home through the cool night air cleared our minds. Once back at the Uhl house, we quietly foraged a meal of pasta with tomato sauce (from a tube, like toothpaste) or bread and cheese before figuring out how many people could sleep in each bed. Anytime drinking was involved, walking was the mode of transportation. Never drive, even if someone had a car, and no one could afford a taxi, so we walked. We even walked several kilometers into Bad Kreuznach if drinking was involved.

Chapter 22
Asbach

═══

After a few weeks of my arrival in Germany and staying at her family home, Angie decided it was time to take Gabi up on her offer to move in with her and Rudi in Asbach. We packed some essentials and our clothes and headed out the door. Angie and I tried to hitchhike, but no one stopped, and we walked several kilometers to the train station in Bad Kreuznach. We changed trains in Mainz and arrived in Darmstadt mid-morning.

While awaiting transfer in Mainz, business people were noticeably upset when an announcement stated the train to Frankfurt would be two minutes late. It's hard to imagine a short delay like this would have such an impact. Back in West Palm Beach, waiting for a bus to take me to class was typically 30 minutes late or even an hour, and my only real option was to take an even earlier bus to make sure I didn't miss a class. When waiting for a train in Germany, a two-minute delay might cause you to miss your connecting train to your final destination, and people are visibly upset. The efficiency of everything in Germany was genuinely remarkable.

We exited the Hauptbahnhof in Darmstadt to a bustling city larger than Bad Kreuznach. From the *Bahnhof,* we found our way to the central plaza and transportation hub to determine which bus or buses were needed to get to Asbach. The pungent smell of diesel hung in the air. Big box trucks and delivery vans crowded the patched cobblestone streets as several *Strassenbahns* (streetcars) followed their tracks to various stops in the plaza. After Angie carefully analyzed the transit schedules and with an answer from a local, she determined that we should take a Strassenbahn to a different plaza to catch a bus to Ernsthofen, the nearest town to Asbach, with a regular bus service. Asbach only had bus service twice daily, early in the morning and once in the evening, to accommodate work traffic.

I had never been on a Strassenbahn before. We stepped into a long, double wagon Strassenbahn, with a flexible rubber accordion-type middle where we stood and held on to the hand loops above our heads. When the Strassenbahn went through a curve, the big circular mid-floor area would rotate to accommodate the turn. As the Strassenbahn made its way through the pedestrian areas, the clanging small bells would alert walkers who always yielded or quickly moved. I was intrigued that when entering the Strassenbahn, you didn't need to give money or a ticket to the driver, who was isolated in a cockpit. Instead, you paid your fare at a machine at the Strassenbahn stop and just stepped into one of the sets of open doors on the honor system. No one checked our small paper tickets, valid for the Strassenbahn ride and the two buses we would need to get to Ernsthofen. After an hour of efficient rides and transfers, we arrived.

Asbach was a 30-minute walk through the woods from Ernsthofen. Woods in Germany were much different than you might experience in the U.S. The woods were thick with trees, but the forest floor was cleared of all brush, dead trees, fallen limbs, and bramble. The state paid farmers to harvest firewood during the winter months, which meant the wooded areas remained remarkably cleared and looked almost manicured. Walking paths were also well maintained and connected every little village. Many of these paths were even paved, especially in the larger communities. This one, to Asbach, was not. It was a well-worn path that looked as it probably did a hundred years or even a thousand years ago.

Angie walking the path from Ernsthofen to Asbach.

Arriving in Ernsthofen shortly after noon, our walk through the woods was brisk and pleasant. As we crested the last hill and left the woods, we passed by the stone-walled cemetery and saw Asbach below in the small valley. Seeing the bucolic village in the distant valley made us feel like we had returned to a scene from a "Grimm Fairy Tale." Asbach consisted of one street, maybe five blocks long, with several short side streets. Each was lined with classic old timber frame houses and working farms on each side of every road. You could see a local swimming pool on a far hillside fed by a natural stream. Surrounding the village were fields of wheat and various produce, bisected by farm roads as far as you could see. Patches of wooded areas and footpaths radiated out in several directions.

In the village, there was one part-time bakery, a post office room in someone's house, a small Wirtschaft (pub), and a part-time pharmacy, but no other business. Walking down the long hill to the village, we were glad to find Gabi's and Rudi's house on the main street closest to the path. The sea bag I was carrying was taking its toll on my shoulder, as was Angie's bag and guitar on hers.

Asbach house. Fachwerk (timber frame) construction, built in the late 1800s.

Gabi embraced Angie in a big hug. Her exuberant smile and excitement were infectious. I was introduced to Gabi as Rudi came down the stairs and joined us on the back steps. It was a pleasant surprise to hear both Gabi and Rudi greet me in English, and they both firmly, in turn, shook my hand. They invited us in, and we all walked back to the kitchen table to rest and share some homemade cake while Rudi brewed a pot of tea.

We left our bags in the living room, and they walked us around the house and the grounds, followed by a tour of the old place. The long front of the house was separated from the street by a narrow sidewalk, and there seemed to be almost no traffic on this main road. The house was over 100 years old and in a livable state of disrepair. Architecturally, this was called a *Fachwerk* or timber frame house. Rudi and Gabi agreed to make the necessary repairs to the house instead of paying rent. The owner provided the materials, and they provided the labor. We walked through a set of large double wooden gates from the street to a working courtyard with several pieces of old farm equipment parked inside.

Several unused and musty stalls and pens inside the gate preserved the smell of wet hay and droppings of the previous inhabitants and added to the general farm smell of the entire working town. The outhouse was a room beside a stall across the courtyard from the house's back steps. The odor, as we passed, as said in the cult comedy album "Child's Garden of Grass," would "knock a buzzard off a shit wagon." You had to pay to have it emptied, and money was a rare commodity, so defecation was done quickly, with breath held, or sometimes a more creative solution, say a morning walk through the deep woods. Although there was no plumbing for sewage, there were three sinks with water, one in the kitchen and two off the bedrooms upstairs. They all drained directly to a rough, unused area behind the house. There was electricity throughout the home and cold running water to the sinks. The heat sources were wood-burning stoves in the living room and bedrooms.

Outdoor shower (with a watering can) at Asbach house.

The kitchen also included an electric cook stove but no refrigerator. Instead, we kept perishable food in a small dark closet on the north side of the kitchen, which remained cooler than the rest of the house. Perishable food that was not needed as often was stored in the small, cool earth dug-out cellar.

On rare occasions, we obtain milk from one of the owner's dairy cows. We collected it and kept it in an old-fashioned metal milk container with a small plate as a lid. I once tried my hand at milking the cow, but Gabi was the best. It took her maybe 10 minutes to get a liter, whereas I got a shot glass full in the same amount of time. We kept the cheese, milk, leftovers, and other perishables on small shelves in this cool kitchen closet.

Rudi and Gabi each had rooms on the second level, and the room on the third would be for us. Our room had a mattress, a small table, and, like each room, an even smaller wood stove. Now, getting wood for the stoves was another matter. The owner, who lived next door, allowed us to use the slag lumber left over from milling boards. We quickly cut the scraps into lengths suitable for burning in the small wood stoves with his table saw.

This is a view of a harvest parade from Angie's and Bert's room in Asbach. In the background, a neighboring commune (with the closest telephone) is visible.

Rudi and Gabi had furnished much of the house from *Sperrmüll*, or things left on the curb to be carted off once every couple of months by the *Landkreis* or county. Rudi had five or six overlapping oriental carpets on his floor, well-worn but still soft and warm. Basket lights hung in comfortable nooks in each room. Antique or just old furnishings were throughout the house, and the woodwork on the curved stairway, doors, and windows was worn but gorgeous.

One thing about the place that bothered me was that the windows had no screens. Gabi insisted on leaving the kitchen and living room windows open to allow air to circulate. She would return from wherever, fling open the windows and exclaim, "*Frische Luft,*" or fresh air, and inhale a deep breath. This announcement was an invitation for an onslaught of flies to invade our space, which would bug the daylights out of me. The farm smell accompanying these open windows was fertile but something we got used to and not offensive. However, I never accepted the flies.

A week or so later, as Angie cooked a nice dinner to be ready when Gabi and Rudi returned from town, I closed all the windows and decorated the kitchen with several rolls of sticky fly paper. I took a rolled-up newspaper and killed hundreds of flies. I was so proud of ridding the place of these vermin before our lovely meal. Still, this pride quickly vanished upon Gabi's return when she flung open the windows again and invited every living fly from the farmyard back into the house. Oh well, it was their house. What could I otherwise do?

We spent nights talking and listening to albums on a small but decent stereo and turntable in Rudi's room. We'd sit on the carpets, shifting now and again. With Angie's translation help, Gabi and Rudi's rudimentary English, and my minimal knowledge of German, we carried on many varied discussions and story recollections. Gabi, always adventurous, detailed the many exciting wonders of her solo hitchhiking trip to Nepal and back. Here she was, a 20-year-old, attractive, long, red-haired woman, catching rides through some of the most unsafe countries in the Middle East. Gabi did pay for long bus rides through parts of Iran and Afghanistan but mostly made it on the kindness of strangers. Once, while traveling by bus through Afghanistan, her bus was stopped by armed bandits who searched the luggage strapped to the roof, took some valuables, and then released them on their way. The trick was to carry nothing of real value, which Gabi followed.

She loved Istanbul, the Grand Bazaar, its culture, and its history. She told us we should go there ourselves, and by doing so on the cheap, we might only need to spend a few hundred dollars or so. I wasn't sure how long I might even stay in Europe, or for that matter, how long Angie might want me to stay. I hoped I'd remain long enough to travel and see as many different places as possible, then persuade Angie to return to the States with me. We hadn't discussed our future yet.

I have always been passionate about traveling to Greece, strolling through the land of the great philosophers and the classic civilization. After listening to Gabi's idea, I realized that such a trip appealed to me. Maybe we could hit Istanbul first and experience a different culture, then on to Greece. Angie, always a good money manager, had saved a couple of hundred dollars and was convinced to join in planning this new adventure.

While living in Asbach, we took the bus into Darmstadt to look around and get familiar with the place. We found an army surplus store, bought two sleeping bags, two canteens, and ponchos, and started planning the trip for real. I purchased a used European travel guide in English at a college swap meet that cataloged youth hostels and site descriptions of where we might travel along the way. It was a few years old but probably generally accurate.

While in town, I met two U.S. Army soldiers stationed at the local *Kaserne* (Army Post) and formed a new friendship. Randy and Larry were young, Private, First-Class soldiers stationed at Cambrai Fritsch Kaserne in Darmstadt. Randy was single and lived in the barracks, and Larry was married to Sherry and lived off-post. They both had cars and would provide transportation when we occasionally got together. Angie got along well with these new friends as well. We would typically hang out at Larry and Sherry's.

A few weeks later, Angie and I were ready to begin this new journey along what many would call the "Hippy Trail." We borrowed a couple of framed backpacks, stuffed them with all our needed provisions, and decided to hit the road. I told my parents of our plan through a collect phone call from the local post office, and Angie shared our trip plan with her friends. By late June, we would be off.

We called Randy from the phone of our neighboring commune in Asbach. He agreed to meet us in Darmstadt and drop us off at a busy Autobahn entrance to begin our journey. Full of excitement and more than a bit of apprehension, we made the leap, hopefully with no turning back.

Hitchhiking was not new to either of us. I had hitchhiked between Florida and Michigan quite a few times, as well as many shorter trips like a hastily planned trip to Key West once, even though I had a car. Hitchhiking was cheaper, and you met interesting people along the way. Angie had hitchhiked with Christhilde to Austria and back as two 16-year-olds. Hitchhiking in the 1960s and 70s was quite normal. Most hitchhikers were young, but a fair share were older, and probably 90 percent were male. It was common to see someone with their thumb out for short or long distances, summer or winter.

You'd give 'em a lift if you had the room in your car or van. It was also not uncommon if you picked up a person down on their luck to give them a couple of dollars when you let them out; someone better off would give you a dollar or two to help with gas. More often than not, you'd share a joint, and the stories would flow. It was nowhere near as dangerous as it might seem. Sure, there was always the possibility of some stranger hassling you, but you'd brush it off and move on. It is amazing how everyone behaved within a set of social norms and feared to break them. There was a slight bending here and there, but we followed these norms for a reason, and everyone counted on them to be respected. But also, to some extent, everyone was just plain ole lucky. Thumbs out, we were on our way.

Chapter 23
The Bavarian Scene

———

Day 1, June 27th, 1976

Randy helped us with our packs and said goodbye at the Darmstadt Autobahn entrance heading south. Randy thought, wow, what a trip, but they are crazy. Angie and I had similar thoughts but pushed them to the back of our minds, having already decided. We were prepared to make the long journey. It would be an adventure, and worse comes to worst, we would turn around. It was a warm afternoon. Sun and diesel fumes greeted us as Randy disappeared.

We stood at the edge of the road, packs at our feet, and both our thumbs out, looking at each driver as they began to accelerate. From my experience, making eye contact with passing drivers improved our chance of getting one to stop for us. Each location presented a different challenge. Hitchhiking at the entrance of an Autobahn was good, but it was essential to stand where the cars were going slowly. Few drivers would stop when they were accelerating to merge with fast-moving traffic.

There was plenty of weekend traffic, and it didn't take long to catch our first ride from a nice man on his way to Mannheim. Typically, when a couple hitchhiked, the man would sit up front for safety considerations, but since Angie spoke German, she sat in the front seat. I climbed in the back seat with our packs, and we began the routine of conversing with the driver. Setting a friendly tone with these complete strangers, who were nice enough to give you a lift, was essential. The driver could always drop you at the next exit if things became uncomfortable or he did not like you. More often, in my past, a driver went out of their way to drop you at a more convenient location to catch your next ride. Having a friendly conversation was helpful, regardless. The main topics are traffic, weather, where we were from, and going. Our first driver spoke some English but mostly talked with Angie. It was interesting how predominantly single people stopped to give us a ride.

With two or three shorter lifts, we made it to Heidelberg, a place I was interested in seeing, and we used our outdated travel guide to find a youth hostel in a classic old building not far from the city center. Most of our money was in *Deutsch Marks*, which equaled fifty American cents each. The hostel cost us 20 DM, and spending our money at this rate wouldn't get us out of Germany. We needed to rethink the youth hostel plan, especially in the more developed countries. We paid for a room and left our packs in a safe space behind the front desk while walking around the city. Not wanting to spend more money, we just meandered around, looking at the sites and watching people. Sightseeing was OK because everything was new, and we never knew what exciting place we might see.

Heidelberg castle was off in the distance, and the Neckar River flowed nearby, but we mainly experienced sub-urban congestion and a somewhat foul, industrial-smelling air. We returned to the hostel a bit disappointed but still excited for what must lie ahead. We played with a life-size chess board on the lawn and sat in a double swing to re-evaluate our expectations and how to make our money last. It could still work, we surmised, but we had to spend only on essentials, which meant minimal food and sending postcards to the closest people in our lives. Forgoing souvenirs, our actual mementos for this trip would live in our memories.

Day 2, June 28th

Waking up from the somewhat comfortable stay at the Heidelberg hostel would be our last good sleep. We had a small continental breakfast, included in our stay, before returning to the Autobahn. As we waited for a ride on the entrance ramp, the Monday morning traffic was a flurry of quick cars racing to join the quest for the hectic life ahead at their jobs. Angie and I were looking forward to escaping this rat race to settle into a more relaxed pace of countries to the south and east. A couple of rides and many hours later, we were dropped off near Munich. It was time to get our walking legs in shape. This trip was to be more than just getting to Istanbul and Greece.

There was so much to see along the way. To me, everything was new and fresh. Traveling in a region where every country had its language, money, and customs was exciting. Traveling within the United States was similar no matter where you went. Money and traditions were consistent, and the language was understandable even with a strong dialect. The little things I observed in Germany differed from how I grew up. The way people swept and washed the sidewalks every morning, all the food smells that changed every hundred meters or so, how small cars could squeeze into the tiniest space, and the constant noise of trucks, street cars, horns, loud voices, and there were few public bathrooms anywhere. When I did find a public toilet, I had to pay 20 *Pfennigs* (pennies) to use it. To beat all, an older Turkish cleaning woman might be mopping right behind you while you relieve yourself at a urinal. It's all fascinating. Angie was more experienced in these ways. She had lived in Germany her whole life, traveled to Austria twice, and made a trip to Paris with friends, but this trip would be equally new for her, and we wanted to experience our journey at a slower pace.

When traveling in the US, I went straight there as quickly as possible if I made a long trip. Stopping along the way for anything other than gas, food, or to stretch my stiff body was considered frivolous. Here, with everything new and different, we wanted to take our time and see more than just Autobahns and rest stops.

With a quick check of the map of European motorways we purchased before we started this journey, we headed to the Munich city center in the early afternoon with many hours of daylight left, wondering what we would see along the way. We spent 12 DM (*Deutsche Marks*) for this rather large but highly durable map. In the United States, almost every gas station had a rack of free maps anyone could take. Our destination in Munich was the English Gardens, which we located on the back side of the whole map of Europe in the city insert portion for Munich. English Gardens was similar to Central Park in New York City. We would look there to find a place to discreetly roll out our sleeping bags for a night at the end of our exploring.

Taking a Strassenbahn into the city center would have been quicker but cost a few Marks each. Sure, we could hop on without a ticket and steal a ride, but there was always the risk of the transit police getting on and checking everyone's ticket. Riders without a ticket paid a 25 DM fine on the spot, as we found out recently in Darmstadt. No, we would walk. Nice day, new surroundings, and that's why we were on this journey, to experience life, not just visit places.

Our meals along the way were simple and cheap. Restaurants were out of the question, so we carried a few cans of tuna, a jar of peanut butter, a jar of puszta salad, and a small bag of Brötchen. Every two or three days, we would find a grocery store to replenish our stock. Tuna Was our favorite meal. The tuna came packed in oil with small peas and a slice of white onion. Delicious spread out on a piece of bread or Brötchen. Peanut butter was almost non-existent in Germany, but since I was a vegetarian and peanut butter was a staple of my diet, I had found some in a specialty shop before we left to bring along. Puszta salad was a mixture of sliced peppers, onions, celery, carrots, and pickles packed in a light vinegar mix you would spread on bread. These foods, except for peanut butter, were cheap but tasty. And they provided the sustenance we needed to make the journey.

Inside the city ring, there was more for us to see. Huge pedestrian avenues of shopping streets, the *Glockenspiel*, Baroque churches (free to enter), statues and monuments, and finally, the English Gardens along both sides of the Isar River. What a beautiful space, trees, meadows, paved trails everywhere, flower gardens, statues, small lakes with islands, and every so often, the smells of cooked food emanating from carts or kiosks. After all the traffic and waiting for rides the last two days, it felt good to be in the open nature area.

Couples with blankets spread out, locked in passionate embraces, a few dogs chasing around, a few nude sunbathers, and no one in a hurry or speaking loudly. What a pleasure to drop our packs and sit and enjoy. It was late evening, and we were seriously thinking about where to find a spot to sleep. There were small stands of trees, but the grounds were all cleared and well-maintained, with nowhere to hide. We found a place somewhat private between a stone bridge and some tall bushes, but there was too much foot traffic. Someone was sure to see us sleeping there, we thought.

We talked with two young women passing by and asked if they knew where we might discretely sleep in the park. They were friendly and "hippyish" and told us it was not a good idea, but they offered us their couch where we could crash for the night. Great! The two women had just left work and would meet friends at a club. They invited us to join them. After, we would head to their apartment for the night. Being on such a tight budget, we were reluctant to go to the club, but we joined them in return for a safe place to sleep.

With evening upon us and the light fading, we walked to the club on the edge of the English Gardens. The club was a good size, with jazz music drifting onto the tree-covered lawn. Small groups were mingling outside the entrance, all minding their own business. It was more crowded inside the club, with busy conversations at each booth and standing groups. Smoke smothered the air, and abstract videos were projected on a wall in a dance area in one room with a few single and couples swaying to the music. They all seemed trance-like while they moved to the offbeat tune.

I was hesitant to leave our packs with the staff person at the front counter, but they assured me they would be OK, and there was no room to keep them at a table. We slid into a large U-shaped booth with the women's friends. It was a tight squeeze but doable. Introductions rarely happened with groups of young progressive people, and it wasn't necessary or expected. You might tell or ask for a name once you initiate a substantial conversation with someone, but otherwise, names are unimportant. Most everyone said "hallo" or nodded. A few had drinks, and everyone was smoking. A young man emptied the tobacco from a single cigarette and mixed it with a small amount of crumbled hash. He repacked the cigarette, lit it, and shared it with some. The discussions involved heavy conversation and spontaneous laughter, which rounded out the scene. We had nothing to drink, and the hash never made it to our side of the table.

After 15 minutes, a girl squashed between me and someone else passed out. Her head hung limp, breathing still, I hoped, and if not for the cramped quarters, she would have collapsed into a puddle on the floor. I tried to alert some of the party about her dire situation, but between my English and everyone else's intense conversations, no one seemed aware. I nudged Angie to make a path to the aisle, pulled the young woman to the edge of the large booth, lifted her in my arms, sleeping baby style, carried her out the front door, and laid her on the grass.

By this time, several people had started paying attention and joined me, showing genuine concern for the girl. One said she was a paramedic and would help her. No one seemed too concerned, as if this was almost ordinary. One person said, "She'll come down soon," and fetched a bottle of Sprudel (carbonated water). Angie and I decided it would be better to take our chances for the night back in the English Gardens and went to grab our backpacks. Now, after 11, the Gardens were mostly empty. We found our way back to the semi-secluded large bush by the stone bridge and rolled out our sleeping bags underneath the thick branches, almost wholly covering our existence in the dark. I slept as I could almost anywhere, but Angie was awake all night on constant vigil, hearing each passing footstep until the earliest light of day.

Chapter 24
Caravan Luck

Day 3, June 29th

With rolled-up sleeping bags and packs secured, we hiked through the early morning bustle of the inner city and, with our map and helpful directions from several people, found our way to the large entrance/rest area of the southbound Autobahn leaving Munich. The entrance was a big parking area with restaurants and gas stations for cars and trucks. A long entrance ramp to the Autobahn started on the other side. Our journey would begin here. I pulled out an 8" by 20" cardboard sign I had spent several evenings making, with "Istanbul" neatly and colorfully labeled on the face from my pack. Now the question was, where would be the best place to stand? We hoped to catch a long ride into the Alps and, possibly, beyond.

On the road, hitchhikers should follow basic rules to be courteous to other hitchhikers. When there were multiple hitchhikers, you would always go to the end of the line and leave a respectable space from the last one. Drivers would then have time to assess each hiker before deciding who to stop and pick up. A single guy was typical and got a ride the quickest. Two guys was a more difficult ask, and three or more was near impossible, but a guy and a girl was a safer bet for a driver. We might get picked up by another couple or even an older person. Rides from these were usually the best and safest.

After several minutes of assessing traffic patterns and checking out the other hitchhikers, we walked to the farthest end of the entrance ramp, beyond the other hitchhikers. We exchanged a brief greeting with the pair and then the single guy we passed. We propped our packs beside us 30 meters beyond the last. I pulled out my Istanbul sign, and we stuck out our thumbs and waited. It was morning and still cool from the air of the nearby mountains.

Car after car passed up the pair and single hitchhikers and us. No one gave us more than a glance. I began to doubt the effectiveness of Gabi's shared strategy to make a destination sign. Maybe potential long-distance drivers would not want a hiker going that far. When you would catch a ride, it wasn't unusual for the driver to be somewhat cryptic about how far he or they were traveling in case the chemistry was not good. If the driver did not feel comfortable or safe, they could drop the hitchhiker at the nearest intersection and claim this was where they needed to exit. The more we thought about catching a long ride, the more it seemed impossible. The idea of someone going all 2,000 kilometers saying, "Hey look, they are going all the way to Istanbul, same as us, let's fit them and their packs in our small car and have a great three-day trip with people we don't know," was beginning to seem unlikely.

Back in the parking lot, apart from all the other cars, stood a group of multi-ethnic men looking our way. These men shuffled around a lot but didn't appear to have much purpose for their gathering. Must be waiting for someone or something, we thought. They seemed suspicious, but it was hard to tell from this distance. Two from this group walked a hundred meters up to the pair of hitchhikers, talked with them briefly, and pointed back to their group. The hikers packed their sign, grabbed their packs, and returned to the parking area to join the awaiting group. The two men then strolled up to the single hiker, another 30 meters or so, and the same thing happened. He folded his sign, packed up, and walked to their cars.

What the heck, we wondered. Maybe the two men were some officials, and hitchhiking here was not allowed, but we thought this wasn't very likely. Perhaps they had some scheme and were looking to hire accomplices, or who knows? Our suspicions were growing, but we were becoming curious. About then, the two men continued toward us, and I said to Angie as they approached, "Stay cool. Let's not give them any information." I slid our Istanbul sign back into my pack. The two men arrived, said they needed a driver to take a car to Istanbul, and asked if we would be interested. "Right! What's the real deal?" we thought. Somewhat hesitant, we declined, saying we might only go as far as Salzburg. The two turned and returned to the now-growing group at the parking area.

Angie and I tried to determine if the offer might be legitimate or a dangerous scheme. The offer of a long ride seemed to be a gift horse, and should we look at it in the mouth? A possible opportunity was passing, and no cars were stopping, so we decided to walk back and talk to them, get more information, and check out the overall vibe before deciding.

We arrived at the group of men and older cars and talked briefly to the three other hikers, who seemed happy about the deal. We spoke to Liaqat Ali, the group leader, about the offer. Ali, a Pakistani businessman, said he traveled to Germany twice yearly to buy cheap Mercedes to resell in Pakistan for a hefty profit. He knew people in Istanbul who would recondition them on their way. I asked if we could look at the car we would be driving, and Ali obliged. Our first thought was that maybe we would be transporting drugs, but if they wanted us to be drug mules, we would be traveling in the other direction.

We examined the 1964 Mercedes diesel with a four-speed stick shift on the column. It was clean and empty except for a large television in the back seat. The trunk contained an assortment of neatly folded, brand-new Levi's blue jeans, new-in-box cassette recorders, and several other household items. We saw no drugs, assault weapons, or blindfolded, tied-up hostages, so maybe this would work.

Liaqat Ali seemed friendly, and his compatriots were congenial and somewhat excited. I agreed we would take one car but told Ali I had no international license. Ali said this was not a problem as long as I knew how to drive. Ali had four vehicles. He led the way in one, his younger brother followed with the next car, the pair of hitchhikers took the third, and we drove the fourth. Johan, a South Afrikaner looking to make a profit, had two more cars, and another Indian man had one more. The single hitchhiker drove Johan's second car. Every car had a driver, and we would soon be on our way.

Ali talked with us all about the ground rules. He would pay for all the gas and car-related expenses, and we would provide for our food. We could sleep in the cars or outside if we prefer. The caravan would travel together, and if anyone got separated, everyone else would wait at the next rest area or gas station for the ones separated to rejoin the group. That was about it. We hopped in the front seat of the old Mercedes and thought, "Sweet, just the two of us." Ali asked me to be the last in the caravan, watch for others who might stop or pull off the road, and flash my headlight, signaling him to stop. There would be no need to engage in small talk with random drivers or be extra careful with what we say. Only the two of us were in the car all the way to our first major destination, 2,000 kilometers away.

I had never driven a diesel before and couldn't figure out how to start the car. I turned the key, but nothing happened. Ali came over and showed me how to hold in the glow plug heater button, which warmed the spark plug heads, for several seconds before turning the key. That worked, and we pulled out, taking the last place in the caravan of seven cars to begin our long journey with excitement and uplifted spirits. The manual four-speed on the column was odd, but I picked it up quickly, and shifting became smoother with some practice.

We were off in the early afternoon, windows down, into the cool breeze from the Alps. The Mercedes had a radio, but with a quick check, nothing was worth listening to, so we discussed what we anticipated in this new experience. Our heads were calming, and our hearts lifted as we settled into this classic, comfortable car with just us! This peaceful solitude was a relaxed feeling that was a welcome surprise. Now, we could focus on what we might see and experience on our journey and leave the somewhat stressful task of getting a string of unknown rides from strangers out of our minds.

It wasn't long till we reached the Austrian border. Each car waited in line to present passports to the border control agent. Vehicle inspections and searches were rare, but with keen eyes, officials looked intently at each driver and each car as it passed. The line of vehicles moved quickly, and as we pulled up and presented our passports, I wondered what would happen if they asked for a driver's license. Most tourists planning to drive in Europe would go to a recognized travel agent to obtain an international permit by showing their valid license and paying a small fee. I had only my Florida license, which was in English and intelligible in other countries. As luck would have it, the official quickly looked at our passports and waved us through. The entire border crossing was like going through a toll booth on a turnpike, fast and easy.

As we ascended into the Alps, traffic became lighter, and we began to appreciate the beautiful mountains rising in front of us! The Autobahn passed many towns and villages that looked quaint and storybook-like. Rushing crystal-clear rivers flowed through meadows of wheat fields and stands of trees with snow-capped peaks above. Most stretches of the Autobahns had no speed limit, but our caravan maintained a steady speed of around 110 kph. Newer, faster cars passed us like we were crawling, so I had to stay focused constantly. Once, I needed to pass on the four-lane, divided Autobahn, which became a somewhat harrowing experience. As our caravan, one by one, made their way around a bus going up a mountain incline, I took my turn as the last car. Immediately after a fast car zoomed past the bus, I pulled into the left lane to pass, but a car, quite a distance behind me, repeatedly flashed its lights at me. I saw their flashing headlights and wondered what they were thinking. They were right on my tail within a few seconds, the driver pounding his steering wheel and cursing that I slowed him down. I won't make that mistake again. If they flashed their lights, I'd pull back behind and let them fly by, no problem. This is how it worked on the no-speed limit Autobahn, and our only hurry was to ensure we didn't get separated from the caravan.

The caravan group stops for a break in Austria. Angie, Liaqat Ali, and his brother are on the right, and the other hitchhikers are on the left.

It was time for a group gas stop, so we followed the caravan off the Autobahn to a nearby gas station, where everyone filled their tanks, and Ali took care of the payments. We got out and stretched our legs, filled our canteens, and talked a bit with each of the others, who shared plans for their journey. The pair of hitchhikers that started this journey with us from Munich were young Germans from Hamburg, hoping to reach Istanbul and maybe farther. The single hiker was also German and on his way to meet a friend in Istanbul. Everyone else was intent on making a profit, selling their investment cars in Pakistan, as Ali did. This group consisted of the Pakistanis, Ali and his brother, one Hindu Indian man, the South Afrikaner, and his young friend. Before the trip, this group knew each other and hung out together each time we stopped. Angie observed that everyone in the group was male except her. Driving a car by ourselves made this imbalance seem more comfortable.

We were all bound for Istanbul or beyond. For the three hitchhikers and us, this journey was following the hippie trail. Ever since the Beatles became interested in Indian music, culture, and philosophy, many rock music lovers (hippies) decided to make the journey east themselves, and this trek became known as the "hippie trail." I was interested in traveling to India or beyond one day, but with limited funds, this trip to Istanbul and Greece was more than enough for us now.

After this 30-minute pit stop, we were all back on the road, trying to sync up as we drove through the busy traffic and headed to the next Autobahn entrance on the other end of town. Traffic became more congested, and as we waited to turn right over the railroad tracks back to the Autobahn, the light changed to red. The rest of the caravan made the green or bright yellow light, but I had to stop, and the cross traffic followed the caravan. Once a space opened, I turned right on red, trying to see the caravan way up ahead. A right turn on red was legal in most states back in the US, but nope, not in Austria. A police car quickly pulled us over, and with a flurry of statements, questions, and hurried talk from all parties, I got a ticket for running a red light and had to pay directly to the policeman right there on the spot. No way, I thought, you don't do that. The policeman accepted that my Florida driver's license might be an actual driver's license but couldn't read it. Angie understood most of the policeman's Austrian dialect and assured me that paying on the spot was standard. Twenty Marks poorer, we were back on the road. We hit the Autobahn southbound, but the caravan was nowhere in sight. Our group was waiting at the rest area a dozen kilometers down the road.

We drove on till early evening, where we all stopped at a cozy, rural rest area and shared time eating our light food at a picnic table. Ali told us how he had been making this trip for almost twenty years, twice a year, which provided a decent living for his wife and kids back in Lahore. Everyone spoke at least some English and combined with gestures and visual aids; we managed to communicate with each other pretty well. It was a friendly group, and everyone seemed legit. We all had more questions for Ali about what might lie ahead and what to expect. He asked some light questions about each of us as well. We were all feeling more comfortable about this evolving, shared experience.

As we headed back on the road, the Autobahn ended, and we proceeded on a minor two-lane highway with less traffic. We drove through the mountains, passing through small towns and villages until dark. Ali, in the lead car, pulled over at an off-road parking area where we would spend the night. Angie and I pulled out some Brötchen and a can of tuna for our big meal, then settled in for the night. Doors locked, and a window lowered slightly to let in fresh air. We talked until we felt sleepy. The seats could recline but only one or the other because the big TV would need to be behind one.

The close snuggling lasted for a while, with an unrolled sleeping bag providing just enough warmth to hold off the night chill. Eventually, we would each find our position to stretch out as much as possible. At least the gear shift was up on the column, and our legs had more room to move.

Part 5
A Peculiar Passage

Chapter 25
The Frontier

———

Day 4, June 30th

Everyone awoke with the breaking dawn. Some lit portable stoves, boiled water, and made coffee. Each nibbled on bread or whatever food they had. Angie noticed Ali and his brother walking away from the group, looking around and pointing, then kneeling, prostrating themselves in prayer. I commented to Ali about the prayer shortly before we got back on the road, and he was firm and adamant about the importance of the moral code that guided his life. Ali shared how his wife and children owed all they had to Allah's Grace. He mentioned how his wife ran the house at home in Lahore. What she said was the hard and fast rule. Neither he nor his children questioned her guidance, including religious orthodoxy, but he was the boss on the road. Ali seemed genuine, and I took him at his word.

We drove out of the Alps and into the lower mountains and the eventual foothills. The breadth of the Alps surprised me. I had always equated the Alps with the Rockies, and those would take a couple of days to traverse. The Alps were high and beautiful but relatively narrow where we crossed.

The Yugoslav border was coming up in the next hour, so Ali led everyone to a nearby gas station even though the cars had half-full tanks. I thought the early stop might be because gas prices would increase once you cross the border. It turns out there was a different reason. We approached the border by mid-morning to find the two southbound lanes backed up for several kilometers. Sometimes we didn't move for 5-10 minutes. Other times, we crept along at a snail's pace. Periodically, we would get out and lean on a car to talk or complain. Once we reached the border crossing, we could see each car taking several minutes to clear the border station. The border guards directed several vehicles to a different lot for further questioning and possible searches. This long border delay was the reason for the early gas fill-up. It was now our turn to cross the border. Ali, in the first car, talked with the Yugoslav agent for a moment and pointed at each vehicle in his caravan. No one knew what he said, but we all were able to proceed quickly through the checkpoint after showing our passports. That was a relief. This crossing was nowhere near as smooth as crossing into Austria, but still not too bad. It only took a couple of hours.

There was clear traffic for the next two hours on what became a more narrow, two-lane road. The habits of too many drivers were erratic, and some were dangerous. Sometimes, a car would come up quickly behind you and pass into the oncoming traffic lane, flashing their lights at approaching cars and wildly honking their horn. The oncoming vehicle had a choice. It could move to the dirt shoulder or get hit head-on. Head-on collisions were less common, but they did happen. If the oncoming car refused to yield, the passing vehicle would again force its way back into the proper lane with loud honking and wild gestures. The oncoming car was forced to swerve to the shoulder, going full speed and honking its horn repeatedly.

We all pulled off into a small village gas station sometime after midday. Across the street, there appeared to be a grocery store in a residential-looking house. You would never know it was a grocery store without a small sign tacked next to the door.

We all needed food, and this rural store was a perfect place to buy what we needed, and it wasn't too expensive. We were happy to find out they accepted Deutsche Marks. As it would turn out, almost every business would welcome Deutsche Marks and American dollars at an appropriate and favorable (to them) exchange rate. We entered the store in shifts as it was small, and several local customers were also there. One medium-sized room with three walls of shelves with food products and one long counter blocking anyone from reaching anything.

Each customer would tell the store worker what they wanted, and the worker would turn, grab it, and place it in their pile on the counter, keeping a careful eye on them and everyone in the store. This restriction limited any possible theft but required a long wait before our turn to purchase the groceries we needed. When the clerk asked Angie and me what we needed, he was impatient, and the language barrier became insurmountable. We would point, make air pictures with our hands, and try a variety of words in English and German to express our wants. Each time the clerk retrieved an item that was not what we wanted, he would become visibly annoyed and return it to its place, back on the shelf. We eventually walked out with a couple of jars of puszta salad, some hard rolls, a large bag of mixed nuts, two cans of tuna, two apples, and a one-liter bottle of bubbly mineral water, which was a treat.

Back on the road, we drove through more traffic and passed through several bigger towns south of Zagreb. Johan, the Afrikaner, had been pulled over by local police. We all waited an hour for him at the next gas station on the edge of town. When he and his friend caught up, he explained what happened. He told us how the police accused him of crossing the center line in traffic and demanded he pay an immediate 100 DM fine. They argued, and Johan snapped a picture of the police, saying he would post this with the ADAC's (Top German travel agency) main office to warn travelers about this corruption. A struggle ensued between them. The policeman forcefully grabbed Johan's camera and ripped out the film. Johan lunged to retrieve it, but the policeman unspooled the film, exposing it to the light and erasing all the pictures on the roll. Their arguing subsided, and they eventually settled on a 50 DM fine, which went directly to the policeman's pocket.

In addition to this incident with the police, a rock shattered his windshield as they drove out of town. They had to remove the glass entirely so they could see. Amazingly, through all the anger and frustration they experienced, they could laugh about it. Johan put on his oversized aviator sunglasses to deflect the rush of air, and the trip went on.

Johan and the Indian man in the car with no windshield.

The two-lane road we were on was in poor condition and became much busier. Some drivers were just plain nuts in the way they drove. Speeding cars, screeching brakes, and frequent horn blasts were the norm. You started to see more disabled vehicles along the roadsides and off in the fields. Many cars had severe damage and seemed abandoned. Some were rusted frames that had been there a pretty long time. One passenger bus we saw was burned entirely and left, with smoke still rising from the carcass.

Smoke rising from another traffic accident in Yugoslavia.

At the next stop in a small town, the pair of hitchhikers in our group decided they had seen enough. One chose, on the spot, to leave and head home. The other made some excuse and walked toward a gas station. I have no idea what he eventually did, but he also left the caravan. Ali followed him and tried to persuade him to continue but to no avail. The guy was fed up and left.

Now, there was one car with no driver. It was getting late and would be dark in a couple of hours. Johan's friend had never driven a car, but he relented when Ali asked, more like begging him to. They spent about 10 minutes explaining the fundamentals, giving him a quick behind-the-wheel practice, and we were all off again. Ali was in the lead, Johan with his sunglass's windshield next, his new driver friend behind him, then the turban-wearing Indian man followed by Ali's brother, the remaining hitchhiker, and Angie and me bringing up the rear of the caravan.

As darkness fell, traffic backed up once again. As we slowly moved, we had to creep into the oncoming lane to get around an incident on the road ahead. We saw an older woman bicyclist who was hit and killed by a car, lying on the side of the road. As we passed, people were covering her face with a blanket. After a few more hours driving in the dark, our caravan pulled into a truck stop on the outskirts of Belgrade to spend the night. Between all the parked cars and some continually running semi-tractor trailers, we slept as best we could. At least there were public toilets here, and it was worth paying ten Pfennigs to use the facility.

Days 5 and 6, July 1st and 2nd

The following morning, Ali gathered everyone to explain his interrupted, new plan. After talking with some truck drivers on their way to Istanbul, he learned that to enter Bulgaria with any business agenda, you must now obtain the appropriate visas before arriving at the Communist border, or you would not be allowed to cross. He said he would need to visit the Bulgarian Embassy in Belgrade to obtain the necessary visas. We were suspicious. Ali told us he had made this trip many times, and only now has he learned of the required permit. We wondered what his real motive was. Our best option was to wait it out and stick with the caravan to Istanbul.

We waited several hours in the hot and smelly cement resting place. Ali returned to the truck stop and told us the Bulgarian Embassy was closed for the day. With this unexpected delay, several of us went into the city, but there was not much to see or do there, especially without money to spend. Angie and I tagged along with Ali and his brother through a part of the city center. Ali commented many times about how people smoked and drank alcohol and how immoral they were. He chastised some for tossing aside a half-eaten bread roll when so many worldwide were hungry and poor. Ali enjoyed pointing out these faults as they walked through the crowds. No one paid attention to him, and it seemed he did this all for show.

Belgrade was drab, and a busy sort of lifelessness gripped the people. These were the last years of Josip Tito's rule, the Yugoslav national ruler for decades after World War II. Tito, Prime Minister and President for Life, had unified the various Slavic nations in determined resistance to the Nazis. His leadership during the resistance movement cemented his endearment to these Slavic peoples. Tito was a master negotiator who somehow kept the Slavic nations out of the Warsaw Pact and out from under Soviet domination during the Cold War period. He had agreed to many Soviet demands for a Communist-type economy and mostly closed borders in return for some autonomy from Communist rule.

Belgrade Yugoslavia 1976

The entire Yugoslav economy stagnated much like its Communist neighbors after WWII, and Belgrade now showed this all too well. Architecturally, one structure stood out. A massive, modern-looking apartment complex rose from the horizon just outside the city. It looked like a two-dimensional pyramid visible from many kilometers away. As far as I could tell, this seemed to be their crowning achievement. Every other building, road network, and mass transit system looked old and run down. The Yugoslav people did have some freedom of movement, which was not available to those in other Communist Bloc nations. Many Yugoslavs migrated to Western Germany, including Angie's best friend's family, Helga Felde, back in Bosenheim.

Back to the truck stop for another sleepless night. There was nothing on the radio, and it was too dark to read, but we did notice a pattern of nocturnal visits to some truck drivers by nicely made-up young women for an hour or so each. That was it for our evening entertainment.

We spent the morning hanging out at the truck stop, talking with the others. Angie and I played two-handed spades in the front seat of our car to pass the time. It was scorching hot outside, and we would keep the front windows down as long as possible, but the diesel fumes would become overwhelming, and we shut them again. It was finally starting to feel like Summer. We walked around as much as possible to stay cool, but the truck stop was off a busy highway amid a smelly industrial area, and there was nothing of interest to do nearby.

Ali and his brother made another trip to the Bulgarian Embassy, so we caught a ride with Johan and returned to the city. We found some green space near the Sava and Danube Rivers and rested comfortably. Walking back into the city center to meet Johan, we spotted Ali and his brother sitting at an outdoor cafe. Ali had a lit cigarette in his hand, feet propped up on another chair, and glasses of beer were on the table. I told Ali, "I thought you didn't drink or smoke." He brushed this comment off, saying, "Ah, that was before. Sometimes you needed to live differently, no matter," like this was no big deal.

As Angie and I walked away, we made connections about Ali's and his brother's behavior over the last several days. They were nice enough, but it seemed they would often say something quite opinionated and then contradict this with their behavior not long after. It became usual to hear them say or do things the complete opposite of their truth the day before. We decided it best not to count on anything they said or promised, which was a good decision. They were big talkers and liars, but they made this all seem normal. I asked Ali about the visas, and he said there was some Bulgarian holiday, and the embassy was still closed. My suspicion of his truthfulness was growing. We contemplated heading to Istanbul alone but decided it would be safer to remain with the caravan.

In the days ahead, we trusted our trip would get more exciting or at least we would find more interesting places to visit. However, except for some coastal cities we heard about, Yugoslavia could be skipped entirely. You had to endure the entire 800 km frontier road to reach your desired destination. Back to the truck stop for another noisy night. We locked our doors, with windows slightly cracked to keep them from fogging, and spent another hot, restless night smelling diesel fumes. At least there were toilets.

Day 7, July 3rd

Ali and his brother were making another trip to the Bulgarian Embassy. The Indian man and I decided to join them early this Saturday morning. We arrived at the embassy to find the doors closed and locked. We waited till nine and tried again. No answer. Crap, we walked around the building knocking on every door until some man finally answered. Ali explained how he needed visas to transport his cars through Bulgaria. The man told Ali he was crazy, "Just go to the border crossing and get them like everybody else!".

We wasted two full days in this drab city smelling the diesel fumes at our truck stop, temporary home. Let's get the heck out of here now, we thought. Angie and I had been on the road for seven days and hadn't even reached Turkey. Fortunately, we were spending very little money. We never did figure out what Ali was really up to concerning this long delay in Belgrade, but we suspected there was more to the story.

Chapter 26
Sneaking Through the Iron Curtain

There were more single-lane roads, potholes, and our share of crazy drivers over the following hours, but we approached the Bulgarian border sometime in the early afternoon. Bulgaria was a Communist Bloc country totally at the mercy of the Soviet Union. Two Eastern Bloc countries, Hungary and Czechoslovakia, attempted to assert some independence in 1957 and 68, respectively. The Soviet Army violently crushed these moves toward self-rule. The other Eastern Bloc countries, Including the smaller, less powerful Bulgaria, learned from this and remained loyal partners of the Soviet Empire.

Our caravan would be allowed to travel through the Communist country and even encouraged to stay and spend money for a while. However, Bulgaria's citizens led lives of strict government control in a fixed command economy with little personal freedom and were not allowed to travel outside the Communist states.

Border crossing, Bulgaria

As our caravan again waited in a long line of cars approaching the border, we saw a tall, maybe three-meter high, double row of chain link fence. The fence lines were about 40 meters apart. Each fence had strands of barbed wire on the top, stretching as far as we could see in both directions. There were no trees or structures on this barren landscape for several hundred meters from the road in both directions. People in Western countries knew this border as the "Iron Curtain." This formidable, heavily guarded barrier separated the Communist Eastern European countries from the Western Democracies. The only way to pass through this Iron Curtain was at a tightly controlled border crossing like we were about to enter.

After several hours of waiting in line, our caravan approached the border crossing and guard stations. When we got close, Ali instructed us to park in a lot while he and his brother walked to a checkpoint to get everyone's passports stamped, buy transit visas, and exchange about 20 DM each into *Levs*, the local currency. The Lev must be spent in Bulgaria as no bank in non-communist countries would convert Levs to any other currency. After gathering everyone's passports, Ali said not to worry, as he had done this many times. No one was certain about what he was up to. By this point in our trip, Angie and I had become quite suspicious of Ali and his motives, whatever they might be. Our passports were essential for our journey, and we never let them out of sight or touch. Giving them to Ali was a considerable risk.

While we all waited in the parking area, I followed from a distance and watched Ali and his brother, who now had all our passports. I wandered around, keeping them within sight. I looked at the barrier fence, the guard posts, and the many, mostly women, soldiers with machine rifles strapped over their shoulders. There was a small store and gas station near the official window stations where passports were stamped, and Western money exchanged for Levs. Many people had parked their cars and were busy getting documents checked or visiting the store. I looked around the area and ensured I could remain in visual contact if things went sideways. I had no idea what I could do if something odd happened, but I felt observing them was in our best interest.

I watched as Ali stood in line chatting with his brother. I noted how slowly the line progressed and strolled around in this tight, secure environment, trying not to draw attention to myself. Every guard and soldier looked at each traveler with intimidating suspicion. The travelers either looked down or away to avoid any potential problems with their crossing. I had my camera and snapped pictures of the fence and guards. Still, I did so by holding my camera at waist level, nonchalantly pointing the lens in a desired direction, and clicking from the hip unnoticed.

I saw the line moving faster, and they stepped closer to the control house. I saw people stepping up to a window to have passports stamped, buy visas, and exchange money. Ali and his brother stood in line a bit apart now as if they were not together. His brother approached the window first and handed a stack of passports, paperwork, and money to the uniformed women in the booth. As she turned her back to record the transactions, Ali's brother slipped out of view, and Ali, older but looking similar, stepped in his place. The woman returned to the window and handed Ali the completed paperwork and passports. Ali made a terrible fuss about how he had given her all this money and shoved his stack of passports at her. He lamented how she had not stamped his passports and what a travesty it was to be poor and taken advantage of in this way. His brother poked his head back, saying how she cheated him. Together, they got the uniformed woman so flustered and confused with their ranting and raving that she finally gave up and stamped all the passports, shoved them back, and said something to the effect of, "Here, now get the hell out of here" or likely worse.

Ali and his brother promptly returned to the group with everyone's passports stamped and a slight smirk on their faces. We were all relieved to have our essential passports back in hand and lined up the caravan to show them to the final guard. After a quick physical inspection of our car and with stern looks from the other guards, we were motioned through. Now, it would be a short trip to Sofia, the capital city of Bulgaria, where we would stay the night.

We drove into Sophia and parked in a well-maintained parking area surrounding a large building with multiple round domes. Late Saturday afternoon at Saint Aleksander Nevski Cathedral, an Orthodox Church, we all parked and got out to enjoy the summer afternoon while Ali, his brother, and Johan met to discuss something that appeared clandestinely necessary. The church didn't seem open, but dozens of youths, primarily boys, were hanging out around the parking lots. There were green spaces with benches and statues mixed within the parking areas. There are many shade trees and some picnic-style tables around the grounds. Some of the many teenagers and young men in their 20s slowly came to get a closer look at our cars and the people in our newly arrived caravan. Ali and the others were all out, stretching their legs and breathing in the fresh air. Soon, they started talking with a couple of the local youths. Angie and I followed a short distance but did not want to be far from our locked car. We were happy to be in a place so quiet and peaceful for a change.

Two young men approached Angie and me, speaking fair but broken English, and Ali joined us, seeming eager to engage with them. After maybe five minutes, he led them to the trunk of his car, opened it, and began showing the young men things he had brought to sell. Another young man joined the discrete transaction while others, obviously interested, kept their distance for the moment. Everyone was playing it cool, not drawing unwarranted attention. Little by little, other locals would stop by to see the wares in his trunk, and if you did not know what was transpiring, you would think they were all chatting about the weather. Ali closed his trunk, and within two minutes, Johan opened his and joined the process, followed, in time, by the Indian man and, eventually, Ali's brother. You could not see money exchanged in the open, but we knew it was as several people walked away with a cassette player or Levi's blue jeans.

Ali approached the 64 Mercedes, asked me for the keys, opened the trunk, and sold its contents. After maybe 90 minutes of selling, the caravan market ran out of supply. Two young men hung around and talked with Angie and Me. One offered me 100 American dollars for the Levis I was wearing. Although tempted, I declined. I had another pair in my pack, and an extra hundred dollars or two could afford us more travel time or allow us to spend more freely. I did not want to take financial advantage of them and knew that the use of US dollars in Bulgaria was outlawed. Should officials observe us selling goods for dollars or Marks, it would mean jail time or a hefty fine for them and an even heavier penalty for us. I was reluctant to take advantage of the situation, and my two pairs of Levis were all I had to wear, so I rebuffed their offers.

Ali's brother, who had left earlier, now returned with a key to a hotel room. We gathered, and Ali told us it was not allowed or safe for us to sleep in the cars in Bulgaria, so he had rented a single room in a nearby hotel for us all to sleep that night. He explained how it would be essential to slip into the hotel discreetly. We would enter a couple at a time, using a side door, and be very quiet once in the room. His brother had paid for a room for only one person, and if the hotel found more were in the room, we would be evicted or even turned over to the police. After dark, we did as instructed and slipped quietly into the room.

All eight of us were now together in one relatively small room. The danger of violating the rules in a strict, Communist country was exciting, but again, we were suspicious of our situation. Over the last several days, we had become more comfortable with the group, but we still were not confident with everyone's motives and ethical standards. We were afraid to share these close quarters, as Angie was the only female. We had no other option, so we followed their plan and stayed. Ali decided that since Angie was the only female, she and I would share the single bed, and everyone else would sleep in the two stuffed chairs or on the floor.

In hushed voices, our compatriots talked about the earlier sales and how much profit they each made from the clandestine sales. Johan told us about following one young man on a circuitous route to the teen's home with a portable cassette player, valued at $20, tucked under his arm. They entered the boy's home, and he was briefly introduced to the boy's mother, then led up to the boy's bedroom.

The boy flung back a carpet and worked a loose floorboard open. He removed a small box, pulled out a stack of American dollars, and gave Johan $120 for the cassette player. It was apparent how scared Johan was, but Ali said as long as you were careful and didn't see anyone follow you, you'd likely be alright.

As everyone settled in, a loud knock on the door startled us. Ali's brother held up a hand to suggest, freeze, don't move, and placed an index finger in front of his mouth to say, no noise. He opened the door, a crack at first, and slipped into the hallway. We could hear their muffled voices, but no one knew what was said. A moment later, the brother returned, motioning to remain silent. After a minute, when the man who knocked left, the brother said it was the clerk from the desk checking on some vague complaints. The brother said he assured him all was well and left satisfied. The looks soon after between the brother and Ali suggested some money likely exchanged hands for the clerk's silence.

Even though Angie and I had the bed, and she slept between me and the wall, she had another uneasy night. Angie was the one who felt the most skeptical about our evolving circumstances with the group. Being German, the wishy-washy truth Ali seemed to live by made her tense and apprehensive. She was used to people saying what they plan on doing and then sticking to it. With this group, stories and plans changed constantly, sometimes at a moment's notice. Truth had a different connotation for Ali and his group. It was more story than factual. Very discomforting. The men of the caravan were OK and respectful, but she still refused to allow deep sleep to overtake her.

Day 8, 4th of July, America's Bicentennial

After leaving the hotel room, a couple at a time, we all met back at the parked cars down the street. We visited the city in the morning before heading to Istanbul and the Turkish border crossing. We did need to spend the Bulgarian Lev we were required to exchange for Western currencies. We piled into two cars and left the five other vehicles in the quiet neighborhood.

Johan looks down a street in Sofia, Bulgaria. July 4, 1976

After driving for about 10 minutes, we arrived in Sofia's city center. It was Sunday, and almost every store was closed. Many people were on the streets, but only a few restaurants and tourist places were open. Ali told us to return to the cars in two hours. He warned us to be very suspicious when talking to anyone and, under no circumstances, to spend any Marks or dollars.

Angie and I walked down a street following an old streetcar to an area with taller buildings and lots of traffic. There were giant billboards, high up on the buildings, of Soviet and Bulgarian leaders or other heroes, all in decorated military uniforms. I recognized one as Vladimir Lenin and another one as Joseph Stalin. They each had well-defined jawlines and determined looks on their faces. While maneuvering through a crowded sidewalk, a car with big megaphones on its roof stopped dead in the busy intersection ahead. An announcement was made in an unyielding tone, repeated, and then it moved on. Strangely, everyone stopped in their tracks, and no one spoke.

After the 20-second announcement, the car and the people moved on as if nothing happened. We looked at each other, "What was that?" I asked. I then shared with Angie, "You know, today is the Bicentennial of the United States. There's no sign, banner, or American flag anywhere. The Bicentennial is a big deal today in the US, but what would you expect in a Communist country"?

We walked on. As we went down a side street, a well-dressed, middle-aged man approached us, saying he was Austrian and on his way to Istanbul. He claimed his car broke down here in Sofia and asked, then pleaded with us to exchange his Bulgarian Lev for dollars or Marks to pay the garage as they wouldn't fix it on a Sunday otherwise. The man tried to be convincing, but we had a pretty good notion he was likely a government undercover agent attempting to entrap us, so we walked off. We knew those caught exchanging Western currency with locals would be arrested by authorities and heavily fined before being released.

Hunger is almost always present but is now getting more noticeable, increasing each time we pass a restaurant. We looked at the chalkboard menus outside the restaurants and understood little, but the large numbers, no doubt, were too expensive for us. We had hoped to find a grocery store, but none of the few we saw were open. Our hunger continued when we stumbled upon Ali and the Indian man who said they were going to a cafeteria not far from there, and they said it had reasonable prices. It was where the locals ate in large numbers.

We arrived and stood in line with several dozen people waiting to make our selections. The place was a simple, large dining area with dozens of large round tables. Every table in the restaurant was full, so people with their food trays stood behind each diner, waiting for the soon-to-be-vacated seat to open. Angie got a bowl of goulash and bread while I finally splurged on a piece of fish and boiled potatoes. We had nothing to drink and paid the equivalent of a few Marks for both meals with our remaining Levs. I hoped all four of us could sit at the same table, but new diners waiting for a seat to open up were quite competitive, and pushing their way behind a patron about to get up was common. Angie spotted a table with several almost-finished diners, so we stood behind what appeared to be a couple on the verge of getting up. Soon, we were seated together, but Ali and the Indian man were still waiting behind diners at different tables. We had eaten half our meals awkwardly while standing and waiting. We weren't seated long before we finished, got up, and vacated our places to others awaiting our departure. This meal was excellent, and my hunger was satisfied for the first time since our trip began.

Angie and I returned to the cars earlier than the others and took advantage of the time to roll and smoke a Drum *Tabak* cigarette before the others returned. We talked about how Ali, ahem, wink wink, opposed such behavior. Drum Tabak was the preferred cigarette of German hippies. Mainly because it cost five times less than a pack of cigarettes, but also because it had a good flavor. You could roll it full and loose for a robust taste, but I preferred a smaller, tight roll. It made it mild tasting and lasted longer because it burned slower. Angie rarely smoked, but today, we both enjoyed the tasty poison.

Our caravan pulled out of Sofia, now led by Johan, with his missing windshield, followed by his friend, who was now a much more experienced driver. Finally, Angie and I followed the pack, taking the rear position as usual. We stopped for gas, and I talked with the Indian man for quite a while. His name was unpronounceable to me, and like several others, I never referred to them by name. He spoke some English but with a heavy accent and described meeting Ali the year before. Ali persuaded him to join his business venture, and he borrowed money from a relative to fly to Germany, buy the car, and follow Ali's lead. He explained his simple lifestyle in India and how this risk might help his young family. The thousand-dollar profit he hoped to make selling his car back home would improve his family's lifestyle for many years.

I finally felt comfortable asking him how he wrapped his turban so neatly and kept it together. He promised to show me several different ways he wrapped the turban and explain the significance of each style when we had more time. Maybe once we reached Istanbul.

At this point in the trip, Angie and I seriously considered skipping Turkey altogether, abandoning the caravan, and heading straight south to Greece. We had been gone eight days and felt we were not progressing enough. If we did, we would leave Ali with another driverless car, and the thought of being alone in this Communist country might lead to other problems. We said nothing and stayed put with Ali and his group.

Chapter 27
Welcome to the Bizarre

By mid-afternoon, we approached the Turkish border. The line of cars stopped ahead and stretched as far as we could see. I recalled crossing into Austria was a breeze, Yugoslavia took maybe two hours, and Bulgaria took six. Angie was sure this would take longer, and she was right. With all cars stopped for extended periods, many people got out and talked, passing the time till they saw movement ahead, then jumped back in to creep along again. After a couple of hours of barely crawling along the two-lane road, we passed the final Bulgarian checkpoint and another double row of tall fencing with little attention paid to us beyond a look for Bulgarian citizens who were not allowed to leave. They checked our passport stamps, matched our passport pictures to our faces, and looked in the trunk.

The caravan group is waiting to approach the Turkish border from left: Ali, Johan, Ali's brother, Angie, and the Indian man. Angie and Bert drove the white 1964 Mercedes, which was second in line.

With the border control cleared, we entered a prolonged area of nothingness. Along this stretch, there were no towns, no houses, no anything, just a road widening into two lanes going our way, allowing for a little better progress. Cars still jockeyed for position, and any slight space left between cars would find a vehicle from the other lane squeezing its nose between them. The cars in our caravan stayed in line, but somehow, Ali slipped back a car or two behind Angie and me in the next lane. Cars were bumper to bumper and quick to close even the smallest gap as small movements occurred. Cars even moved to both shoulders to pass others, becoming a three- and four-lane traffic jam.

Tensions were high in all the drivers, and horns blared in a constant sequence near and far. With Ali getting closer, I waved for him to come up, cut in front of me, and allowed a half-length space to open up in front of our car. Just then, a car on my right took advantage and slipped its nose in front of us. This intrusion caused me to be even farther behind the rest of the caravan drivers, with Ali still stalled to my left. I was infuriated and finally lost my temper. I burst from the driver's side door, yelling and cursing at the bold driver who had cut in front of me. Angie held the back of my shirt and tried to calm me, but I refused to calm down. The man who cut me off was equally enraged and yelled back at me, shaking his fist and waving his arms, but after a short minute, it was apparent nothing would happen with either of us or the car's progress. We settled down.

We crept forward slowly, and the road ahead expanded, looking more like a vast parking lot 6-8 lanes wide. We could not see the front of this massive jam. On both sides of the extreme congestion, we could make out some structures, more shacks, and tents with people milling about. The two lanes had already added both shoulders with cars and were now opening wider again to more pavement with no lane markings, which every vehicle used to its advantage to get ahead. The cars were like liquid spreading across the hot pavement, almost touching the shacks on each side as they slowly progressed.

Hours passed as we crept forward, and as we approached this widened pavement, the noise of horns, yelling, and loud Middle Eastern music mixed with the yelling vendors walking through the stalled traffic, hawking their wares or food. This commotion was too much. The evening was hot, but we rolled up our windows anyway and suffered from the intense heat to dampen the constant noise.

We could still see Ali's car, now several rows left but now a bit ahead of us. The other caravan cars were all blended somewhere in front of us. We could no longer see them. We pushed along, bumpers bumping, and people constantly jockeying for position. This extreme traffic jam was highly stressful, but we stayed vigilant and kept up with the slow flow.

Time moved glacially, but eventually, we neared other buildings or small structures up ahead. There were dozens of wooden huts in clusters on both sides of the road. Some sold food and beverages, others t-shirts and sunglasses, and basic car supplies. Young Turkish boys weaved between the cars, talking with drivers as we closed in on the buildings ahead. A boy with a broad smile gently rapped on my window. I rolled it down halfway as the boy said many things, but neither Angie nor I understood. The boy repeatedly said, "Pass, pass," and "Passport." Many other young boys were doing the same thing near other cars, and there didn't seem to be any real threat. We cautiously pulled out our passports, thinking to show the boy, when he, quicker than lightning, grabbed both and darted off, running into the village of small shacks.

I sprang from the car, giving chase. People were thick, moving quickly in all directions. I, fearing the loss or likely resale of our all-important passports, pushed through the crowds, watching the boy running ahead. I emerged in another world utterly foreign and caught up with the boy in a few minutes. The boy arrived at what must have been a family operation, all sitting at a table in one of the primitive structures, stamping our passports and returning them to the boy. They spoke to me, but I had no idea what they were saying, and the boy smiled and returned our two passports.

Dumbfounded, passports in hand, I turned to find my way back to Angie in the sea of cars. The boy gently tugged on my shirt, smiled again, and held out his hand, wanting some payment or a tip. Not sure why or what happened, I pulled out my handful of change, including coins from several countries, and split it with the boy. I am unsure how much I paid him, but I knew it could not have been much. The boy and his parents seemed content. With passports securely deep in my Levi's front pocket, I meandered back to the sea of parked cars, where I found a relieved Angie.

We had been in this rolling traffic jam for ten hours and had almost reached some semi-official-looking buildings. These extended hours of jockeying for position and constant noise were exhausting. The fact that you had to remain ever vigilant to stay right on the car bumper in front of you to avoid being cut off meant no looking around and nothing but the most basic conversation with Angie. I spent more time complaining about other drivers than talking with Angie. We were both at our nerve's ends. The excessive heat emanating from the blacktop road, constant yelling, loud music, and continuous honking was unbearable.

The cars were now beginning to form actual lanes, each lane entering what looked like bays of a self-serve car wash but was the Turkish border control. Ali, who had already crossed the border, appeared, rapped on my window, and asked me to let his new friend in the back seat of the 64 Mercedes. Ali explained his Turkish friend, who had come from Istanbul and walked from the Turkish side of the border, would claim to be Liaqat Ali as we went through the checkpoint.

Ali had given this man his passport with instructions to pose as him, the owner of the 64 Mercedes, and the big TV in the back seat. If Ali were to bring multiple cars, especially a TV, into Turkey, he would need to pay expensive tariffs. This new man, impersonating Ali, could complete the crossing by claiming the Mercedes as his car and his TV, tax-free. The man was Middle Eastern and looked vaguely like Ali, but this was a stretch. Next in line to enter a bay with a Turkish customs official, a sense of relief swept over Angie and me. We could see open roads ahead and several gas stations and stores, all open near midnight and bustling with activity. But first, we had to clear Turkish customs.

We pulled into the drive-through bay, where an official held up his hand to stop and signaled me to turn off the car. Turning off the diesel engine was a problem because the 64 Mercedes could not restart once warm or hot until it cooled down for 30–60 minutes. I'm not sure how, but with the help of emphatic hand gestures, we seemed to have convinced the official to let us leave the car running. We all stepped out of the car and stood near the official with a clipboard, understanding nothing of what he was saying. The stranger, Ali, talked with the agent, obviously claiming to be Liaqat Ali, and presented his (Ali's) passport. The official already had Angie's and my passports in one hand and proceeded to argue with stranger Ali. We watched the unfolding drama intently without understanding a word or why our new guest had to impersonate Ali. It seemed apparent the official doubted the authenticity of Ali's impersonation. The arguing went on for ten minutes.

I interrupted the officer who raised our two passports, exclaiming, "German," pointing at Angie, and "American," pointing at me. He indicated it was no problem and said we could exit and go. We decided to wait but considered taking the man up on his offer. After another ten minutes of arguing, hand waving, and walking around the car, the authentic Ali appeared and spoke with the agent. The tone of the conversation moderated, and the two negotiated a solution, which we found out later involved the agent's tales of a big family to feed and assorted health problems. In return for a cash donation, we were quickly on our way out of the bay, crossing into Turkey. It was no wonder it took so long to cross the border, and it was undoubtedly a lucrative side business for the officials, who softly extorted this kind of money. This perpetual traffic jam and the development of the micro-economy of business shacks hired messenger boys and extorting officials was a boon to the local economy. Ali said several other cars were still in line, so we should park ahead at the store and wait for everyone to catch up.

Day 9, July 5th

We parked in the busy gas station/store lot around two in the morning, dead tired, and slept for about 90 minutes. Ali woke us with a heavy rap on the window and said, "All ready, come on." I replied that we were too tired and that I could not possibly drive without more sleep. I needed to sleep after 12 hours of extreme stress and congestion. Ali persuaded us to go as long as I could, and we would all stop to rest soon. We all filled our tanks for the last time and returned to the road in the wee morning hours. Impersonator Ali was fast asleep in our back seat. Traffic thinned but was still busy as we drove along the dark two-lane road. We continued until 4 AM when I finally flashed my headlights at Ali.

Soon after, we pulled off at a quiet but busy parking/rest area. I told Ali I could no longer keep my eyes open, and he said, "Stay here and sleep for an hour, then meet us in the next town at daybreak." It sounded good. Ali went on, and Angie and I settled into the front seat for well-needed shut-eye. Impersonator Ali, who was uncomfortable in the back seat with the TV, signaled with hand gestures that he would sleep outside.

I went into the nearby bathroom. In the quiet dark of the early morning, several men went to the hut I assumed was the bathroom. I followed them in but saw no toilets. Now alone in the dimly lit place, I looked all over, but none were there. After stopping at a bush outside for relief, I returned to the car, passing several people curled up and sleeping in the grass. Angie unlocked the door and listened as I told her the bathroom had no toilets. She said except for more urban and tourist-friendly places, toilets like the ones we were used to didn't exist in this region. I likely missed the holes in the hut floors serving as the toilet.

Sleep came quickly, but the early morning glow soon startled Angie awake. She said, "Wake up. We slept too long. We've got to get going and find Ali and the caravan." "What about the fake Ali? We've got to find him?" I replied as I stepped out of the car to look around. Surprisingly, I saw a dozen or more people sleeping on the ground, but none looked like fake Ali. I called out in a loud whisper, "Ali! Ali!" Several times. Some stirred, but none responded. Back in the car, we both agreed that fake Ali must have gone ahead with another caravan member. The diesel started with repeated loud efforts, and we slowly pulled out. I looked over my shoulder for fake Ali and lightly honked the horn several times. Seeing nothing, I accelerated onto the two-lane road, anxious to catch up with the group.

Chapter 28

Crash

———

We hurried down the two-lane road, hoping to see a sign for the next town or village where the plan was always to meet the others at the first rest area or gas station. The few signs we did see were confusing, but the kilometers were clear. We figured the next town was about 30 minutes ahead and raced on. It was now full daylight, about 8 in the morning, and we feared, running late, we would not find the group. As we approached a small town, a tractor-trailer pulled in front of us. There was no other traffic, so I accelerated and passed the truck on the two-lane road just in time to see a signal light turning red. A car waiting on the cross street for the light to change was ready to pull out, so I hit the brakes, stopping in time, but the tractor-trailer behind me wasn't so lucky. He braked too, but not quick enough, and plowed into our rear end. The jolt pushed the 64 Mercedes into the intersection. Everyone was OK, but we were startled. I got out to assess the damage. Except for the one other car, which did not stop, no one else was there to witness the accident.

We suffered a crumpled fender, broken tail lights, a pushed-in trunk, and a damaged bumper. The truck driver climbing down from his cab had much to say, but I didn't know what he was saying. He was young, maybe in his late twenties, of Middle Eastern descent. We both tried talking but wound up relying on hand gestures and pointing. After looking all around and seeing no one, I indicated to the truck driver with hand motions to follow me into the small town ahead to get help. The truck driver had no idea what I was describing but seemed very thankful.

Just then, I noticed, down the block, a group of excited children surrounding a uniformed man, walking towards the scene. The truck driver quickly returned to his driver's seat and attempted to pull out and around our damaged Mercedes. I stepped into his path, arms raised, and waved for him to stop. The officer, with the gang of kids, arrived and directed the truck to pull over. We all stood there looking over the damage while the kids mingled on the roadside and offered lots of comments. The truck driver and what turned out to be a local police officer could communicate, but not with me or Angie. We tried English, German, and extended gesturing with no luck. After a few moments, the policeman made it clear we were to follow him into the town to attempt an analysis of the crash.

Back in the car, we slowly followed behind the policeman and the group of kids down the tree-lined, shady couple of blocks to the small village center. We arrived at an assortment of residences, maybe apartments, several businesses, and a three-story, sizeable, white stucco structure with lots of architectural character, which fit this near Middle Eastern culture. After parking, we waited with the policeman at the entrance of the large building for the truck driver to join us, and then we all proceeded inside.

This large building was a municipal center. It was not too busy this Monday morning, but people were working and moving up and down the corridors. Some wore Western professional attire, but most wore a more casual, loose-fitting dress or robe for women and pants or jeans and shirts for men. Moving through the halls were young boys dressed in an old style, traditional loin wraps, bare-chested, with close-cropped turbans. They were carrying silver trays suspended by three silver chains, tiny steaming hot glasses of sweetened tea for sale. We wanted to try one, but the business at hand took precedence. We wondered what we would do about finding Ali, the real one. We had his car with his passport in the glove box and should have met with him hours before. Oh well, first things first, I thought.

We walked down mosaic-tiled hallways with plants and small potted trees decorating the lovely interior. Finally, we ascended a curved stairway in this open atrium-style main room to a second-floor office, waiting for someone or something to happen. No one talked except for brief comments between the truck driver and the policeman. An employee who could speak a little German entered the room and told Angie that the town's mayor spoke fluent German and could mediate, but they had to find him first. Today was when he was to begin his vacation and head to Germany. She said they were looking for him at his home and around town to see if he was still there.

We settled into comfortable, overstuffed chairs in the nicely decorated office and waited almost an hour before a man entered the room. It was the mayor, and now we might sort things out. The mayor was a short, rotund man dressed in casual vacation attire. Everyone stood as he introduced himself to each person in a most friendly manner. We all stood and formed a loose semi-circle facing each other in a particular order. I was on the far left, then Angie, the mayor, in the middle, followed by the policeman, and finally, the truck driver on the far right.

The mayor started by asking each of us how the accident happened. He directed the truck driver to speak first. The truck driver told the policeman, in Lebanese, his account of what happened. As he began, his voice rose and fell with emotion, and he waved his hands over his head in apparent outrage. With less emotion, the policeman translated this to the Mayor in Turkish, who translated this version to Angie in German. Angie turned to me doubtfully and translated what the truck driver said. "He claimed I stopped at the light in front of him and quickly reversed and crashed into his truck," she said. I laughed at the preposterous notion and told my rendition of events, which translated back down the line. The truck driver refuted my story with anger, which came back down the line to me, where I again emphasized my account.

This exchange went on like a kids' game of gossip, back and forth, for several minutes until the mayor raised his hands, finally indicating for all to stop. He had heard enough, saying the truck driver was at fault, and believed the fair thing would be for him to pay me 600 Deutsche Marks. Once the translation reached the truck driver, his hands flew up again, and he threw a fit. The mayor briefly translated the truck driver's comments about how unfair this was, how honest he was, how corrupt Westerners were in general, and a dozen other excuses.

After more back-and-forth, the mayor decided we would all walk over to the local auto repair shop to see what the actual cost for repairs would be. Once there, the garage owner assessed the damage and said he could "fix it brand new for 500 DM." The mayor agreed and told the truck driver to pay me 500 DM. Not at all happy, the driver gave the mayor the 500 DM and left in a rush. The policeman followed him out.

The mayor gave me the 500 DM and attempted to excuse himself to begin his long-awaited vacation with his family. Not familiar with customs in this part of the world, but not stupid either, I peeled off a 50 DM bill and placed it in the mayor's hand with great appreciation. The mayor thanked me profusely, and we all walked out happier than when we arrived.

It was now afternoon, and there was no way to contact Ali. Angie and I returned to the garage to arrange the repairs. The garage owner took great care in showing us his previous work and some current body repairs. The language was a barrier, but the shop owner proudly showed us nice cars with shiny repaired fenders and one where he was so proud to have used a 7-Up can and a Coke can to mold into a damaged area of one car smoothly. "All very nice," I said, but I finally got across to the man, "Quick fix, good brake lights, must go, and how much"? The man showed two fingers pointing to a clock and wrote down 300 DM, rubbing his finger over his thumb. I said OK, and Angie and I decided to look for something to eat while we waited.

I turned to the owner, rubbing my stomach, and pointed to my mouth with an eating motion. With a slight wave, he motioned across the square to a small storefront and rubbed his belly. "Good," he said, so that's where we went. It was nice to escape the day's rising heat into the small dining room, which had a half dozen tables and ceiling fans that created a gentle breeze. These fans both cooled the place and kept the flies at bay.

Angie and I entered and made our way to a glass display in the rear, where two cooks fiddled with eight large, round, shallow pots of simmering food behind the glass. With no menu nor a common language, we realized we should point to what we thought looked good and indicate how much we would like with our hands. We both attempted to inquire about "No meat, no moo moo, no baa baa" and shook our heads, but nothing. The cook looked at us like saying, "Make up your mind. I've other things to attend to." Angie ordered a delicious stew and rice combination first. She poked around and saw there was pork or maybe beef, so I kept analyzing each pot, looking for something with no meat. Every option seemed to have meat visible except one covered with over-easy eggs. I chose that one. We paid and even got a small bottle of mineral water to share. The egg dish also had a fair amount of ground beef, but I picked it out as best I could and gave the meat to Angie.

After eating, we walked around the small village in the steamy heat, rested under a shady spot on the grass, and smoked another self-rolled Drum cigarette. After the promised two hours had passed, we returned to the garage, hoping we'd finally be on our way. The mechanic had barely started. "What the hell?" I exclaimed as I motioned, with my shrugged shoulders and outstretched arms and spinning my finger in a circle. I began tapping my wrist where a watch might have been, indicating to get a move on, as well as sharing lots of words I knew he did not understand. After 5 PM, we were finally on our way, still two hours from Istanbul and no clue where Ali and the caravan might be.

It was a beautiful evening ride following a ridge where we could see the Sea of Marmara's coastal water from up high. We slowly passed or stopped at almost every gas station and rest area, hoping to see Ali or someone left behind to greet us. But no one, and soon it became too busy to hope we would find anyone. We saw a big sign saying the equivalent of Welcome to Istanbul, including a population number of around four million, and thought we'd never find Ali in this urban jungle.

We reflected on our eventful and strange day sarcastically with amusement. It has taken us more than a week to get to Istanbul, and looking back at the many unreal events, we could only shake our heads and be thankful we were still sane and not locked up somewhere. It was getting dark in an hour or so. We had Ali's car and passport and no idea where we might find him or the caravan.

We drove up and down many busy roads, skirted the big city center, and finally returned to a campground I had spotted earlier. It was too busy of a city, and I did not feel we were safe sleeping in the car somewhere, so against Angie's advice, I used some of the remaining money meant for Ali to rent a campsite for the night. The night air was thick and hot, and even though we had no tent, I attempted to sleep outside, first on the small patch of grass at the site, which became wet. Next, on top of the picnic table with the sleeping bag as a thin mattress. Finally, stiff and uncomfortable, I rejoined Angie in the car's front seat for a sweaty night of little sleep.

We discussed and relived all the events of the last several days. We wondered what Ali would think or do should we not find him and return his car and passport. Was he connected With some mafia types who might track us down and, GULP, dispose of us? Maybe he'd find us and only break my leg as punishment. Ali didn't seem like that type of person. Sure, we had his car and passport, but we had no phone number to call and no idea how or where to find him in a city of 4 million. Tomorrow, we would search for him or any clue about what to do with his car. On the bright side, we were together and had reached our first destination. We would worry about finding Ali tomorrow.

Chapter 29
Finding the Needle

<hr>

Day 10, July 6th

Awake with the morning sun, we took advantage of the campground's simple bathrooms and showers. Heidelberg was the last time either of us had a proper shower. Gas station sink baths were our typical daily wash. We did not shower in Sofia in the small hotel room we shared with six other men. Refreshed, we drove out of the campground, down the busy four-lane road, toward downtown Istanbul. We had no idea where to look for Ali, so we cruised through parking areas, tourist spots, and city streets, hoping to spot one of the caravan cars. Finding Ali among four million people in an area of more than two thousand square miles would be a challenge, but we remained hopeful.

Talk about finding a needle in a haystack. Our odds were even worse than we knew. We suffered the constant noise of car horns that played tunes like the first part of the "Battle Hymn of the Republic" or "I Wish I Were in Dixie" or just an "awooga" sound (like an old Model T Ford) for no conceivable reason. There might be a pedestrian crossing the road a block down, a great time to mash the horn and play the loud and annoying song piece, what the heck, maybe twice or three times. To many Istanbul drivers, signal lights, stop signs, lane markings, and sidewalk curbs were mere suggestions. They drove where, how, and as fast as they wanted. Double parking was also fine. Blocking the road parking was another excellent reason drivers played their horn songs.

Driving along, looking down every side street, I got into another shouting match with an unruly driver who cut me off. I gave up quicker this time, and Angie didn't need to restrain me. We needed a break from this urban driving nightmare with seemingly no rules. Parking was nowhere to be found unless you were willing to pay, so we decided to go east into Asia. Taking the bridge across the Bosphorus to Istanbul's Asian side was an unlikely place to find Ali, but while we still used the car, I wanted to say we visited Asia at least. Still, there was no Ali. Stopping at a waterfront store across the bridge, I insisted on buying a pack of Turkish cigarettes with good Turkish tobacco as our pouch of Drum tobacco was almost gone. We sat on a bench looking over the busy Bosphorus. I lit a cigarette, but oh man, was it harsh. The tobacco flavor reminded me of an unfiltered Camel or Lucky Strike cigarette from back home, but stronger. The one cigarette was enough. We never smoked the rest of the pack.

It was mid-afternoon, and we decided to drive back to the large, park-like square in front of the Blue Mosque. The Blue Mosque was an architectural wonder, surrounded by beautiful old trees and shaded sidewalks. Across from the main entrance was a grassy park with more footpaths and benches. We drove around this city block-size central square looking for a parking space directly on the street to abandon the car. The plan was to lock the keys in the car, place the leftover money from the accident settlement with his passport in the glove box, and continue our journey. We hoped he would find it, for he must be looking for it. After all, it was valuable, and life without his passport would make his travel home near impossible.

Bert is looking for a place to park and leave Ali's car near the Blue Mosque in Istanbul, Turkey.

We drove around the big square three or four times before we were lucky enough to see a car ready to pull out of a space just ahead. Almost out of gas, I parallel-parked the 64 Mercedes in front of the grounds of the Blue Mosque. Before I could even shut off the engine, a car pulled up next to us and, through his passenger side window, Ali said, with the calmness of a casual friend, "Hallo!". What a relief. After a brief, incredulous conversation, Ali told me to follow him. He said the caravan group was staying at a friend's hotel, and we should get a room there too, "Very cheap! Almost free".

Following Ali through the crazy traffic to a noisy industrial area, we parked at the hotel lot. We grabbed our things and knew this was the last time we would see the 64 Mercedes. We followed Ali into a small room/office on the ground floor of this skinny, six-floor hotel. Ali spoke with the man at the counter for a minute, possibly in Arabic, and the clerk, or perhaps the owner, told us he still had a lovely room facing the back for us if we wanted. "Cheap, almost free" turned out to be the equivalent of 20 DM a night. Tired and needing rest, we gave the man 20 DM, which he gladly accepted. We took the room key and climbed the stairs to the third-floor room to crash.

The room had a single bed, a small table, and a hard-backed chair. There was also one electrical wall outlet, but we had no use for it. A table fan would have been a welcome addition. The back wall was all glass from the sill about a meter off the floor to the ceiling, with a small part that would open from a lower corner. The air coming through was barely detectable, but it alleviated some heat. The large pull-down shade could block your view but did not stop daylight from filling the room. There was barely enough space between the bed, against one drab wall, and the other wall, to walk from the entrance to the window. There is no bathroom, not even a sink. Angie looked in the hall, barely big enough for the four doors to different rooms. There is no bathroom there either. We wondered what a better hotel might cost but agreed we would not stay here long and decided to live without some amenities.

Ali's room was one floor down, and we visited him to explain what had transpired over the last two days. Angie asked him about the bathroom situation, expecting the worst, but discovered a shared bathroom on every other floor. There is no shower or bath, only a toilet and sink. Ali's brother and another man we did not know were there. We later learned he was Ali's friend and business partner in Istanbul.

For the next 30 minutes, we explained the car wreck and how we searched for him. We described our plan to park the 64 Mercedes in the conspicuous place near the Blue Mosque had we not run into him. I handed Ali the remainder of the money from the accident settlement with a brief explanation of the accounting, and then we returned to our room.

We checked out the bathroom on our way back and saw it was small, with barely enough room to open the door. It included a tiny sink and a wall-mounted water faucet near the floor with a short hose attached to spray over the recessed, porcelain toilet. The toilet was just a hole, with two raised portions for your feet while you squatted. That was it. A recessed porcelain area to do your business, then rinse it down with the hose. This porcelain toilet was a step up from the "toilet hole" back at the rest area near the Bulgarian border, but not by much.

Back in our room, we slept for a couple of hours. It was hot, and we awoke in a sweat with no fan. It wasn't quiet, even in the back of the building. A big construction project was being started right outside the window. At about 6 PM, we decided to check out the city around the hotel. There wasn't much to see, mainly an industrial area. Still, we bought a small city map, which showed we were within walking distance of the old city center, where we hoped we could find some of the exotic markets and sites Gabi had told us about in the Grand Bazaar. At a small corner food kiosk, we bought a doner kebab, or gyro, for Angie. The meat for her kebab was scrapped from the well-done outer surface of a turning rack of lamb, cooked by a single vertical electric element. The vendor served the meat in a pita bread slice with a light sauce. I settled for a large portion of fries, heavily seasoned.

As the sunlight disappeared and the city lights came on, we returned to our room to rest and assess our trip. We were finally relaxed enough to see the humor in the calamity that had overcome us the last few days. We sat on the bed with our liter bottle of mineral water and celebrated overcoming the many taxing obstacles. A little pride invaded our recollections, having survived so much excitement. It was time to plan our Istanbul visit, assess our money, and decide how long to remain here. Angie looked through our used travel guide while I looked over the map. We decided to stay one day, maybe two, and chose some areas to explore.

Ali knocked at our door after 9 PM and invited us to his room as several other caravan people were there. We told him we'd be down in a few minutes. Stowing our packs under the bed, we carried our money and passports and went downstairs to Ali's room. For the next 90 minutes or so in the cramped quarters of Ali's room, we regaled the others with tales of the accident and ensuing communication puzzle and how we tried to find Ali in this vast city.

The fake Ali was there and claimed I had abandoned him at the early morning rest area. Upon hearing the 64 Mercedes take off, he ran after us as fast as he could, waving his shirt above his head, which he said we completely ignored. He had to beg for a bus ride back to Istanbul without money. Ali's brother told us that he was sure we had stolen the car and were driving it to Greece. But in the end, everyone was OK, and there were no real hard feelings.

Ali remained somewhat suspicious about the accident settlement money and said, "You should have just driven the damaged car after the accident to meet up with the rest as planned." He said they had waited several hours in another town and even sent someone back to look for us.

Ali's Istanbul friend, whom we had met earlier, was still there and invited everyone to his place for dinner the next night, which we all accepted. He lived in a nice neighborhood on the outskirts of Istanbul and promised a feast and an enjoyable time. Exhausted again, we returned to our tiny room, wedged the hard-backed chair under the doorknob, and fell deep asleep for the first time in quite a while.

Part 6
In The Footsteps of the Ancients

Chapter 30
Bazaar

Day 11, July 7th

The sun was beginning to lighten the morning sky when we were startled awake by the construction crew right outside our open window. We closed the tiny window, but the heat quickly made our small room uncomfortable. After dressing, we ate the little left in our food supply and headed out. Part of the day's plan was to find a grocery store to replenish our staples.

With a map and dog-eared travel guide, we walked the streets leading to the old part of the city. Busy roads gave way to pedestrian avenues, more retail shopping, tourist shops, and even some green areas. We sat by a cool fountain and, while orienting ourselves, indulged in a couple of purchased pastries before walking several kilometers into the old city and the Grand Bazaar.

Once we found the area of the Bazaar, we spent the morning perusing the various market booths and merchant stalls. They were interesting to visit and had many unique items for sale, but with little money to spend, we passed through without purchasing their wares and trinkets. There was no doubt that this city and its culture were very different. The Middle Eastern influence was evident in the dress of the people, the architecture, the food, and the language.

Although mostly foot traffic, there were many small delivery trucks. Each one had a pin-up girl picture in the side window behind the driver's window. The images were of nude Western women in suggestive poses. Seeing these photos and experiencing the leering stares at Angie from many of the men we passed was a fair indicator of their prevailing view of Western women.

Our assumption was also reinforced frequently by the working-class men's behavior. With her beautiful long, auburn brown hair, wearing shorts and a t-shirt, Angie attracted the unwanted attention of almost every working-class man on the street. It's probably good neither of us could understand the men's comments, but their eyes and expressions said enough. Several men brushed a hand along Angie's arm, shoulder, or even her butt as they passed. I kept my arm around Angie's shoulder the whole time, but that did not deter some.

My long hair and beard were also an object of interest to some. They would pinch some of my hair between their fingers and thumb and say things we did not understand, but they seemed more curious than threatening. This behavior went on the whole time we were in the old city.

Finally, we started seeing structures that showed we had reached the part of the ancient city with ruins of old buildings and a large section of the old and very tall city wall, well worn by the ages. Near a gate in this city fortification, along a cobblestone road, we stopped to look at a business along the old wall where many people drank tea or coffee from tiny cups. People smoked hookah pipes while they chatted away in a most relaxed attitude. Tables spread around the grassy area surrounded by a picturesque low, wrought iron fence. Several small tables stood in recessed features of the old wall a meter or two above the ground. This open-air cafe/hookah bar looked appealing, but there was no way we could spend the money to participate.

A bit later, we passed another open-air business surrounded by a low stone wall. There were no separate rooms; everything was in a large open area divided by low stone partitions. It was a broom-making business with mounds of straw on one end, bundles of long wooden sticks piled high, spools of twine scattered about, and one person, presumably the owner or proprietor. He was frantically using a wet blanket to try and beat out a growing, smoldering fire in his work area. Oddly, no soul seemed interested in helping the man as the small fire resisted the wet blanket. There were hundreds of people witnessing this, but none lent a hand. I wanted to help him but was uncertain and unfamiliar with customs and expectations, so I did not, and we moved on.

Walking for several kilometers, we saw many interesting buildings, smelled good food cooking, and watched the people go about their daily routines. Whether they were tourists, shop owners, or business people finding a lunch place, the city's rhythm started to make sense. Like any significant urban area, there were so many things going on at the same time that individually, some seemed peculiar, but taken as a whole, we started to make sense of what we were seeing. People looked different, dressed differently, and spoke differently, and many behaved differently, but the city life was vibrant and lively. It was all so foreign to us, but these people who had been doing this their whole lives made these everyday tasks seem curiously exotic.

Exhausted from the heat, we ducked into a food market and purchased enough to eat for several days and two one-liter bottles of carbonated water. We carefully loaded our purchases into a smaller backpack, which we carried for daily use while exploring. Now, it was time to return to the hotel. Having walked so far, we took a short break to rest and plan the return to our hotel, which we had carefully marked on our city map. We followed a different return route to see another part of this vast city. We arrived at the hotel with some time to rest before meeting with Ali and his brother to attend his friend's dinner.

I crowded into the back seat of Ali's newer Mercedes with Angie on one side and the turbaned Indian man on the other. Ali and his brother, in the front seats, talked about many things, some in English, but primarily Pakistani. As we exited the central city and drove into the suburbs on the north side of Istanbul, the area became hilly and packed with houses and several high-rise apartment buildings. It was a clean and well-maintained residential area. The traffic/noise was much lighter here, a welcome pleasure. We traveled onto so many different and smaller streets that finding our way out of this area would be difficult. Fortunately, we trusted Ali but wondered what we would do if something "unexpected" happened. We might be stranded and exposed to the whims of people we did not know. For the moment, things were good, but we remained cautious and alert. We bounced around in the back seat as the Indian man finally explained one of the many ways to wrap a turban in severely broken English. We swapped stories about each other's home lives and what we missed the most.

I imagined this dinner we were about to attend might be an outdoor barbecue like friends back home might throw in an outdoor garden. I was wrong. After parking on the street and walking several blocks, we entered a medium-sized apartment building and walked up to the fourth-floor flat. A stranger greeted us at the door, bowed, and welcomed us all in. After removing our shoes, I noticed the group sitting around on carpets but not a stick of furniture anywhere. The overlapping Persian-type carpets were soft; some used pillows to prop against a wall, but no couch, chairs, table, or anything.

Angie and I sat down, and the ensuing conversations, in Arabic, Turkish, and fair English, were both friendly and somewhat engaging. A man came from the kitchen with a mortar, pestle, and a handful of dried roots, spices, and lots of garlic. As he sat and ground each ingredient to a fine powder, the conversation turned to food and food prep. It started to smell delicious and exotic, which caused me to ask what meat was in the recipe. Trying not to be rude, I emphasized my practice of not eating meat. The cook smiled and said, "No meat, all good food you like." I, unsure the cook understood me, turned to Ali to emphasize my concern. Ali said, "No meat, all will be OK," and "You will love the dish." Several others grinned, laughed, and poked fun at me about my diet with no meat. I explained how I did eat some fish but no pork, beef, or chicken. My new Hindu friend was supportive, but the others thought I was odd and let it go.

Once again, Angie was the only female, but everyone was well-behaved, not like the city truck drivers, and they included her in conversations. They asked her good questions about life in Germany and what she thought of Istanbul. I made a trip to the bathroom. Hurray! I found an above-floor toilet.

On my return to the living room, I cut through the kitchen and briefly conversed with a man who lived in the apartment about hashish. The man didn't take long to show me a large kilo slab of hash wrapped in aluminum foil he took from a paper bag. He asked me to smell it and, if I wanted, to smoke some. Ordinarily, this would have been an excellent idea, but not here, not now, I politely declined. The man asked me if I would like to buy this, "very cheap" to sell in Germany. He told me he could arrange for more in the future as well. Again, I declined but did ask about what "very cheap" might be. My asking encouraged the man, and the price he insisted was at least 20 times less than it would have been back in Germany. If I learned anything during this trip, I realized everyone in the caravan and the locals I met lied about everything. Not so much to cheat but to embellish or make themselves look better than they were. This fact and the possibility of a Turkish prison ensured I stayed away from anything illegal.

Shortly after I returned to the group, two men came from the kitchen and passed large bowls of food out to each person. The food smelled wonderful, and the portions were large. Angie tried hers first, chewed and tasted, tried another bite, then turned to me saying, "Be careful, I, uh, think there may be meat." I analyzed my warm dish, stirred it with the spoon, noticed small round pieces like ground meat, and took a small taste. Yup, there was meat here. Again, not wanting to be rude, I asked Ali, and one of the cooks replied, "Not really meat or only a little, but lots of other that's no meat," with a laugh, he said, "Eat, enjoy, good food." Even though I had been a vegetarian longer than a year, I was pretty particular and wouldn't eat anything with meat-related ingredients. Without appearing too picky and remaining hospitable and appreciative, I picked around the meat as much as possible and discreetly gave these meaty parts to Angie. This was now twice in a few days I had consumed a dish that included meat. Oh well, I'd live and continue my meatless diet in the future.

Day 12, July 8th

Another day began, and we woke up to the concert of trucks, jackhammers, and many loud workers working outside our hotel window. We stood at the window and watched the activity from three floors above. The tiny-looking workers dug ditches for footers for this large building by following lines spray-painted on the dirt. Cement was being mixed by hand and hauled by wheelbarrows. What a job, and soon, the temperature would become unbearable.

This day, we went down to the Bosporus and watched large and small ship traffic traveling to and from the Black Sea a bit farther north. We sat near a large granite historical sign that described, thankfully with several embedded pictures and maps, how a huge chain was stretched across the Bosporus many years ago. The chain forced shipping into one narrow channel where they would pay tariffs, a significant revenue source for the Ottoman Empire. The historical sign also pointed out how Istanbul was a critical crossroads on the Silk Road. The park along the water was a nice place to rest and watch the boat traffic. We sat under shade trees and enjoyed the cool breeze flowing off the turgid water, which relieved the day's scorching heat. We savored quite a bit of time there. After almost two weeks of stressful travel, we could finally drop our guard and relax.

Blue Mosque, Istanbul, Turkey 1976

Looking up the hill toward the city, we could see, not far from us, the unique dome and spires of the Blue Mosque. Before Muslim rule, the Mosque was a Christian church known as the Hagia Sophia. First constructed in 537 AD, it was the world's most significant open dome structure and changed the history of architecture. Many other large buildings surrounded the compound, and minarets poked above the many trees. We would have loved to visit, but our travel guide listed admission prices that were too expensive for us, so we walked some more and began contemplating our next day leaving Istanbul.

Hitchhiking back to Bulgaria, then south through sparsely populated Northern Greece, was not appealing. We inquired about ship passage to Athens at one of the travel offices along the waterfront and found we could not afford it. Angie suggested that we ask Ali when we returned to the hotel. He has experience and may know a better, cheaper way to get there.

We continued walking along the seaside promenade and stopped at a market catering to tourists. I negotiated a reasonable price for a small pair of shoes to send to Kimberly, my daughter, back in Michigan. These were ancient-looking, sequence-covered shoes with pointed, turned-up tips, like Aladdin, might wear in a fairy tale, with elaborate, colorful decorations. They looked expensive, but I paid only the equivalent of 2 DM for them. I would place them deep in my pack and wait till we returned to Germany to send them.

We then sent a handful of postcards to family and friends. I sent a card of the Blue Mosque with ISTANBUL printed in large letters to my favorite literature professor, Watson B. Duncan III, in the care of Palm Beach Junior College. Professor Duncan always talked about the three words he loved most: Timbuktu, Xanadu, and Istanbul. He had a collection of postcards sent from all over taped to a wall in his office. I remember looking at them while I waited for him to review my paper and dreamt of future travel. In class, he would sometimes repeatedly say, "Istanbul," with dreamy, rolling eyes and get us all laughing.

We contemplated staying longer in Istanbul and driving Ali's soon-to-be-reconditioned 64 Mercedes to Lahore, Pakistan. It would be a free ride, and India was a place I would like to visit. The idea of spending more days of wishy-washy plans with a group of people who were culturally different from us didn't sit well with Angie. Her German sensibility needed to be grounded in some more truth and permanence. Our money was about half spent already; even by hitchhiking back on the cheap, we wouldn't have enough, and the thought of visiting India faded away.

Chapter 31
Road to Izmir

<hr>

Day 13, July 9th

With Ali's assistance and the knowledge of the hotel manager, Angie and I devised a plan to get to Athens, Greece, the cheapest way without hitchhiking. We figured we would need at least 50-75 DM for our return home once we left Athens, and we'd like to have a hundred or more while we were in Athens. We still had a couple hundred Deutsch Marks left. This tally did not include the fifty dollars I had tucked away in my backpack tube frame for an emergency. The hotel manager suggested we travel south along the coast and book cheaper passage across the Aegean and mentioned how ships from Istanbul charged inflated prices. A ticket for a boat from a southern port would be much more affordable.

Looking at our map, we saw the city of Izmir, 500 km away, and the hotel manager said, from there, we could take a ferry to the neighboring Greek island of Chios to find a cheaper passage to Greece. Traveling from Chios to Greece sounded perfect, but getting to Izmir was another challenge. We were hesitant to hitchhike through an unfamiliar region of Turkey, and Ali recommended taking a regional bus line. The hotel manager told us there was a bus terminal a couple of kilometers away. Taking a bus sounded like a safe plan, and after carefully reassessing our remaining funds, we decided to begin the next leg of our journey, walking to the bus depot. I appreciatively shook the manager's hand, and we hugged Ali, saying our final goodbye.

We walked about four kilometers that morning, picked up more provisions at a market, and briefly stopped at a local bakery for breakfast. The bakery was packed with locals elbowing their way to the counter where one of several young men would quickly transact each purchase. Angie waited outside with the packs while I pushed with the crowd to reach the counter. Ignored for several minutes, I finally shouted like the others and waved my hand at a young man who stopped long enough for me to point at items in a case that looked like egg sandwiches and held up two fingers. The young man quickly retrieved them, loosely wrapped them, and placed them on the counter in front of me with a hand extended for a quick payment. Not wanting to spend a Turkish Lire bill, I pulled out my now large handful of coins from various countries and searched for the amount I thought it might be. The young man impatiently repeated an amount, but I had no idea. I held out my hand full of change while the young man started picking out many Turkish coins from a mixture of German, Yugoslav, and Bulgarian coins. Once I felt like this coin mining went on long enough, I pulled my hand back. The young man made a mischievous smile and moved on. As we have seen many times with the attitude of the locals, if you are dumb enough to be cheated, so be it. I elbowed my way back outside to Angie, and we ate while we walked.

Like everywhere, the regional bus depot, small and cramped, was busy and loud. No one spoke English or German, but by repeating Izmir several times to the ticket agent, we bought two tickets for a bus leaving within the hour. While waiting outside, we smoked the last of our Drum Tabak. The buses, coming and going, looked decent, and all had the name of their destination taped to the inside of the windshield near the door. The buses stopped in several different spaces, so I walked to see each new arrival while Angie stood with our packs to ensure we didn't miss our bus.

The bus to Izmir arrived after noon, and we joined the growing crowd to stow our packs under the bus, get on and show our tickets. There were a few male and female single riders, but the majority were either older women wrapped like Russian babushkas or middle-aged women with one or two young kids in tow. We did find two seats together midway back and settled in for the long ride. Due to the day's heat, all the double-sash bus windows were open. The smells were interesting, not offensive, like heavily spiced leftovers mixed with the ever-present diesel fumes.

As the big bus navigated the narrow streets heading out of the city, I noticed the outside of the old wall we had seen two days before with the hookah bar. The old wall was littered with pasted paper signs and ads. Finally, the twists and turns, the stopping and accelerating, gave way to a faster ride on a highway. We settled back into our double seat and looked out the open window to the ever-changing scenery. The landscape changed from city to industrial, commercial, residential, and finally, farm fields and forested patches. The ride was smooth except for the occasional braking and random horn blasts. We dozed off several times, but not for long. A bump or swerve quickly startled one of us awake, usually Angie. The bus was hot, as was the outside, probably well into the mid-30s Celsius or 90s Fahrenheit, but with open windows, there was a pleasant airflow. Our canteens were getting low, and a bathroom stop would be nice, but we rode on till mid-afternoon.

Three and a half hours after we started, the bus pulled off at a wide spot in the road in the middle of nowhere. As we came to a stop, several traditionally dressed women approached the sides of the bus. Some had trinkets for sale, others beverages, and others sold some rolls with meat. One head-covered and robed woman was holding up peeled cucumbers for sale. Following the procession off the bus, we took a few minutes to stretch our legs and shake off the stiffness after the long ride. One of the vendors approached us after others had concluded their business, and we bought two cucumbers for a few pfennigs each. These were almost wholly peeled and quartered lengthwise with the white juicy center lightly sprinkled with salt, which tasted amazing. These even quenched our insatiable thirst for the first time since we had left Istanbul.

The city water in our canteens was barely tolerable and almost gone. I still had a half-finished bottle of carbonated mineral water I pulled from the bottom of my pack with the fizz gone. It would suffice in a pinch. The rest area had a shaded lawn area and bathrooms behind tall bushes. The holes in the ground toilets were no longer new to us but still a bit of a challenge, and these, unlike the porcelain ones at the hotel, were hard-packed clay surfaces, and it was difficult to aim for a clean hit. The bathrooms themselves were walled halfway up and then open air, which helped with dispersing the smell. A water tap, mounted outside, was used to rinse your hands, but we decided to wait for a cleaner source to fill our canteens down the road.

After maybe 20 minutes, everyone responded to the driver's call and gathered to re-enter the bus. Another four-hour ride, with a brief stop for a diesel fill-up and bathrooms, brought us to the small bus station on the outskirts of Izmir, Turkey. This station consisted of an office with a Dutch split door where the top half opened to expose the small office counter space and a glass-walled waiting area that held a dozen people. The sun had set over the city in the valley below, and dusk was beginning to turn dark as we arrived.

We grabbed our packs and entered the waiting room as the bus pulled out for its next destination. As we watched the bus drive away, I realized my straw hat, the one I found in Nannie's (pet goat on the Florida ranch) stall, was left on the luggage rack above our seat on the bus. "Crap!" I exclaimed that it was hot in these parts and I would suffer. Oh well, it was too late now, and our immediate concern was to find a place to sleep before dark in another unknown location.

Within minutes, the other disembarked passengers were gone. We were alone in this glassed waiting room, not even an attendant. The only living person around was a cab driver, sitting beside his cab, smoking a cigarette with hopes of a paying passenger. Our map was of little use; Izmir was a mere dot, and we could see no details of streets or landmarks. We could see the city lights down the hilly slopes by the sea, 4-5 kilometers away. The bus terminal was in a residential neighborhood with no woods or other discrete places to sleep visible.

We decided to look for a cheap hotel nearby instead of trekking to the city. Angie suggested I ask the taxi driver if he knew of one. I approached him, asking about a cheap hotel. He jumped up, eager to get me into his cab, but didn't speak English or German. Angie joined us, and we tried several ways to communicate, but all he seemed to understand was "hotel." I motioned by rubbing my fingers and thumb to say how much and pointed to his taxi. He responded with a shrug and opened the rear door for us. I said, "No money," and he repeated, "Yes, yes, no money," we were loaded and off we went. In broken English, the driver pointed out the city lights down in the valley and many other places that must have been significant sites in daylight. I expressed hurry and no money from the back seat, but on we went. The ride took longer than we had hoped, and we started to notice familiar buildings and shops.

As we finally arrived at a large house with a small hotel sign at the top of a staircase, the eager driver pulled our pack from the trunk, set them on the walk, and said, "600 lire." The exchange rate was 40 lire to the Deutsche Mark, and with a quick calculation, an argument ensued between the driver and me. Neither of us understood the other, and I finally turned to Angie and said, "Let's go, we're outta here," without paying. We walked up the long, open-air, wooden stairway to the hotel sign on the second floor. The driver followed us, ranting and saying, "600 lire, nice ride, you pay", but after 10 minutes of arguing below, we ignored him and climbed the stairs.

Ringing the bell, with the driver still ranting, the attendant opened the door and welcomed us all in but with a shushing sound and a finger over his mouth. It was now almost 11 PM. The driver and clerk briefly talked, but the clerk shrugged his shoulders and turned out his arms as if saying, what can you do? The driver then said 500 lire, to which I shook my head no and waved him away. The 500 quickly reduced to 400 in stages, and Angie pulled out a 10 DM bill, which he accepted. The driver stormed off, but this amount was almost as much as we each paid to get from Istanbul to Izmir, and we were not happy either.

Turning to the hotel clerk, who spoke a little better English, he quoted a 400 lire room charge for the night. We decided not to stay for the six-hour rest and would try to find another option for the night. Back down the long wooden stairs, we headed toward the city lights below, looking for a secluded place to unroll our sleeping bags. Before we had walked 15 minutes, we came upon the same glass-walled bus station waiting room where we started. As expected, our suspicions were confirmed. The cab driver had taken us on a circuitous route to the hotel to jack up the cab fare. What a racket. 10 DM turned out to be too much to pay him. After 1 AM, we curled up in two hard plastic chairs in the "bus station" waiting room, leaning on our packs, to sleep the four more hours till daybreak.

Chapter 32
Full Moon Voyage

—————

Day 14, July 10th

A couple entered through the swinging glass door of the waiting room and startled us awake. We gathered our packs, rubbed our weary eyes, and headed to the street. Things were feeling surreal now. It was still Turkey, but the culture was different. People were dressed similarly to those in Istanbul but less modern. We could see the city below from this hilly suburban neighborhood and the sea beyond. There was less congestion, and the morning traffic was light and much quieter than the assault of horns so prevalent in Istanbul. The street had few pedestrians, and some we passed even smiled. The smell of food wafted through the air and tickled our noses, but we had spent enough. We'd live from our bread, puszta salad, and canned tuna till we arrived in Greece. This is where I wanted to be.

The day was quickly heating up, but a nice breeze came off the nearby seawater that cooled the valley. We visited a travel agency on the main road into Izmir and stopped to inquire about passage to Greece. A nice young woman who spoke some English and fair German talked with Angie for twenty minutes. This conversation was a welcome pleasure for Angie, and soon, she was booking passage for us to Piraeus, Athen's port city. We knew this would be expensive, but Angie had asked many questions and purchased the cheapest tickets in a simple interior transit room on a lower deck of a passing cruise ship. We would need to get to Chios, the Greek island 100 km away, before morning.

We wanted to look around Izmir a bit but decided we better get to Chios as quickly as possible to avoid missing our passage. It took us almost three hours to hitch a few rides to the seaside town of Cesme, Turkey. We arrived at the end of the long peninsula into the Aegean Sea, this side of the water to Chios.

Cesme was a quaint village similar to a French resort or a Florida Keys town, except it was much more casual. We found the ferry going to Chios left every hour, so we had time to look around the relaxed little village. We walked around the area and sat on the small beach, watching the waves splash onto the sand. We waded in the shallow water and picked up a few small shells. Our jeans got wet but would quickly dry since the day was so hot. How nice. Angie thought it would be relaxing to spend a day or two here and recharge, but we already had tickets to leave the next day, and we obviously could not afford such a stay.

The ferry ride to Chios was a short trip across the water, and an onboard customs agent handled passport control leaving Turkey. Chios was both the name of the Greek island and the name of its largest town. We arrive at a bustling port and tourist town with many hotels, restaurants, and beaches. We sat on a bench in the town square while contemplating where to spend the night on this rather expensive-looking island. These hotels were expensive, and unless we wanted this to be our last day on our journey and head home tomorrow, a hotel stay was out of the question.

Chios harbor

I had heard about Greek ouzo, a licorice-flavored liquor, and wanted to try some. We were window-shopping in a cafe and gift shop when I noticed a board with ouzo prices. While Angie was at the other end of the shop, I paid a man two DM for a bottle. The man grabbed an empty, clear bottle from a large basket, filled it up from a cask in the back, popped a cork, and gave it to me. I slipped it into a tight space in my pack, unknown to Angie. Back out on the bench, I couldn't wait. I Pulled the bottle out and surprised Angie. I removed the cork, and we each took a sip. Yuck, it tastes like kerosene. It might have been kerosene. Who knows. We dumped the contents in the sand and discarded the bottle.

Walking past some beachside huts, we overheard a long-haired young man ordering a yogurt from one of the tent-like stands in British English. Except for talking with Angie, this was the first person I had heard speaking English in quite a while. Back in Germany, some friends spoke fair English, but this guy was British, and I started conversing with him. His name was Robbie Swinerton, and he was waiting to board the same ship as us. As we stood there, Robbie ate his yogurt while we each told the other our stories of how we wound up in Chios. He hung out with us for the rest of the day. Strolling from the port to the north side of town, we shared more details of our backgrounds and journeys here.

The evening was ending, and the after light was fading. Robbie already had his room booked on the ship, but enjoying each other's company, we all decided to walk past the edge of town and camp along the hills by the beach. Robbie did not have a sleeping bag, but I explained how our two bags, when zipped together, would hold us all when the chill of the night arrived. Angie wasn't too fond of this idea, but I said I would sleep in the middle position. As darkness approached, we left the town and found a spot in the sea grasses, up on a small hill looking out over the water toward Turkey.

It was a gorgeous night; the stars were out, and the temperature cooled, so we needed long-sleeved shirts. No structures were visible except a small grouping on the town's edge, maybe a kilometer away. In the cool sea breeze, birds swept in momentarily to check for potential gifts of food. The birds were disappointed, but not Robbie, Angie, or me. We made a campfire and used an empty can from the night's bean dinner to heat water and make tea from the tea bags Robbie always carried.

We stayed up late into the night exchanging stories. Angie's and my account of our journey was pretty cool, but Robbie's was genuinely unique. He described how he had left England two years prior, fed up with life, hitchhiked on the cheap through Spain, across Gibraltar, and followed the Mediterranean coast across North Africa. Robbie first lived with a settlement of Western youth in Tunisia for six months, then continued through a brief stay in Egypt and joined a kibbutz in Israel. He never even told his parents that he had left.

Robbie and Angie by the fire on the island of Chios.

After working in the Israeli kibbutz for over a year, Robbie became homesick and called his parents to explain his journey. They were relieved he was still alive and insisted they send him money to return home. Robbie was ready, and his parents booked him the ticket, with a private room on the cruise ship from Istanbul to London. Robbie found boarding at Chios easier, and here we all were.

Angie and Bert at the fire on the island of Chios July 10, 1976.

We slept intermittently but cozy in the early morning under a cloudy sky. A light rain fell, but our sleeping bags kept us dry. It was such a tight fit in the sleeping bags that rolling over without significant disruption to each other was impossible. After the clouds cleared and the chill left us, we pulled down the zippers halfway. A little breathing room was nice. We slept until sunrise when the heat forced us to get up earlier than we wanted.

Day 15, July 11th

Angie and Bert watch the sunrise from their morning camp on Chios, July 11, 1976.

The sunrise burned off the dampness from the previous light rain as the bank of rain clouds headed deep into the Aegean Sea. Turning my back on the bright sun, I saw a rainbow glimmer over the dunes to the southwest. I pointed this out to Angie, and we agreed this was a good omen and hoped the next stage of our journey would reflect this good fortune. Sleeping bags, now dry, tightly rolled, and tied to the bottom of our backpacks, we returned to the waiting ship in Chios. It was seven or eight stories tall, and you could see its smokestacks from the edge of town.

Ship that takes Angie and Bert from Chios to Athens.

While boarding, signs directed us in different directions: Robbie to his private room on one of the upper decks and Angie and me to the large, windowless transit room on the main deck. Robbie and I planned to find a way to meet on the ship, but when we finally did see each other, it was through the bars of a locked metal gate on the main deck. There we said goodbye.

Angie waited in the large interior transit room full of non-tourists, many with small kids at their sides. With only rows of plastic and metal chairs, comfort was impossible. The air was rather stale and noisy. A hard tile floor rounded out this Spartan atmosphere. We claimed two seats along a wall and sat there patiently waiting for the ship to depart.

Once we felt movement, leaving our packs on our chairs, we walked down a short corridor and stood at an interior rail with a limited view of the water. As the ship slowly made its way from the port to the main channel, we reflected on the highs and lows of our journey.

We looked back on our life in Florida and discussed how this trip brought us closer together. We even touched on those many nights laying on the waterbed in our tiny trailer when Angie sorted through our budding relationship and her loneliness while I reluctantly listened.

View of the previous night's campsite on Chios from the departing ship.

We relived the pain of her leaving Florida and the surprised joy of our reunion when I left everything behind to find her in Germany. We talked about how she no longer felt lonely and how working together on this journey helped us get through some rough previous experiences by talking more about our situation and our relationship in general. I still found opening up and diving deep into my feelings challenging. Still, I was starting to appreciate how Angie's determination to analyze our life together strengthened our relationship. During this time at the rail, we discussed that today was the first anniversary of our hastily arranged marriage. With everything that happened on this trip, dates were unimportant.

Looking at my transit ticket, I confirmed July 11th and remarked to Angie, "Happy anniversary." We both smiled.

We tried to settle into a "comfortable" position back in our seats, as we would not arrive in Piraeus until early tomorrow. Passengers occupied every chair with their luggage securely stowed close to their chairs. Several children chased each other through the rows with playful laughter, providing pleasant background sounds or, obviously to some, annoying chatter. Few people talked, and some tried to sleep. I tried to stretch out in a vacant corner on the floor with my back propped against a wall. That was no better than the plastic chair.

═══════

Restlessly, I decided to roam around the limited space just before evening set in. I walked down a hallway and found a metal interior door with a stair-step symbol stenciled on the heavy door. I opened it and found the empty stairs. Climbing several decks, I approached another big metal door at the top, which opened to a medium-sized working deck.

I found no chairs, tables, or anything for passengers, only a large mast with flags and antennas rising from the middle of the deck. The ship's gigantic smoke stacks channeled the engine exhaust into the evening sky and consumed the entire middle portion of the vessel. No one was there. The deck was empty. The floor was oily, likely from the diesel residue released by the smoke stacks. Tall locked containers with heavy coats of white paint created a perimeter connected by wide metal storage benches along the rails looking over the churning sea. While sitting on the bench, I looked out at the fantastic view of the sea. The open air, blue sky, and azure sea created a vastly improved atmosphere from our passage room below. I waited, maybe 15 minutes, and not seeing a soul, excitedly returned to get Angie.

I returned, sat beside Angie, and casually asked her to grab her pack and follow me. I slowly grabbed my pack while ignoring her many questions. She calmly grabbed her backpack, and we left the seating room. Angie was apprehensive but followed my lead. I quietly opened the big metal door, and we entered the stairwell unnoticed. The sound of our feet ascending the metal stairs was light but still echoed in this enclosed space. We waited for someone to appear and tell us to return to our seats below, but no one ever showed. I opened the door to the upper deck, and we proceeded into the open air and fading sunshine. We were both feeling like kids who had found an open door to a private candy shop with jitters, awaiting the return of the proprietor.

The view from this top deck was incredible. Looking out over the heavy metal wall side rail was the blue Aegean Sea, softly rolling along about five stories below. We saw islands scattered about in the distance and some smaller vessels making their way to points unknown. At first, we were reluctant to relax, but we finally dropped our packs and sat on a bench between the locked cabinets with the best view over the sea. I propped my back against a large metal storage cabinet, and we used our sleeping bags for seat cushions on the hard metal bench while Angie nestled in front of me with my arms wrapped around her. The salt air was refreshing, and the cool breeze was amazing. Time slipped by, and no one else came to join us or ask us to leave. This bench became our private perch, where we gazed at the sea, and neither spoke more than a word or two as darkness fell over the Aegean.

We rolled out the sleeping bags on the top of the metal bench and used our packs for pillows. As the air cooled, we lay there side by side and watched over the sea. A vague brightness gently appeared on the horizon, slowly turning to a rising full moon reflecting off the shimmering water. As it slowly rose above the edge of the earth, dozens of islands appeared like diamonds under the moonlight. We watched the soft light reflecting off the dark water as we floated through the Aegean Sea on the voyage to our future.

We lay in each other's arms, dreamily watching the changing seascape as the giant ship slowly rocked us to sleep. We could have planned the whole year but never had a better first anniversary than this. One year ago, we couldn't imagine still being married this long. Fate has a marvelous way of making subtle decisions for us sometimes, and now, this act of kismet showed us the value of our relationship. Our love took a big step forward.

Chapter 33
The Grecian Yearn

———

Day 16, July 12th

Arriving in Piraeus, we disembarked and were disappointed to find only a large port facility with cruise ships, cargo ships, military ships, and an industrial area stretched for miles, as far as we could see, in both directions. I guess I was hoping to see ancient ruins and old-style urban streets. We made our way with the crowds through passport control and customs offices, then into the busy port facility where everyone was connecting somewhere. There were taxis and buses and wide streets filled with cars. Signage was in Greek but usually included an English, German, and French translation in smaller letters below. We found a shuttle bus to Athens's city center, bought tickets, and arrived somewhere in Athens just before noon.

We had already circled several potential youth hostels in our European travel book on dog-eared pages. Now it was time to get some fresh water, a city map, and maybe a snack. Sitting outside a small grocery store on a stone wall, we pinpointed a few hostels on our new map. We calculated their distance from our current location and how far from the Acropolis and other major sites we wanted to see. We cross-referenced this information with the cost from the travel guide for each hostel's nightly charge. Soon, we were off on foot to find our first lodging choice.

What a change from Istanbul! Sure, Athens was busy but more organized. Traffic flowed smoothly, and we rarely heard a horn. Cars followed the rules and politely stopped to allow pedestrians to cross the street at intersections. Many people smiled, and we heard laughter from groups of pedestrians. Many other young people, like us, wore backpacks and spoke several languages. We heard English, German, French, Greek, and other languages spoken as we walked through the crowds.

The air was hot and dry. We walked through the city, passing parks with trees and flowers and public drinking fountains whose water tasted good. Athens seemed to be an urban paradise. Angie said, "What if we had come to Athens first, then to Istanbul? How different would it be"? I agreed. Had we done that, Athens may not have seemed this wonderful. But here we are, Athens, a culture that made us feel welcome and comfortable. We arrived at the land of the ancient Greeks, followers of the "golden mean." We couldn't wait to start exploring.

The hostel we found for the first night was quite charming. There were two bunks with soft beds in a clean room, green space outside, and a couple of tables and chairs. The price was the equivalent of nine or ten DM for the night for both of us. At this rate, we figured we could afford two, maybe three, nights in Athens before our money ran low and we needed to head home. It was a bit far from where we wanted to be, but this whole trip was walking, and we were both young and fit. With our traveling diet, we both lost weight as well. The following morning, while visiting a market, another hiker told us about their hostel, which was just below the Acropolis and cost only five DM a night for two beds. I put an X on my map for this new hostel, and Angie and I grabbed our packs and moved to spend our remaining nights there.

The hostel below the Acropolis in Athens, where Bert and Angie stayed.

Days 17 – 21, July 13th – 17th

Athens was our trip's highlight and primary focus as tourists or explorers. We both loved it here. Time spent here did not disappoint, and although we would see and experience so many exceptional things in Athens, this is not the real focus of the story of our journey. These fantastic days blend into one significant experience that doesn't need detailed accounting. We traveled only by foot and walked all seven city hills. We walked from morning to sunset, following in the footsteps of the ancient philosophers and innovators. During our six days in Athens, we shared a wealth of experiences in ruins, museums, cemeteries, and theaters. Each night, we returned and collapsed into our single bunk, exhausted but fulfilled.

This new hostel was more Spartan, but exactly where we wanted to be. Five sets of bunks in a larger room with two shared showers and two toilets. Clean, with a small balcony, you could see a bit of the Apollo temple at one end of the Acropolis when you leaned out over the railing and looked up. Spartan quarters were ok, as we planned to spend very little time here. After our first night, sleeping together in the same lower bunk, we figured we could share and pay for just one of the beds and save about 3 DM a night. This savings was enough to extend our visit.

The hostel provided a place for a daily shower and to hand wash some clothes. After wringing out most of the water from our freshly washed items, we hung them on the balcony railing to quickly dry in the Athenian heat. We each carried two pairs of Levis, four or five shirts, underwear, socks, light pullover sweaters that lived untouched in the bottom of our packs, one pair of walking shoes, and sandals. Angie also brought a pair of shorts, which she usually wears. This hostel stay was the first time we washed clothes beyond our underwear in some bathroom sink.

Seven or eight other young people shared this same room with us, but it was rare to all be there simultaneously. Usually, when it got late and exhaustion set in, other travelers would return, and we might offer each other a suggestion for someplace to eat or something to see or do. Relaxing on the bed or walking around the room was typically done in underwear or wrapped in a towel returning from a shower.

Dressing discreetly in a corner with backs turned to the others wasn't unusual. We had all become comfortable strangers.

Angie and Bert on the steps to the Acropolis.

Angie and I returned to take a short nap one hot, exhausted afternoon. We were alone, dead quiet, and collapsed on our lower bunk. It did not take long to realize a horrible stench was coming from somewhere. It was so bad we could not sleep. I looked and sniffed: out on the balcony, in the bathroom, the trash can, and eventually, I found the source. Some guy's tennis shoes, neatly arranged under a bed. We knew we would never sleep with the horrible smell, so I carefully, touching only the shoe laces, removed the stinky shoes, placed them on the balcony, and closed the double doors, even though this made the room warmer. Better, now we both slept, only to be awakened by four returning hikers speaking French. They were Canadians from Quebec. The group arrived, probably discussing their morning and making plans when I noticed a guy looking everywhere for something: his shoes. A girl from their group was teasing him about the smelly shoes as now several were searching under beds. I waved, pointed to the balcony, and pinched my nose with a sour look. They all laughed, but his shoes stayed outside.

Angie at the site of Plato's Academy.

Later that evening, another hiker told me I could get the equivalent of $20 by donating blood, so I decided to do that the next day. I followed the directions to an immaculate, professional medical facility, where they gladly took my blood. I was looking forward to the glass of orange juice and cookie they gave the other donors as they left. They removed the needle from my arm, taped an alcohol patch in place, and thanked me. When they said goodbye, I asked, "What about the money"? They reluctantly gave it to me, but no juice or cookie. I felt a little bad expecting the money, but this meant we could stay longer in Athens, and it was worth it.

Bert finds his ancient Doppelganger at the Theater of Dionysus.

That same hiker from our hostel told me he had traveled through Iraq and got $100 for his blood, but the conditions were far more primitive. He extended his arm through a hole in a wall where they drew his blood, sight unseen. He said they probably took way more than they stated, and the sanitary conditions were worse.

After several more days of walking everywhere possible, Angie and I decided to take it a bit easier for a change and meandered around the shops nearby. I wanted a small statue of a seated Socrates, but even the cheapest figure was more than I was willing to pay. After sharing with the owner how much I wanted one but couldn't pay the price, he told me to wait while he retrieved one from the back. He showed me one that came out of the mold with a bit of a squashed head and said I could have it half price, "GREAT!" I exclaimed, and off we went, prized possession in hand. Sharing my happiness, Angie and I talked about what she might like as a memento from our trip, paid for with my blood money. She had seen a small silver cross necklace at a store the day before but was not sure where the store was. We had walked to so many places all over the city it could have been anywhere. Angie had a pretty good idea, so I followed her lead, and we searched for the silver cross. Amazingly, we found the store and, like everywhere, were able to negotiate a better price. Now we each had our prize to remember this visit forever.

Angie at the Olympic Stadium in Athens.

Bert contemplates outside Socrate's prison.

The Acropolis, Socrates prison, Theater of Dionysus, Olympic Stadium, Temple of Zeus, and grounds of the former Academy, we saw it all and, along the way, snapped pictures on the one roll of film I brought for the 35-millimeter camera. This entire trip turned out to be quite a blast looking back, especially once we had boarded the ship in Chios and could let our guards down a bit. We needed to get home before our money ran out, so it was time to start planning our trip back to Germany. No Ali and a caravan to lend us a 64 Mercedes for our personal drive and sleeping quarters. As dangerous and uncertain as driving a car in Ali's caravan was, it had been a stroke of luck. Going back, we would stick out our thumbs on the highway going north and hope for the best.

Chapter 34
Last Ride in the Fast Lane

———

Day 22, July 18th

With an early start, we found a local bus that took us to the northern suburbs of Athens. We were dropped off in a small village and caught a short ride to the highway's north entrance ramp. Our packs were heavy from full canteens, and each backpack had an extra liter bottle of water. We loaded up on food before we left Athens, as we had no idea when we would find another grocery store. Our stay in Athens was seven days, and during that whole time, we only carried enough for our daily outings. This time, our packs overflowed with extra water, and our bulky sleeping bags strapped at the bottom of our frames. The weight of everything was noticeable, and with the dry heat beating down on us, we worried our journey back would break our spirits and maybe our backs.

Another hiker couple was already at the highway entrance, hoping for a ride. We hung out with them and spoke for a bit. They were from Ireland, on a similar journey, and finally on their way home. I was happy to speak English with someone again, but their Irish accent was so heavy I could understand only a few words here and there. We all smiled a lot, though. We walked a respectable distance, about a hundred meters past them, dropped our heavy packs, and waited. After 30 minutes, a car finally stopped for the Irish couple, and they got in the back seat. They waved heartily at us and gave a big thumbs-up hand gesture to say GOOD LUCK!

Alone on a near-deserted highway, Angie and Bert wait in the dry heat north of Athens, Greece.

Alone, we waited one hour, then two, then three. Maybe five cars had passed us by without even a second look. It was a dry, hot day on the dusty side of the road with nothing around. No houses, shops, gas stations, nothing. We were starting to get worried. We decided to move farther down the entrance ramp so cars on the highway would see us, and hopefully, one might stop for us. Waiting so close to the fast-moving traffic was risky and probably illegal, but we were desperate.

After noon, a speeding box truck, seeing us, decelerated and slowly pulled over a distance ahead of us. Could it be? We grabbed our heavy packs and ran several hundred meters to the waiting truck's passenger side. The driver leaned over, rolled down the window, and spoke to us in Greek. We said, "Germany, Deutschland?" The man shook his head no but motioned for us to jump in anyway. I handed him our packs, and he stowed them behind the seat on top of his things. We had no idea where or how far he was going, but anywhere was better than here, so we climbed into the cab.

The truck cab had two single seats and a thinly covered, hot engine between them. There was a small area behind the passenger seat full of his tools and our backpacks. Angie sat closest to the passenger door, and I sat half on her seat and half on the covered motor. My position was uncomfortable and quite warm, but the driver was exuberant and friendly, and off we went. He talked the whole time and laughed, seemingly, at himself. What a nice guy, but we, understanding nothing, smiled and nodded affirmatively back at him.

After three hours or more of searching for common words and using hand gestures, we finally understood he would take us all the way north and drop us at the Yugoslav border. Going to the border was out of his way, but he knew there was no good place to catch another ride, and he wanted to help us. He would then backtrack for 30 minutes and continue heading east to Thessaloniki. He slowed down as he passed another hitchhiker couple we recognized as the Irish couple from earlier.

Hearing our excited comments, he pulled over to pick them up, too. After their previous ride, they waited at this barren location for hours and were glad to get this ride and see us. There was, however, one obvious problem. Our space was tight, and I was hot and uncomfortable sitting half on the motor. We stowed their packs on top of ours and shared the one seat. I slid over the engine close to the driver, the Irish girl between Angie and the door, and the guy on the floor facing us all. Angie and the Irish girl rested their feet on the seat and hugged their legs. We spent the next hours talking and laughing but rarely understood each other. The driver drove a couple more hours with us crowded in this tight position, and we finally arrived at the border.

The driver pulled over in the vast parking area before the border crossing. We all piled out, stretching our stiff bodies, and retrieved our backpacks. The still, exuberant driver motioned us all to the rear door of his truck. While we all helped each other strap our packs on our backs, he insisted we wait while he climbed in the back, opened one of the plastic barrels, and gave us Greek olives to sample. They were tasty but huge. One bite was not enough. They still had their seed and were very salty. We all sampled the olives, complimented and thanked the driver, and said our goodbyes.

The Irish couple walked ahead while Angie and I entered the small store and gas station. The long ride and salty olives made me quite thirsty. We had finished off all of our water many miles ago. I insisted on buying a carbonated, sweet beverage from the store, against Angie's better judgment, before we proceeded to the border station. This beverage did nothing to quench my thirst. It made me thirstier, just as Angie told me it would.

We refilled our canteens and spare bottles from an outside water tap. Sitting in the shade on a curb, we ate a bit from our packs before showing our passports to the border guards and continued to the highway ahead. Crossing this near-deserted border and getting our passports stamped was a breeze compared to our previous border crossings on the way down. There were no lines of cars jockeying for positions or custom agents to pay off. Sometimes, there were no cars at all.

The road entering Yugoslavia snaked on ahead around hills and curves, and we settled into the nearest space along the highway north and stuck out our thumbs. I was still sore over our little spat about buying the soft drink at the store. Barely settled on the shoulder of the road, a German couple picked us up in their sedan. Wow! What a stroke of luck. It only took a few minutes, but what happened to the Irish couple?

As we pulled out, I exclaimed, "Who were all those hitchhikers up ahead"? As we made some initial small talk with the German couple, we passed four sets of hitchhikers, with the Irish couple being the last. They glared at us, shaking a fist or a single finger. It seems we broke a fundamental rule of hitchhiking. When you are the newest hiker, you are to go to the end of the line so the earlier hikers have the first chance for a ride. Getting this ride happened so fast, and I was already grouchy, so we never noticed the others up ahead. I'm so sorry, I thought, but it's too late now. We were on our way.

The German couple was going all the way to Germany. How lucky, I thought, but they told Angie, truthfully, they would give us a ride but didn't want company for that length of time, but they'd drop us at a better spot to catch another ride. They seemed sorry, but this was at least a ride out of nowhere. We rode with them until dark and were dropped off somewhere in southern Yugoslavia, where there were two stores and a gas station. Traffic here was light, and the chance of getting another ride in the dark seemed unlikely. Hungry and tired, we visited the gas station bathrooms, bought a snack, and then walked down an intersecting farm road a couple hundred meters to roll out our sleeping bags to try and sleep behind a stand of trees.

Day 23, July 19th

Looking at our map in the morning and with the help of a store clerk, we pinpointed our location four hours south of Belgrade. From the gas station, we stepped out to the road, thumbs out, once again continuing, homeward bound. This road had more traffic, and we did not wait long before receiving a ride. The man who picked us up was going to Belgrade but spoke no English or German. It was a quiet and uneventful trip, which suited us just fine. Near noon, a single German man in his late twenties picked us up near Belgrade and said he wanted someone to share the cost of gas with him in return for a ride. He was going to Nuremberg and hoped to drive straight through. We quickly considered our options, and Angie told him we could give him twenty DM, but that was all we had. He agreed, and we were on our way again. I still had my emergency money, and making it to Munich was almost home, so this was our best option.

He was a pleasant man but unusually quiet and seemed preoccupied. He drove all day long with little said between us. There was no language barrier this time. The radio played as he stared straight ahead. Angie and I were exhausted, and sitting in comfortable seats allowed us to take a quick nap. Like most German drivers, he drove fast, and we were making excellent time. The only time we stopped was for gas, a bathroom break, and for him to eat dinner. Angie and I waited outside in the evening while he ate. This diner stop was an odd and uncomfortable scene. There we were, eating a simple Brötchen leaning against the hood of his car just outside the window while he ate a hot meal two meters away. Only the diner window separated us, but we purposely made no eye contact.

After a few more evening hours on the road, he asked me if I would drive while he napped. Angie and I got in the front while he stretched out in the back for a couple of hours. The radio was on low volume and blended into the highway noise. Otherwise, quiet. He awoke and resumed driving, and I returned to the back seat. There was not much talking in the late-night hours, and what was said was in German, which left me out of the loop. Time passed slowly, but eventually, the driver realized he could go no farther at this late hour. We exited the Autobahn near Salzburg, Austria, to check out a country hotel. The man discovered a room for the three of us would cost 50 DM, but we had no money to contribute. Only three or four hours from Munich, we decided to try the three-person, two-sleeping bags trick in the rural thickets near the hotel. This stay was less comfortable than with Robbie, but the night was chilly, and we slept until the break of dawn.

Day 24, July 20th

Back on the road, after daybreak, hungry and broke, we descended the Alps and were let out south of Munich. This part of our trip was mundane and often uncomfortable, but we covered a lot of territory in that one full day and night. Angie and I discussed spending some of our hideout money to return to Munich. With memories of the English Gardens and the Jazz Club, we decided to stay on the Autobahn and head toward Stuttgart and home. After catching several shorter rides to bypass Munich, we took a break at an Autobahn rest area. Our last driver said this rest area would be the best place to catch a long-distance ride.

There were bathrooms, a restaurant, and a gas station with a store where we exchanged our emergency dollars for Deutsch Marks. We bought a simple meal and topped off our water. We relaxed for a half hour after our light lunch before walking out of the large parking area to the beginning of the entrance ramp back to the Autobahn. It was a sunny summer day but nowhere near as hot as Greece or Turkey had been. I sat on the curb with our packs, thumb out, while Angie walked beyond some trees to an apple orchard to grab a couple of apples before our next ride.

Not expecting to catch a ride so soon, a young, fit, bare-chested man screeched to a stop right before me and motioned for me to get in. I jumped up, held up a finger indicating to wait one moment, and stumbled in English and a little German, explaining that my wife, uh Frau, was behind me. The impatient man raced his engine as Angie appeared from the trees, and I held up my hands, pleading for him to wait.

I pushed both packs into the narrow back seat of the sports car, climbing in behind, and Angie sat in the front passenger seat. She barely had the door closed when the driver peeled out. We zoomed out onto the Autobahn and quickly reached 160 kph, as I could see the speedometer from my backseat perch. With mixed emotions and the fact there was no speed limit on the Autobahn, we both became apprehensive and somewhat afraid. At this rate, I thought we'd be home by dinner time if we survived. Angie and the driver talked, but it was mostly a one-sided conversation. Even with my limited understanding of German, I could tell everything said was most uncomfortable.

I observed this man from the back seat, dressed in athletic shorts, expensive sports shoes, and calf-high, white sports socks with no shirt. He was both intense and intimidating. While he talked, not with but at Angie, he repeatedly checked his glove box to ensure it was closed, maybe locked. This glove box was close to Angie's knees, so I paid close attention. Sometimes, while speaking, he would rapidly breathe or snort through his nose like a bull ready to charge. This aggressive attitude was becoming quite concerning. On top of this, the man drove fast and cut lane changes way too close to other cars. He continued to reach over and touch the glove box every minute or two. From his behavior, I surmised he may have had some drug he wanted to protect or secure instead of an interest in Angie's leg. He sure seemed to be high on speed or some amphetamines. I placed a sleeping bag in front of me as a cushion in case we crashed. I wanted to hand the other one to Angie but feared the driver's reaction.

When I spoke to Angie, this seemed to upset the man; his eyes bulged, and he would glare at me. At this point, Angie was no longer talking, and he was telling an intense story about something I didn't understand. He would turn to the quiet Angie and say something in German like, "You don't believe me," while the veins in his neck bulged and his breathing accelerated. The situation was getting scary. On the bright side, if there was one, we were making excellent progress time-wise. If we could only survive this, we'd be home in a few hours, hopefully alive.

We were now maybe 50 kilometers southeast of Stuttgart and coming around a long sweeping curve in the Autobahn doing 160 kph. Suddenly, both lanes of traffic ahead had come to a complete stop. The crazy driver had been going too fast, and the stopped cars surprised him. He braked and downshifted quickly but not soon enough, requiring a last-second swerve onto the shoulder of the Autobahn. We abruptly stopped about a car length ahead of the last stopped car. He missed the stopped car by millimeters. I breathed again, only after we came to a complete, screeching stop. Angie's blood had drained from her face, and she was in shock.

His car was not damaged, so he revved the engine repeatedly and took off down the shoulder to the exit a couple of kilometers ahead. Now off the Autobahn, he raced through a small town, mostly ignoring stop signs and signal lights unless another car blocked his way. It wasn't long till we all noticed the rumble of a flat tire on the rear driver's side. This flat tire infuriated him. Pounding the steering wheel, he jumped out to look at the damage. Angie and I took advantage of the situation and quickly got out. We were relieved to be safe for the moment. While the driver was crouched down and assessing the flat tire, Angie slowly started walking down the sidewalk while I retrieved our packs and sleeping bags. The man stood up with a tire iron in his hand, hitting it into the palm of his other hand. He told us in German, "NO! Stay here. It won't take long…". But we slowly kept backing away, then, from a safer distance, turned and briskly walked on while the man seemed to start arguing with himself. Phew! That was a close one.

Not looking back again, we continued walking straight down this residential street, not caring where it led. Finally, we came to another road with commercial activity and followed it across the Neckar River to a busier part of Wendlingen am Neckar. We stopped to rest, check our map, and reevaluate our situation at a large pond with walking trails and tables. After carefully discussing our last ride and how a few others were odd but nowhere near as harmful or dangerous, we counted the last of our money and devised a new plan to get home.

In familiar Germany, we decided to forego hitchhiking, find the local Bahnhof (train station), and see if we had enough to buy train tickets to Bad Kreuznach or as far as possible. After asking a passerby where to find the Bahnhof, we walked two kilometers into the town center and asked the station clerk the price of the tickets. It was more than we had. Our remaining money would get us about halfway to a stop on the north side of Mannheim. OK, we decided we'd do it. Halfway was better than death by another suicidal driver.

A day after we returned home, I heard a news report on Armed Forces Radio about a disgruntled Munich professional soccer player who had been released and traded to a Hamburg team. We had to wonder if that was maybe our crazy driver. It sure seemed to fit.

The two-hour wait for the train gave us time to settle down after our harrowing ride and reflect on the better parts of our journey. These last days were quite stressful. We opened up and shared how our previous ride scared us, contemplating our possible demise.

We then focused on the many positives we experienced. Everyone from the Greek olive truck driver, who went out of his way to help us, to Ali and his caravan. Overall, this remarkable trip was more than an incredible journey. Those seven beautiful days in Athens will live in our memories forever—the full moon over the Aegean on our anniversary was magical. Crossing borders illegally into communist countries and the twelve-hour crossing into Turkey we will never forget. Even our car wreck and separation from the caravan were challenges for the ages. We survived and are better for it.

We had grown as a couple from surviving these escapades. We worked together, overcoming various unforeseen circumstances and strange events, and became even closer in refreshing ways. From being stuck for hours in the dry heat north of Athens to the insane sports car ride, we now had enough. The seven days with Ali and the 64 Mercedes, with all its surprises and issues, was a dream compared to these last days.

Trip beginnings are new and exciting, whereas the long way home after three full, exhausting weeks of exploration had become a road to travel and not much more. Our journey was a once-in-a-lifetime adventure full of new sites, new people, and many unexpected experiences. Angie and I had walked in the footsteps of Socrates and Plato. We found one man in a city of four million, having few resources, and slept under the stars and a full moon while Aegean islands sparkled, just for us on our first anniversary. Angie and I did it all. Life was good!

Exiting our stop in Frankenthal, we carried our packs off the train and joined the bustling Monday afternoon crowd as a light rain started. In only three days, we had traveled almost 2,500 kilometers, living non-stop in strangers' cars, and experienced our mood shift from relaxed adventurers to desperate vagabonds. Athens's 100-degree dry heat had now turned to cool and bleak tedium. Broke and hungry, we set out to find the best place to catch another ride, with the strong memory of our last harrowing ride seared in our minds. With the temperature in the low 60s, we retrieved our long-sleeve shirts and ponchos from the bottom of our packs. It was a short walk to a busy roundabout where we hoped to catch our next ride. The rain increased from a drizzle to a steady shower. We dropped our packs in front of us with our thumbs eagerly out a safe distance from the slow-moving, circling traffic. This was not a good spot. Drivers were attentive to navigating the circle and were hurrying to get home from their workday and out of the rain. I hoped someone might feel sorry for us and pull over.

The rain, congestion, and too many trucks pushed me over the edge, and I began to nudge my pack closer to the oncoming traffic. Spray from the truck tires soaked my pack, and I pushed a bit closer still. Angie stayed back and kept telling me to come back, but it was like I didn't even hear her warnings. A tractor-trailer making the sweeping circle came to close, and its tire clipped the frame of my pack. I futilely shouted as I kicked the last tire when Angie pulled me back to my senses and away from the road.

Soaking wet, tired, and frustrated, we changed plans. Instead of reaching Bad Kreuznach, we try to make it to Asbach. We moved to a covered area outside a nearby gas station and used the last of our change to call our American soldier friend, Randy, back in Darmstadt. The barracks' duty station private answered the phone and ran to Randy's room, and as fate would have it, found him, and they raced back to the phone. He would gladly pick us up and bring us to our shared house in Asbach. We'd catch up along the way. We would owe him big time for this, but that's what friends do.

Randy 1976

Six thousand kilometers, dozens of rides from strangers, and having spent maybe $300 or 600 DM over three weeks, Angie and I would now have a story of the journey we would never forget. Life is more than good. It's AMAZING!

Part 7
Cultivating German Life

Chapter 35
The Harvest

Angie and I had been back in Asbach, Germany, several weeks after our hitchhiking trip east and back. We were settling into our new living quarters on the third floor of Gabi's and Rudi's house. Our lives were slowing down, and our main concerns were back to the basics of life: what to eat, arranging our room, walks through the woods, and an occasional bus trip into Darmstadt. Compared to our recent 24-day odyssey to Turkey and Greece, living in rural, laid-back Asbach was a pleasant shift for us. Gabi and Rudi were also adjusting to us living with them and were both kind and accommodating. They allowed me to borrow the motor scooter occasionally, and Rudi was OK with me restringing his bass guitar to play left-handed. Angie cooked delicious meals, and we helped around the house and grounds.

Angie, picking flowers in a field across from our Asbach house.

Life in Asbach was simple and good. Every so often, friends visited and usually stayed for several days. With no telephones, these visits were unannounced but welcomed. Heinz and Hari Uhl popped in for a visit, and Angie's former boyfriend, Tobias, with his friends Sammy and a mutual Girlfriend, came and stayed for three days. The three shared a makeshift bed we set up in the living area and didn't mind greeting us from their bed in the nude as we enjoyed our morning coffee. Tobias and Sammy used this time to paint his VW Bug, a brown and beige two-toned finish. Since they did this with paintbrushes, I was skeptical about how the finished product might look. It looked professional and classy after working two days on this paint job. There were no visible brush strokes, and how they combined the various body segments with the two tones looked beautiful.

For the last night of their visit, Angie cooked a special meal of creamed *Spargel* (white asparagus) over potatoes, a traditional German dinner at the end of summer. In Germany, Spargel grows on mounded rows, and the leafy stick plant above ground is cut short and fed to pigs. The thick, tender, white root is cooked in a cream sauce and is delicious. Angie's godmother always had a field of Spargel that Angie helped harvest as a little girl. Life in Asbach was simple and relaxing. Visits from friends were times to share this stress-free atmosphere, slipping back in time and escaping the restless pace of the modern world.

We would return to Bosenheim every few weeks to be with Angie's family and visit friends, mainly at the Uhl's house in Hargesheim. When autumn rolled around, it was time in Bosenheim, and all of Germany for that matter, to harvest the grapes. Bosenheim was a medium-sized village sitting at the base of the Bosenberg, a giant hill or small mountain covered in vineyards. A walk from Angie's house to the top of the Bosenberg took about an hour, and the 360-degree view it offered was spectacular. You could see all the surrounding villages and Bad Kreuznach off in the distance.

The Bosenberg looked like one giant vineyard, which it was botanically, but individual families owned or sometimes leased separate rows of grapes and managed them independently. Angie's parents needed help with their many long rows in the vineyards this time of year. They had several parcels of different types of grapes throughout the hillside. In September, Angie and I returned to

Bosenheim to work with the family, tending the vineyards and harvesting the grapes.

When the grapes had matured to peak ripeness, the Bosenberg was as busy as an ant hill, with harvesters from surrounding villages efficiently robbing the vineyards of its bounty. Each day, we worked on the Bosenberg. Manfred drove the tractor with the family workers riding on the wood-floored, flatbed trailer with all our tools and equipment. The Weyell's three vineyards were midway up the mountain. We bounced along, holding tight as we crossed the stream by a wooden bridge and followed the packed dirt trails to the first vineyard.

Ernst used some of his vacation days to oversee the harvest work. Anita prepared a warm midday meal of boiled potatoes, sausage, and vegetables. She wrapped the lunch metal containers in towels to keep the food warm, which we all appreciated during our midday break.

Preparing to harvest the grapes from the Weyell vineyards on the Bosenberg.

We arrived at a vineyard sore and stiff from the bumpy ride, climbed down from the wagon, and quickly went to work. Angie, Christel, and Jutta went to different rows and began shearing the bunches of grapes into large buckets. With a long plastic container strapped to my back, I walked to each girl's location, where they would empty their full pails into my container. They resumed shearing the grape clusters until their pails were full again. I traveled quickly between each girl until my head-to-knee-long container was full, then returned to the wagon. I climbed a wooden ladder onto the flatbed and another to the top of a vast square metal container on the wagon. Ernst would help me dump the load and send me back for more.

Bert dumps the container of grapes and goes back for more.

The Weyell girls dump their sheared grapes into Bert's container.

At day's end, with a full vessel, Anita, Manfred, and the girls would gather tools and lunch containers and walk home. Ernst and I would wrap up the long day by driving the heavy wagon ladened with grapes to Herr Stum's winery in Bosenheim. Herr Stum's family winery was a local business catering to the region. He arranged with the local farmers to buy their grapes for his bottling enterprise. With Ernst Weyell, at least, the arrangement was to pay him in cases of wine over the next year and possibly some money depending on the quantity and quality of the harvest.

Weyells and Stums prepare to take the grape bounty down the Bosenberg to the Stum winery.

As darkness closed on the day, Ernst and I donned boots and stood inside the vast container of grapes we collected. We used large flat-nosed shovels to move the grapes from the tractor flatbed into a three-meter-long, one-meter-tall, cylindrical mechanical press parked next to our wagon. After scooping the day's harvest into the large press, we watched the screw plate, at one end, slowly turn, creating a waterfall of pure grape juice cascading through the metal grating to collect in the large trough below the long cylinder. Heir

Stum handed us small wine glasses to catch and sample the fresh juice as it poured down the sides of the press.

The collected grape juice flowed from the trough through a large transparent tube into one of a dozen or more 1,000-liter open-topped casks to ferment for 3-6 weeks. The wine was ready once the open cask had a good head of moldy foam covering the top, and the sugar content measured just right. Then, the aged wine drained into four massive, hundred-year-old 10,000-liter closed wooden casks in the cool cellar. These giant oval-shaped casks stood two and a half meters tall by two meters wide and three meters front to back. Here, the wine would sit until next year, waiting to be bottled.

The final step was for Herr Stum's mother, now in her 80s, to fill bottles from the giant casks of last year's properly aged wine. This quiet but still able older woman sat on a small stool in the cellar, in front of the double tap of an old oval cask, filing case after case of bottled wine. She would place the neck of an empty bottle over one side valve spout and release the wine to flow in. Holding that bottle with one knee, she would grab another empty bottle to place over the other side valve while the first was filling. She quickly turned the valve to direct the flow to the new bottle. She removed the full bottle, inserted a cork, hammered closed with a mallet, and placed it in an empty crate. She would repeat this process, filing case after case while a young man (likely her grandson) replaced the full crates with empties and brought new baskets of corks.

Ernst always spent a good portion of his payment for his grapes in bottles of wine throughout the following year. The family shared the meager wine profits with Herr Stum, but Ernst had his wine throughout the year. It took us four long days of harvesting to collect all the grapes from Weyell's three mini-vineyards, but we finally finished the job.

———————

What little money Angie and I had was running out, so it was time to find jobs. Still a German citizen, Angie went to Darmstadt to file for unemployment at Gabi's recommendation. Small unemployment checks would arrive in a few weeks, enough for us to survive in Asbach. Angie would go to at least three businesses weekly to apply for work to maintain her unemployment status. Since she had completed school and had received her business certificate, her referrals were to stores in Darmstadt. Not wanting a job, Angie showed up for interviews dressed casually in blue jeans and a plain top. Stores were looking for more polished workers, and she remained unemployed with benefits until she interviewed at Olitsch gift shop. The manager of Olitsch learned that she spoke excellent English and hired her on the spot. Darmstadt had a rather large U.S. Army post, Cambrai Fritsch Kaserne, and many shopped at Olitsch. Angie would become valuable working there.

I also tried to find work. After almost two years of college, I thought I could be a substitute teacher at the nearby US Army high school. I interviewed, and they said they would keep my application on file, but my long hair and beard probably didn't make a good first impression. After checking with some American businesses around the post, insurance, Stars and Stripes newspaper, travel agencies, and such, I had no luck. In a long shot chance, I contacted the European Space Agency, with their Operation Center, Mission Control, facility in Darmstadt. They spoke English there, and I hoped I might find a menial job, but I couldn't even get an interview. Without speaking German, finding work was proving impossible. Without employment, I might need to return to the States. Life in Germany with no money was getting old. Angie always shared, but I wanted to pay my way. I hoped Angie would return with me, but we had not discussed that possibility.

Angie and my relationship was more solid now than in Florida, but we still had some unresolved differences to work through. I enjoyed experiencing the many differences life had to offer in Germany but was again unable to share the depths of my feelings with Angie. Angie appreciated the many deep discussions she had with her girlfriends. Talking with her friends did help her in ways that I was not able or willing to do.

I have always been a loner. Moving so often as I did growing up did not make me reject others outright, but I learned to protect myself by living within myself. Angie enjoyed life with me, sharing and experiencing many new things together. We laughed a lot and truly enjoyed each other's company, but still, the view of what it takes to share a relationship on the deepest, most meaningful level escaped me, leaving Angie wanting. Some nights, she would talk with me about her feelings, like we did in Florida, but I still didn't quite get it. I no longer felt the boulder was crushing me in these conversations, but I still could not find the words to identify and share.

True feelings were not often discussed in my earlier family life. Growing up, my life was more superficial, and when life in my family got complicated, we moved on. We would never dwell on problematic issues, and those issues rarely resolved themselves. My parents avoided confronting problems, and eventually, those problems ate away at their relationship. As much as they tried to protect me from these avoided problems, I suffered from the lack of stability in my life and never dealing with or confronting issues.

Angie was the opposite. She believed we should discuss every difference to keep our relationship growing. Our out-of-sync communication was the primary obstacle to becoming more intimately connected. We knew we loved each other but needed better communication to cement our relationship. Since living in Florida, however, we had made real progress and felt we were on the right track.

Chapter 36
Perks of German Life

Without a job and the growing thought of returning to the States, my friend Randy suggested I apply at the Army Post Commissary (grocery) or Post Exchange (PX). I talked with the Post Exchange manager, who said they needed a helper in the warehouse. The only requirement was to be able to drive and have a driver's license. The PX hired me on the spot to make deliveries in the large step van to Americans living off-base and to work in the warehouse. They needed me to start the next day, and speaking German was not required.

As a civilian employee at the Army Post, I would have privileges at the PX and Commissary. I could buy cheap food (a carton of cigarettes was $1.25) and visit the liquor store and stereo shop, both tax-free. Once we got a car, I could buy gas on post for one-fourth the price in town. I felt life had dealt me a straight flush, and now I could remain in Germany and contribute financially to our life together.

Angie and I worked in the Darmstadt area, but getting there every day was another challenge. The bus from Asbach left quite early, just after 5:30 AM. When we took this bus, we arrived early enough to share a sweet breakfast at a bakery near Angie's job at Olitsch. Then, I would catch another bus to the Army Post, getting there by 9 AM. If we missed the Asbach bus, we would walk through the woods, 20 minutes to Ernsthofen, where buses ran every hour. It didn't take long for us to realize that living in the quaint village of Asbach was making getting to work difficult. We were making money and started looking for an apartment in the Darmstadt area, near a main bus line or Strassenbahn (streetcar) route.

Our close friend Christhilde, the other "beautiful German girl," had recently returned to Germany and planned to move in with us. Christhilde hadn't intended to return to Germany so soon. Her New York family took her to the Montreal Summer Olympics, and upon returning to the US, Customs noticed her tourist visa had long expired. They allowed her to reenter the US if the family paid a $1,000 bond, which would be returnable if Christhilde left the country within 30 days, which she did.

Finding an apartment was very competitive, and each one we visited in Darmstadt was either too expensive or the landlord didn't seem to want us. After a long search of several weeks, we found an affordable three-bedroom apartment in Ober-Ramstadt, a small town about 10 kilometers south of Darmstadt. It was above an apothecary shop on the main, busy road. It had a shared bathroom with an upstairs lawyer's office, but it was affordable, and the law office hours were from 9-5, so sharing was acceptable. Living here cuts our commute time to work by half. Regular bus service, stores, and restaurants were nearby for a change.

Karl Heinz Ulrich (Boobie) and Bert

In my job at the PX warehouse, I would grow close with my boss Karl Heinz Ulrich, or "Boobie" (his nickname), meaning little boy, because he was short and looked young. He gave us several simple pieces of furniture for our new, unfurnished apartment and said we could have the old Coke machine from the warehouse as a refrigerator. This "refrigerator" was a fabulous table size, antique Coke machine. It consisted of a metal "Coca-Cola" box on four wooden legs with a hinged wooden top. When you raised the lid and put money in a slot, you bought a standing Coke bottle and moved it laterally through the rack to a location where you could pull it out. I removed the inner mechanism, and it made a decent fridge.

Our unfurnished apartment started to look like we lived there once we brought our mattresses from Gabi's and Rudi's, a kitchen table, a few chairs, and a couple of lamps from Angie's parents. Randy was a big help using his car to transport our new furnishings. It was exciting to have our own place, and Angie was happy to have Christhilde to talk to.

With our new jobs and an apartment closer to the city, It was time to buy a cheap car. We purchased a 1965 VW Beetle for 500 DM from an Army Sergeant who was returning to the States. Having a car made life so much easier, and now we could travel more around Germany. Our new VW was also perfect for hauling newfound items to our new abode. About once every several months, people would put big things, including unwanted furniture, on the curb for trash pick-up. Leaving unwanted items on the curb was known as *Sperrmüll*, and we found tons of usable pieces to furnish the rest of our apartment by riding around the better neighborhoods early in the mornings on Sperrmüll day.

To complete our new living space, we decided to get a pet. Living in an upstairs apartment with no yard on a busy street meant a dog or cat would be impractical. Angie decided to buy a white mouse, and feeding it would be cheap. Angie set up a corner in her room adjacent to the kitchen with a small cage for the mouse.

Bert's room in Ober-Ramstadt. Right to left: Manfred, Thomas, Wolfgang, and unknown.

Our apartment in Ober-Ramstadt was fun for the next six months or so. Having a place of our own, with plenty of space, allowed us to have frequent visitors. Christhilde's brothers, Heinz and Hari, would make extended visits. Larry, Sherry, and Randy were often there, along with Angie's sister Christel and brother Manfred.

Bert's best friend, Hari Uhl, with the Coca-Cola fridge in the background.

With two incomes and a roommate, I spent about half of the money I earned building a quality stereo system from the PX stereo shop. Prices were much cheaper here, and I could get even better deals since I worked next door and would see discounted returns or special sales first. I bought four beautiful JBL speakers, a Teac tape deck, a Technics turntable, and a Kenwood Model Eleven II receiver. I used my work status benefits to allow Christel, Manfred, and other German friends to purchase stereo systems, too.

Bert's stereo system takes shape.

Having privileges at all the Army facilities also provided us with many other great deals. Cheap American cigarettes at the Commissary replaced my Drum Tabak. It was Kools for me and Marlboros or Winstons for our German friends. Alcohol at the PX liquor store was dirt cheap, but outside of 95-cent bottles of Andrè champagne and beer, we rarely consumed other alcohol. The relatively inexpensive gasoline meant we could travel frequently as cheaply as mass transit. Mailing letters and shipping packages through the APO (American Post Office) costs the same as mailing from New York. These fantastic discounts and having two jobs opened up a new world for us. Our new standard of living was quite different from living in Asbach on our 10 DM weekly contribution for communal groceries. Those 10 DMs were quite a stretch for us at that time.

Angie peals potatoes in the Ober-Ramstadt apartment.

As I settled in Germany, I wanted to visit more places and experience more German life. Having acquired a taste for good beer and finding this a suitable replacement for pot, I invited Randy to go with me to Munich and experience Oktoberfest together. We would stay with Oli (Olivia), a childhood friend of Angie's from Bosenheim, who lived several blocks from the festival grounds.

Oktoberfest was like a gigantic carnival that lasted several weeks. One night's visit was enough. We drank too much beer and went on too many rides, but we had lots of fun. Each Munich brewery had its tent with music and dancing. We'd join arms at long benches, swaying back and forth to the traditional music. Beer was served in one-liter glass steins by servers carrying eight to ten at a time to the waiting patrons at communal tables. After visiting two beer tents, I got sick and lost my lunch under the table in the third tent. A barmaid grabbed my long hair and got my attention by knocking my head on the table, and she threw us both out. With a quick recovery, Randy and I jumped on a fast-moving Ferris wheel while my stomach recovered. We were shocked when, promptly, at 11:00 PM, everything closed down, and the festival staff slowly rounded everyone off the Oktoberfest grounds.

The night was young, and we were not ready to call it quits yet. While wondering what to do next, we started a simple conversation with two young German hippie-type women whose English was somewhat better than my German and decided to go with them to a nearby bar to resume the night. Frank Zappa played on their VW cassette player, and we quickly arrived at a bar. When I took out money to pay for my beer, the young woman across from me asked, "Who is that?" pointing to the photo in my wallet. When I replied that it was Angie, my wife, the late evening abruptly ended, and the two women left. Randy and I had no intention of more than enjoying a beer with them, but they, apparently, had more in mind. We finished our beer and used my city map to find our way back to Oli's for the night.

Even though our new life was coming together well, Angie and I were often not on the same page emotionally. Drinking was becoming a problem for me. I drank one or two bottles of beer daily at work and, sometimes, cheap champagne from the next-door liquor store. Once home, I'd have another beer or sometimes two while listening to music on my new stereo. We were starting to lead separate lives together. Once again, I enjoyed life but found it challenging to understand Angie's unhappiness. At least Angie had Chris to share her displeasure over my drinking.

Winter in Ober-Ramstadt was beautiful. There were several heavy snows that year, and our forest walks were gorgeous and enjoyable. At Christmas, we cut a small spruce pine from the side of a trail to take home for the holiday. Angie decorated it with candles in clip-on holders, simple ornaments, and popcorn string, making the tree beautiful. We only lit the candles while in the kitchen with the tree. Angie's pet mouse, who often had the run of the kitchen, loved hanging out under the tree. Her mouse was friendly and would eat a dab of chocolate from your fingertip, followed by a light bite when the chocolate was gone. After 10 -15 minutes of running around free, Angie would catch it and return it to its cage.

Tannenbaum in the Ober-Ramstadt apartment, 1976.

After Angie's birthday in January, we went to a Pink Floyd concert at the Frankfurt Festhalle. We arrived two hours before the concert began and stood behind a growing crowd waiting for the doors to open. The show was open seating, and we hoped to claim a spot close to the front. While waiting, the crowd grew, and we were smooshed together so tight we could not move. Everyone was waiting to get through quickly and claim their suitable spots. Jokingly, I said to Angie, "Look, I don't need my feet," and picked up both feet while the packed crowd held me in place. It was that crowded. Once inside, however, the crowd dynamic changed most pleasantly. At an American concert like this, everyone would remain standing and pack towards the stage with little room to move, making it uncomfortable. Once we entered the Frankfurt Festhalle, everyone moved close to the stage but quickly sat down in small groups with a bit of a comfort zone around them. It didn't feel overcrowded at all.

Many US soldiers were in attendance, as evident from their whitewall haircuts and speaking American English. When a group next to us passed along a joint to me, I said, "Thanks, man," and the soldier said, "You speak pretty good English." When I told him I was American, he got excited about my long hair and beard. You didn't see many Americans looking like me in Germany. One other American soldier was the only person seated on the floor I saw stand up during the concert. He stood in amazement when two glowing eyes emerged from behind the stage in the fog, high above the psychedelic video screen, backdropping the band. Then came the snout of a pig snorting out smoke just below the eyes. The glowing eyes and smoking snout turned out to be a gigantic, inflated pig, 12 meters long. As it slowly made its way above the crowd, the American soldier stood with hands on his head and mumbled in total amazement until a polite German nicely asked him to sit down so they could all see. The pig continued above us all, slowly making an about-face, and returned while Pink Floyd played "Pigs (Three Different Ones)." It was a fantastic concert.

Chapter 37
Germany by Bug and Bike

As the weather warmed in late Winter, Angie and I wanted to explore different parts of Germany. I converted our VW Bug into a mini-camper by removing the upper part of the back seat and replacing it with a plywood piece attached to a small 2" by 4" frame. When we stopped to camp, I removed the passenger seat and inverted it over the driver's seat. I then placed the frame on the floor with the plywood on top, where the passenger seat had been. Voila! We had a makeshift bed almost two meters long. Our feet would share the same space in the passenger seat area, but we had ample room for our upper bodies to spread out in the open back. Angie made curtains for the side and back windows, and now we could travel and sleep in our cozy mini-camper.

Northern Germany, Bert, and the camper bug.

Our most extensive trip was to visit northern Germany near the Danish border. Over five days, we saw the massive cathedral at Köln (Cologne), rode the *Schwebebahn*, a suspension monorail dating from 1901, in Wuppertal, and experienced a *Fasching* parade in Bonn, (celebrating the last serving of alcohol before Lent). We would find rural, out-of-the-way places to camp and manage to see quite a bit without spending much money. In the far north, we saw traditional architecture was different. Some house roofs were thick bundles of straw atop stone walls. German dialects were different here as well. Overall, it was a more rural setting than central Germany. In Bremerhaven, we splurged on dinner in a waterfront restaurant, eating freshly caught North Atlantic cod.

By early Spring, we rode our ten-speed bikes from Bosenheim to Worms and spent two nights camping. We had brought a small tent and sleeping bags and camped in a secluded place on farm trails along the Rhine River. Riding bikes on the main roads was challenging, but it was much more relaxed and enjoyable once we got to the back roads, where we tended to travel. Seeing Germany at 20 kph in the open air was much more pleasant than through a car windshield at 100 kph.

The ride to Worms was through rural roads with beautiful, iconic scenery. From Bosenheim, we followed back roads to the Rhine River, where we watched the many large ships traveling in both directions, one after the other. We encountered more traffic as we entered the north side of Worms, but we stayed close to the river, and city riding was manageable. Worms is one of the oldest cities in Germany and has a Roman heritage. We visited the town center and briefly visited St. Paul's Cathedral. Finally, we returned to the rural roads to continue our bucolic route home.

While setting up camp between the farm road and the Rhine, Angie told me to watch closely for cars or tractors while she relieved herself along the bank. There were no vehicles, tractors, or people, but suddenly, we realized a parade of ships going by less than 100 meters away behind her. That was good for a laugh. We spent our night close together under the clear sky and stars until we turned into our small but warm and cozy tent.

This trip was our first long-distance bike ride, and we agreed this mode of travel was a better way to experience new territory. The fresh air and beautiful terrain connected our senses to our experience. We became a part of each small village we passed through. People waved to us and spoke a friendly greeting as we passed. Had we traveled by car, we would have been just another anonymous visitor, isolated from the community. Traveling by bike gave us time to see firsthand, smell, and feel the places we passed through. When we returned to

Bosenheim, our butts were sore and legs tired, but our minds were fresh and clear. This bike trip would not be our last, we were sure.

Having enjoyed our ride to Worms so much, I invited Randy on an overnight bike trip so he could experience rural Germany at 20 kph, too. We went from Bosenheim through Bad Kreuznach, past the 250-year-old *Salinental* (health spas) along the Nahe River, to the 200-meter-high cliffs overlooking Bad Münster. We stopped at a local Wirtschaft for a meal and a beer and played the slot machines. As evening fell, we found a nice spot in a field under an immense oak tree to set up camp. We got the tent up before it turned pitch dark and gathered enough wood to sustain a campfire for several hours.

While we recounted events along the ride, an owl with a vast wingspan swooped down to within a meter from our faces. It sat in a tree the rest of the night with a faint hoot every so often. We were invading its territory. It was chilly sleeping but still comfortable. As soon as the morning light appeared, so did a young farmer who was a little sore about us camping on his apparent property and instructed us to leave. With such an early start, we returned to Bosenheim before noon, happy and in good condition except for somewhat sore butts and a little hungry. Well worth it, though.

Angie and I returned to Bosenheim frequently to hang out with friends and spend time with her family. Long bike rides to visit Angie's very close godmother and day trips exploring other small towns in the Nahe Valley were typical. As Spring turned to Summer, every small village had some small weekend festival or wine tasting. These were always fun to attend.

Manfred (Angie's little brother) and I rode our bikes on a 30-km loop trip one fine Saturday afternoon. We stopped for a break not far from home and bought a snack and a beer each. Manfred was 14 and had never drunk a whole beer before. This one got him a bit drunk, his first time. It wasn't until we finally returned to Bosenheim that I realized the beer's effect on him, but by then, the exercise had weakened his buzz.

The work-life in Darmstadt was stable and manageable for both Angie and me. The consistent paychecks were a pleasant change. Angie's job was slower-paced and more formal, whereas my job at the PX warehouse was with a close-knit, friendly group of workers. Boobie managed me and two other employees efficiently, but we all had fun every day. Four or five times a week, we unloaded goods from large tractor trailers and sorted the products into the proper locations throughout the warehouse rows of massive shelving.

It was typical to open a beer mid-morning and sip on it till lunch. The office worker Jenny did not drink at all, but Boobie, Walter, and I did. We three had another beer in the afternoon as well. Walter, the rotund, Polish middle-aged worker, would often have several small bottles of spiced liquor "to settle his lunch." And sometimes, have another beer or two. He was never much help after that, and more than once, we found him asleep on the giant platform elevator. When times were slow, around the holidays, the three of us guys would drink several bottles of Andrè champagne during the workday. We determined how good it would taste by how many beams the plastic corks would shoot over in the vast warehouse. One beam was OK, two good, but three would be extra bubbly.

A couple of days a week, Boobie would ride with me in the large step van making local deliveries or a trip to another US Army warehouse to pick up some necessary shipment. Beer was consumed on these rides, too, but in moderation. Angie and I socialized with Boobie and his wife at their house many evenings, where Boobie would always insist on several shots of vodka from the freezer.

Boobie and I bonded and laughed together as we accomplished our daily tasks. He shared many personal and difficult wartime memories with me as our friendship grew. These shared stories helped me understand the perils he faced growing up during WWII. He was 16 years old in the last year of Hitler's rule. The Hitler Youth was always trying to enlist him to support the home front, but he managed to hide whenever they came after him. Darmstadt was a central industrial region, so British bombers were dropping thousands of bombs at night, and American bombers were doing the same during the day. Boobie's home, far enough outside Darmstadt, was safe from the bombings, but walking into the city for supplies and rations was necessary and dangerous. Once, walking through a field, he found a shoe. When he picked it up, there was still a foot inside.

A day in town with his older sister brought the typical siren alerts directing all people to hide in building basement shelters till the bombing stopped. Each shelter had an emergency escape, with an outside wall rigged with an explosive charge in case the bombed debris blocked the entrance. Someone panicked and set off the charge, and this was the last time he saw his sister as she escaped his clutch to follow a frantic group out of the shelter to their demise. Several times each week, he and his mother would go into town to search the posted lists of known dead and look at the unidentified bodies laid out near the government building. His sister was never found and, likely buried in the rubble. Even though Boobie was older than me, we became good friends.

By early Summer, Angie and I began to feel things were missing in our lives. Her work was not satisfying, and her close friends were all finding their paths in life. The closeness she had, at seventeen, with her Bad Kreuznach friends had changed. She occasionally saw them, but everyone's focus was diverging. We were floating through life with few goals beyond survival and enjoying life.

I had been thinking about returning to college and finally earning a degree. We traveled to Heidelberg to visit Schiller College. It was a private college with classes taught in English and a fine reputation. After talking with a counselor there, I knew it would be a good experience and thought I could probably handle the coursework. Still, it would take all my GI Bill monthly benefits to pay tuition and school expenses, and the remaining cost of living would be too great for us to bear.

Living in Germany was quite a difference for me. Every aspect of life was uniquely German, and it took me some time to adjust. Many of these differences were improvements over life in the States, but still, I felt out of place. My discomfort came primarily from my limited language proficiency. I spoke German well enough to say what I wanted, and my understanding of German was even better, but my limitations made my speaking sound like that of a young child. People would smile at me politely as I spoke and do their best to understand what I said. On one occasion, after I constructed a lengthy question, one stranger in town curtly said, "Just ask me in English. What do you want?" I had to put a lot of mental muscle into my constant translations and felt it was time to return home. My most pressing reason for wanting to return was to go back to college. Life here in Germany with Angie was the best experience of my life, but I was ready to complete my last two years and get my degree. What I would eventually do with a degree, I didn't know, but I knew that a degree was my best option to achieve a meaningful life. That is what I wanted, and it had to be with Angie.

I was ready to return, so I talked with Angie about how she would feel returning to the States. Angie was content living back home in Germany but had no specific plans or goals. She felt how we were floating through life as well. Over our two years together, we matured to the point where we had fewer doubts about our future stability and were content with life together. Looking around at everyone we knew and even thinking back to our Florida friends, we saw the simple lives of people who were happy in their youth but struggling to make ends meet. They all had a disconnect between their jobs and personal interests and desires. Most of the older people we knew were unhappy with their work. There must be more to life than the carefree existence we were living. Life was fun and exciting, but how long might it last? My wanting to complete a college degree was a realistic goal that showed promise. Neither of us knew anyone with a college degree. No one in our families went to college, no friends had graduated, and no one we ever worked with had a degree. I was sure college was a good bet to help us create a life with more potential and long-term contentment.

Like many life decisions, we decided, "Sure, why not?" We agreed to continue working in Darmstadt till July, then move back to Bosenheim until we flew back to the States. Our return plan would be to stay with my parents, living in Winter Park, Florida, until we could settle somewhere. Doubts remained in Angie's mind. Memories of our past communication problems and many Americans' superficial attitudes gave her reasons to pause. She decided she could change her mind anytime, but this move would be OK for now.

Before quitting my warehouse job at Cambrai-Fritsch-Kaserne in Darmstadt, I took advantage of my US (APO) postal benefits and mailed all our belongings to my parents. Postal costs through the APO were like mailing packages from New York City, much cheaper than international postage rates. Over the next week, we packed and mailed 21 large boxes and shipped them to my parent's address in Florida. It cost us a bit less than $200. Half of the packages contained my stereo equipment and record albums.

We slowly gave our things away or moved what we would keep to the Weyell attic in Bosenheim. Our favorite pieces of furniture, like our Coke machine fridge and lamps from our Ober-Ramstadt apartment, went to the attic. Christhilde moved back with her family in Hargesheim, and we tied up our remaining loose ends before we quit our jobs and moved back to Bosenheim.

Chapter 38
Plans Disrupted

Before returning to the States, we hoped to make one more epic trip exploring another part of Europe to bookend our life in Germany. We had two months after quitting work before we would fly back, so we planned a four-week bike trip. We would follow the Rhine River north to Amsterdam, take a ferry to the United Kingdom, ride north through the Lake District, and take a ferry back across the English Channel to France. Ride to Paris, explore, pack our bikes on a train, and cross the highlands back to Bad Kreuznach. We had the time and barely enough money and energy to complete such a ride. We already had sleeping bags, a small tent, and some supplies, so we purchased saddle bags for each bike and other nylon (think lightweight) bags for every space on the bicycles. We packed these bags full of essential clothes, a small tool kit, extra tire tubes, a flat kit, and other necessities for the trip.

We bought cheap airline tickets to New York City. From there, we planned to take a train to Florida. We were all set to wrap things up in Germany and begin our bike ride of a lifetime. Having some money, we hoped this trip would be more comfortable than our hitchhiking trip to Turkey and Greece. This bike journey would be more of a physical challenge than our earlier trip's emotional ups and downs, but what a way to complete our year and a half in Germany. We were so excited to get underway.

As an afterthought, we contacted the US Embassy to see what Angie might need to reenter the United States. We walked to the Bosenheim Post office (still no phone at Angie's parents) to call the

US Embassy in Frankfurt. They instructed Angie to come to the embassy to complete some re-entry forms. Angie still had her "Green Card," but since she had been away from the US for more than a year, she had to complete the forms to reinstate her Green Card status. Less than a year's absence and nothing was necessary to return. No problem, we had calculated a week or maybe two to take care of Angie's needs with reentry and visit our friends to say goodbye. We would await four weeks in the saddle and new sites to experience.

Frankfurt was a two-hour train ride, and finding our way to the embassy required maps and planning. Arriving late in the morning, we thought we had plenty of time to complete the necessary documentation. The US Embassy was an immense building, but only one large room was open to walk-in visitors who all waited in lines to talk with rather impatient German nationals working the front desks. Finally, after lunch, it was our turn, and we explained Angie's situation to one of these workers and requested whatever paperwork was necessary to resolve her Green Card issues. We hoped to complete the forms on-site and turn them in before leaving. The documents were extensive and required birth certificate info, proof of residency in Germany, and other information we did not have. We needed to return them to Bosenheim, fill them out correctly, get proper official signatures, and then return them to the embassy.

Within several days, we completed the forms, obtained the required signatures, and returned to Frankfurt on a Friday. An embassy worker accepted the documents and informed Angie she would now need a physical done by a local physician contracted by the embassy. She could make an appointment for late next week at the earliest. She made the appointment without a choice, and we began contemplating how we might need to shorten our bike trip. On our third trip to Frankfurt, she completed the simple physical. We returned to the embassy just before closing time, only to find out she had been given the wrong forms to complete the first time and handed another batch of similar documents. Of course, she had to do this at home, not at the embassy. Our bike trip was getting shorter each time we had to travel to the embassy.

Once more, several days passed, and with all the new forms completed and triple-checked, we returned to Frankfurt. This time, the impatient clerk told Angie these forms were incorrect, and she handed her blank documents that were the same as the ones she had completed the first time around, several weeks before. Angie's and my frustration had been building this whole time. I complained to the rather rude clerk about everything we had endured up to this point but was quickly and curtly dismissed. She threatened me with delayed re-entry as I had been away from the States for over a year without official contact. A well-dressed man passed through this enclosed area behind the clerk, speaking perfect American English to a subordinate when I loudly attracted his attention. The startled man, an American embassy official, broke from his task at hand to respond to my interruption. I politely apologized for my outburst but asked for his help to resolve our never-ending predicament. After a brief but exasperated explanation of events and form mix-ups, the man turned to the German national, impatient clerk, and said, "Stamp these forms approved and let them be on their way." A quick thank you, and we were on our way. We were relieved but also saddened because the time and money spent on our multiple train trips to Frankfurt now made it impossible to fulfill our bike tour. Who knows, maybe this was fate and for the best.

Chapter 39
The Ass and the Elephant Win

———

We still had another month before returning to the States, and most of this time was spent in Bosenheim helping in the vineyards or visiting the Uhl family in Hargesheim. We decided to go to the *Jahrmarkt* Festival in Bad Kreuznach, a busy and well-attended regional fair with rides, games, wine, beer tents, and thousands of people. We went to Hargesheim to go with the Uhls and friends. We walked through the fields and Vineyards, five kilometers each way. We had sold our car already, but several others had cars, and when I asked why not drive, Heinz Uhl replied we all would be drinking and walking was the best. Right, he was. Taking the footpaths back to Hargesheim after several shared bottles of wine was a pleasant way to slow down the evening celebration.

Hari Uhl, Angie, and I entered a beer tent with a large sawdust animal ring in the center. The ring leader was a funny, talkative man with a handlebar mustache, a top hat, and a whip, which he frequently cracked to emphasize a joke's punchline. By coaxing and teasing, he would challenge people at the tables to try to ride a young *Esel* (jackass) around the ring three times and win 100 DM. Several tried and either never got to a riding position or lasted only a few moments before being flung to the sawdust ground to the amusement of everyone in the tent. After a beer and with a plan forming in my head, I stood up and volunteered for the next attempt. The ring leader had great fun with me, all in German. He asked if I would grab the Esel by the tail as he pulled my ponytail and teased me a lot about drinking and riding.

He pointed me through the gate with "*Achtung*! and *los*!" and gently pushed me into the ring. The Esel was prancing around the circle like an excited kid. I watched it go by twice, and on its third lap, knowing I had little chance of grabbing it in motion to jump on its back, I leaped directly in front of the charging Esel, clapped my hands real loud, and the startled Esel stopped dead. I grabbed its neck and swung my body up on its arched back, and we were off. After a short gallop, I realized my butt would never survive the Esel's bony back three times around the ring. Instead, I decided to lock my feet under the Esel's stomach and sit erect with my hands straight out to each side while the Esel violently bucked up and down. I rode one full circle to the cheers of the beer tent patrons before I gave up, unlocked my feet, and was tossed into a pile of sawdust to more cheers from the crowd. No one lasted longer than me, but no 100 DM.

After another beer, I decided to try a new challenge in the same ring. This one seemed a bit easier, riding an elephant bareback for three minutes. The ring leader first emptied two bottles of what he claimed was whiskey into the elephant's mouth and had it stagger around a bit before letting me climb up on the kneeling elephant's back. Then, something I missed in the German announcements, two other tent patrons climbed on and sat behind me. Three on its back simultaneously. Sitting just behind the head, I grabbed the elephant's ears firmly. The two people behind held onto me, their only thing to grab for balance.

The elephant stood up, and we shouted out from our high perch as we contemplated the upcoming and inevitable long fall. At first, it was relatively easy. Everyone laughed as the ringleader instructed the elephant to walk around, shaking his head back and forth as he pretended to stumble in its drunken state. The third young man on the back slid off first, but the other guy and I hung on bravely.

After a minute, the ring leader had the elephant kneel and place its forehead flat on the ground, which made sitting on the elephant's neck nearly impossible, but we leaned way back and stayed on for the moment. My legs pressed into the elephant's neck as tight as possible, and I had a firm grip on the ears. The ring leader instructed the elephant to shake its grounded head back and forth quickly. I held until the man behind me, gripping my sides, pulled us both off. As we tumbled to the ground, the entire tent erupted with laughter. I couldn't help but wonder how long I might have lasted had I not been pulled off. We had so much fun that night that when our friend Randy visited a few days later, we returned to Jahrmarkt. Once again, I attempted the elephant ride, this time with Randy, with no more success but just as much fun.

N ear the end of August, with a few weeks remaining in Germany, Angie, Randy, Larry, Sherry, and I drove two hours north to attend an outdoor concert. The concert venue was a natural, bowl-shaped amphitheater high on cliffs overlooking the Rhine River at Loreley. Arrowsmith, Small Faces, Uriah Heep, Ted Nugent, Country Joe & The Fish, and Stanley Clark played till the early morning hours. The first group to play, Country Joe MacDonald, yelled, "Gimme an F" (remember Woodstock "F***"), and it started to pour. What a slippery mess. The mud mixed with the trash, and everyone got soaked. It eventually stopped raining as Stanley Clark came on and played a laid-back jazz set. The rest of the evening was excellent, filled with good music, but finding a dry place to sit was impossible.

The audience remained standing for the rest of the concert, and by 2 AM, we were all quite tired. Anticipating the long ride home in Larry and Sherry's VW station wagon, we weren't too disappointed when Steve Tyler stopped singing "Dream On" right in the middle of his high-pitched refrains and announced, "After eight shows the last six days," he just couldn't hit the high notes this time, and that was it. The music ended without even an encore, which was unheard of. Almost every concert ended with two, maybe three encores. The pitch-black ride back at that hour was a real challenge on all back roads, but Larry got us home safely.

Part 8
The End of the Beginning

Chapter 40
This Time, Together

———

Finally, it was time to say goodbye to Angie's family and head to the Frankfurt airport. Angie was still not sure she was making the right decision. She felt right about living in Germany; There was comfort in being with lifelong friends and family and her familiar culture. She didn't have firm plans or know what else to do with her life, so sticking with me and returning to the States was what we would do. Who knew what the future would bring? Fate had looked kindly on us both so far, so this seemed the right thing to do for us.

I was a different man now from when I first arrived in Germany. My fateful choice to travel half a world away to eventually stand under a dim street light in a strange town with $10 left in my pocket and, knowing not a soul, turned into my reunion with Angie, which became the best decision of my life. Now, I was ready to return to familiar ways and hopefully continue my education somewhere in the United States. Being with Angie allowed me to enjoy living in Germany much more than I imagined. I knew it would be different, but I had minimal knowledge about what to expect living in Germany.

The unanticipated, fundamental things about this culture made me stop, think, compare, and evaluate how things here were different and often better than back home. The way people arrived at a consensus and overcame their differences. Teenagers attained greater personal freedom as they matured and accepted personal responsibility. Rules and customs were followed, not without question, but because they worked and were reasonable for society.

They recycled everything, and the political, social, and economic systems supported these efforts because it was the correct way to behave. The government spent the people's revenue on infrastructure, improving the ascetic quality of life, and supporting an efficient safety network for everyone. Health care, having enough food, decent pay, and benefits for every profession. These benefits included four weeks of paid vacation, end-of-year (Christmas) bonuses, and generous sick leave. Welfare for the less fortunate provided job training, placement, and home visits to ensure enough food in the pantry and a safe environment for those less fortunate.

Several things in the German culture reminded me of American life in the 1940s or 50s. I never understood how direct and impersonal people were when shopping or dining out. Cultural expectations were high for everyone. Everyone knew their place in the order of society and fulfilled their roles as expected. It was rare for anyone to question authority or challenge typical norms. Each town had a Turkish enclave segregated from the rest of the community. The Turks typically had menial trash pick-up or street-sweeping jobs and had little direct contact with Germans.

This whole year-and-a-half experience certainly opened my eyes and gave me much to absorb and reflect upon for many years. My exposure to this life, which was so different and had possibilities I had not imagined, gave me a more mature outlook.

Now turning 25, I have made progress connecting with Angie emotionally. Our relationship had matured, and we understood each other's needs better than in Florida. Angie knew I would keep her safe and respect her emotions. I learned to share myself with her more and engage with her emotional deliberations. I still had a long way to go, but my love for Angie made me understand the importance of expanding our connection. Our relationship was moving in the right direction. I did not doubt my choice to follow my "beautiful German girl" was the right decision, and I would appreciate this decision my whole life.

Tearful goodbyes with Angie's family and bits of advice were given, and then we got a ride from Helga to the train station in Bad Kreuznach to continue our journey. This time, we went back to the United States together. We had our ticket to New York City, but beyond there, it would be by train or maybe bus. We were not sure. We were initially headed to Florida to live with my parents in Winter Park but had found out, in my last phone call home, that my parents had moved to Blacksburg, Virginia, so this was our new destination.

As we lifted off from Frankfurt airport, I stared out the window at the network of small towns and villages, all no more than a few kilometers from each other with woods between, connected by roads, rails, and trails. The terracotta roof tiles on all the stone and stucco houses faded as the clouds made Germany disappear. Now, with Angie's hand interlocked with mine, a new life awaits us both.

It was late evening when we landed at Kennedy Airport and took a bus to Grand Central Station in New York City. We could catch an Amtrak train to Virginia at eight the following morning, so we went looking for a hotel with reasonable rates to spend the night. Angie carried her giant suitcase, which weighed 50 pounds, and a backpack. I still had my Air Force sea bag, which was also 50 pounds, strapped over one shoulder, my hand-made shoulder bag Angie made for me back in Florida, and Angie's guitar. Walking around Manhattan looking for the cheapest hotel was challenging with all this weight and unfruitful. The night-time streets seemed busy to us, and it was still rare to have anyone make eye contact, but several friendly people insisted on helping us with our baggage for a block or two. We asked them for advice on where we might find cheap lodging, and we're told of a Travel-Lodge hotel not far. Around midnight, we checked in for a few hours of sleep.

The following day, Amtrak took us to Roanoke, Virginia, where my dad picked us up and took us back to the Econo-Travel motel they managed in Blacksburg. We lived in the motel's model room, next to the office, for the next several months with our 21 large boxes, which we had shipped from Germany, stacked neatly along one wall. My dad had paid almost $300 to send them to Blacksburg from Winter Park, Florida. He was always kind to those he loved and would not take a dime from us.

Those first several weeks back became a twist of fate neither of us expected, good or bad. Angie realized and announced she was pregnant, which brought tremendous joy to my parents. Angie and I had never discussed having a child, nor did we expect to begin a family at this point in our lives. Having a child after two and a half years together presented many possibilities and even more questions. Our immediate concern was that we were living in another new town with no place of our own. We had no jobs and no money. My parents would help us get settled and assist us however they could, but they were in their sixties and tended to move around every six months to a year. The thought of having a little one around brought joy to our hearts, and we slowly got excited about our upcoming baby. We've handled so much together, and we should also be able to manage this.

Blacksburg, Virginia, was a relatively small, unimposing town in the New River Valley, nestled between the Appalachian Mountains on the west and the Blue Ridge Mountains to the east. Here is a large university, Virginia Polytechnic Institute and State University, or VPI. Thankfully, some years later, this name would be shortened to

Virginia Tech. You would see the university's unusual combination of orange and burgundy colors everywhere in town. Even the motel shag carpeting was a blend of burgundy and orange. Room telephones had a burgundy base and an orange receiver.

It didn't take long to get familiar with the small town, and with so many young people, it was a fun place to start a new chapter of our life together. Mr. Fooze, a bar on Main Street, served the best subs in town. On College Avenue, Gillie's vegetarian restaurant had the best meals. Next door, Carol Lee Donuts made fresh donuts every morning that you could watch, dropping off a conveyor belt into hot oil from their front window right next to the Lyric Theater. Our memorable dates would be grabbing a couple of Mr. Fooze's subs and two donuts from Carol Lee. At the Lyric, we'd sit in front-row seats on the balcony with our meal on the ledge. A root beer would wash it all down while we laughed at Animal House' or, a bit later, Ferris Bueller's Day Off.

With as many bars as other stores, Friday and Saturday nights were always scenes of Bacchanalian pleasure in this college town, with more students than locals. Around the corner on Draper Road, books and the best assortment of records could be bought at Books, Strings, and Things. I spent many fond hours looking through the racks of albums there. Mish Mish was the place for office supplies and graphic arts material.

Our home, the Econo-Travel Motel, was at the far south end of Main Street, next to the best dance place in town, the Holiday Inn Motel and Lounge. There were three or four traffic lights from the motels into downtown, two miles away. We arrived in Blacksburg shortly after the big back-to-school festival and crafts fair, "Deadwood Days," which would later become "Steppin' Out." The town was an eclectic mix of locals, hippies, college students, professors, and shaved-headed cadets from the considerable ROTC presence on campus. This simple, laid-back town was the economic draw for the entire Virginia region west of Roanoke and home to the state's largest university.

After living at the motel for a week, a Virginia State Police officer stopped at the Econo-Travel office asking for me. I came out from our adjoining room, and he asked to speak with me privately. Angie and my parents were there, and worry crossed all our faces. I led the officer into our connecting room, the model, and closed the door. With a small tear in the officer's eye, he told me the bad news. My daughter, Kimberley, had died in a tragic accident two days before. He shared the few details that he knew. At her mother's house in Jackson, Michigan, my three-year-old daughter stood on a chair looking out a window. She slipped off the chair with the curtain cords wrapped around her neck and accidentally strangled herself. I was in a state of shock and could not speak.

When we arrived in Blacksburg, I sent Peggy a letter telling her we had returned from Germany and were staying at my parents' Econo-Travel Motel in Blacksburg, Virginia, but included no phone number or address. As horrible as this news was, I had the suspicion this might all be nothing more than a ploy of my ex to make me suffer with a made-up story. She had never done anything this shocking, but I knew how hurt and angry she must be at me. I wasn't ready to believe this devastating account quite yet. We all talked as soon as the officer left, then I called Peggy's parent's house. Peggy answered, and the story was true. Peggy was devastated, but having a few days for this tragedy to set in allowed her to discuss the details with me rationally and mostly held back her crushed emotions.

Angie and I took my dad's Cadillac to Michigan the next day, in time for Kimberly's funeral and an unhappy, brief reunion with Peggy and her family. This sad visit would be the last contact I would ever have with Peggy. Looking back on my past life, I knew I had never given my old life with Peggy a chance. We were both too young for marriage and a child. Our situation at the time made marriage seem like a good idea, but it would have been best if we had instead remained friends. I often wondered if and how Peggy dealt with this tragedy, and I was remorseful.

———

Within the past month, life had changed drastically for Angie and me, and again, our future was full of uncertainties. Now, we live in a new place, thousands of miles away from friends, with a baby on the way. My parents helped us immensely with jobs at the motel, living rent-free until we could afford a place of our own, and using their car when we needed transportation. Our relationship was more stable now. Having a child would bring us closer as we set up a house, and I found a better-paying job. We had six months to establish ourselves as Virginia residents so I could pay cheaper tuition as an in-state resident. We took this time to find furniture and save money because we had no maternity insurance. We rebuilt our lives again by working together and managed to make life work.

———

You could have always done some things better in a perfect world. Still, we had no regrets from what started as Angie's journey to experience a new culture in an exotic land an ocean away from her familiar home, only to find a man so different from herself with whom to share life. Likewise, my journey across that same ocean went in the opposite direction, following the woman of my dreams to experience a different culture and share the same life. We became one, bound by our love for each other and the new life we created in Angie's womb.

Angie had grown from being an inexperienced 17-year-old, fixed in her need for emotional stability, to growing systematically into a contented life. I had grown from a carefree and experienced young man with no firm home or philosophy to a willing partner to work for a life with my "beautiful German girl." In the year and a half since leaving Florida, our paths had merged into one journey. Our hitchhiking trip and life in Germany had shown us who we were becoming and how much we meant to each other. The obstacles we had overcome and the challenges we faced created a firm foundation for our life ahead.

Exotic Florida provided the exciting setting for our fateful attraction, and we learned of our potential together. Germany gave us the stamina and appreciation to see each other as complete people who would work hard to build a life together. Now, back in the United States again, we found an environment far different than the never-ending, superficial sunshine of Florida and the old-world culture of Germany. The mountains of Virginia and the people we would grow to love were entirely different. Between the age-worn peaks and ridges of Brush Mountain and Peak's Knob, the New River Valley would become the cradle of our continued journey together. New challenges awaited us, and our relationship continued to mature. Our new life was similar to the Riesling grapes we harvested, and it would age and evolve into an enjoyable tonic. Early in our young adult lives, we were both influenced by totems that guided us to where we would meet our soulmates. Angie has her dolphin, and I have my seagull. We have continued a lifetime journey of shared pleasure together as the Gullphin.

A ngie and I settled in Blacksburg and the New River Valley, taking turns working at Pizza Hut or attending VA Tech

University for me or nearby Radford University for Angie. While one of us worked or attended classes, the other stayed home and cared for our three children, Daniel, Marcus, and Katrina. Angie made several life-long friendships, which fulfilled her need to share lives of kindred emotions. I would eventually mature enough to enjoy life without pot or beer and come to terms with the actual impact these habits were having on our relationship.

We both became lifelong, respected public school teachers and raised our children to each follow their journey. Life was never perfect, but we always remained faithful to each other and worked hard to keep our journey alive. We earned everything we ever wanted with no gifts from anyone. Life was never opulent nor lavish, but life was even better; it was real and ours. We reaped the reward of a well-traveled journey and remained happy together in this life and, if fate allows, into the next.

Our journey continues into our golden years. Nothing in our life together would match the fateful story of our newspaper-arranged meeting at Big Daddy's Lounge in Florida or our hitchhiking trip to Turkey and Greece. Like all good relationships, we would work through our share of problems and lack of understanding of each other to build an incredible life together as we raised our three children.

I fulfilled one of my dreams for us: building a log cabin on the bank of the New River. According to regional legend, it is the second oldest north-flowing river in the world. With the help of our eldest son, Daniel, we prepared the foundation, finished the decking and subfloor, and hired an Amish crew from a neighboring county to stack the logs and build the roof. Angie, Daniel, Marcus, and Katrina helped finish the inside over the next several years.

This journey, which began in Florida, from our New Moon trailer with the painted window of the Cat Stevens, pictured hammock under the tiki roof with a bottle of wine and two glasses looking out over the ocean, wound up in our log cabin in the mountains of Southwest Virginia on the banks of the New River amidst the Sycamore trees, ever closer to our colorful rainbow. As it turns out, we were the pot of gold and are now rich (but not in money) beyond anyone's expectations. The Gullphin lives near all three kids and five grandkids in Charlotte, North Carolina. And oh, we still have the log cabin on the New River. Thank you for the inspiration "Foxfire."

Remember the Gullphin, the seagull, and the dolphin? He soars through the air, seeking new adventures not tethered to anything on the ground. She uses her intelligence and intuition to navigate all life has to offer in the ocean of life. She rises to the surface and meets the seagull skimming the same water. Together, we envision a rainbow of vibrant colors covering life's spectrum as we journey together through rain and sunshine to follow our prism of light. Ultimately, we know the rainbow was not our goal but our guide. Instead, our journey is the goal, directed by our rainbow. As long as we let the rainbow guide us, even though we will never touch it, we know it exists, and our goal is our journey, which is infinite.

The Gullphin's Journey
still following our rainbow

The End?

About the Author

Bert is a retired public school teacher now living in Charlotte, North Carolina, with friends and family.

After ten years of on-and-off college, extensive travel, and various jobs, from dishwasher to mobile home sales and service, fate set a new course for his life, as revealed in this book.

Once he settled down at 28, he taught 7th-grade Social Studies for 14 years at Dublin Middle School in Dublin, Virginia. For the next 12 years, he taught World and U.S. History and Human Geography at Patrick Henry High School in Roanoke, Virginia. In two of those years, he served as the director of the Center for Humanities and became a National Board Certified Social Studies teacher. His last ten years were devoted to his passion for teaching human geography at New River Community College as an adjunct faculty member for evening classes, and he was an instructional technology resource teacher during those ten years. He assisted classroom teachers with integrating various technologies across many Montgomery County, Virginia public schools, with extended placements at Blacksburg High School and Christiansburg High School.

Bert was active with the Virginia Geographic Alliance as the Director of the Southwest Region of Virginia for ten years. He received the Virginia Outstanding Geography Teacher award in 1996 and the National Council for Geographic Education Excellence in Geography award in 1998. In 1996, he was a Teacher Consultant with the National Geographic Society in Washington, D.C., and the following year, he became an instructor to the next group of educators from every state, Canada, and Puerto Rico.

Bert now spends his retirement years with his wife, Angie, sons Daniel and Marcus, their wives, Kristen and Jaclyn, and five grandchildren. He has finally learned to play guitar left-handed and has been an avid sports card collector for 65 years. Playing pickleball keeps him active, but his favorite activity is spending his life with Angie, to whom he owes eternal happiness.